Teaching and learning early number

Second edition

Teaching and learning early number

Second edition

Edited by
Ian Thompson

 Open University Press

Open University Press
McGraw-Hill Education
McGraw-Hill House
Shoppenhangers Road
Maidenhead
Berkshire
England
SL6 2QL

email: enquiries@openup.co.uk
world wide web: www.openup.co.uk

and Two Penn Plaza, New York, NY 10121-2289, USA

First published 2008
Reprinted 2009

A catalogue record of this book is available from the British Library

ISBN-13: 978-0-33-523411-0 (pb)
ISBN-10: 0-33-523411-9 (pb)

Library of Congress Cataloging-in-Publication Data
CIP data applied for

Typeset by RefineCatch Limited, Bungay, Suffolk
Printed in the UK by Bell and Bain Ltd, Glasgow

Fictitious names of companies, products, people, characters and/or data that may
be used herein (in case studies or in examples) are not intended to represent any
real individual, company, product or event.

The McGraw·Hill Companies

Contents

To my wife, Barbara, and our children, John and Anna, my mathematical guinea pigs.

Notes on contributors

Julia Anghileri is senior lecturer in the Faculty of Education at the University of Cambridge. She has an international reputation for her research relating to children learning arithmetic and has published a number of articles in professional and research journals. She has been a consultant to the National Numeracy Strategy and the Primary Strategy and works on national test development with the Qualifications and Curriculum Authority (QCA) and the National Assessment Agency (NAA). She has extensive experience with both pre-service and in-service teachers through undergraduate and postgraduate courses as well as in-service courses.

Carol Aubrey is professor of early childhood at the Institute of Education at the University of Warwick and Director of Research. She trained first as a primary school teacher and then as an educational psychologist. Later, she spent a number of years in primary teacher education with a particular focus on the early years, first at University College Cardiff and then at the University of Durham. Thereafter, from 2001, she worked at Canterbury Christ Church University College where she led the Centre for International Studies in Early Childhood (CISEC). Her research interests lie in the area of the policy to practice context of early childhood education, early learning and development with a particular interest in early mathematics and inclusion/special educational needs. She has been convener of the British Educational Research Association (BERA) Special Interest Group for Early Childhood Education and Care and a member of BERA Council (2004–2007). She is the UK editor for *Journal of Early Childhood Research*.

Patrick Barmby is a lecturer in mathematics education at Durham University, with a particular interest in primary mathematics. His areas of research include examining what we mean by understanding in mathematics and the role played by reasoning. Prior to lecturing at Durham University, Patrick was teaching in a rural secondary school in Kenya, working with wonderfully enthusiastic students of mathematics, physics and chemistry. He has been researching attitudes in science, stemming from the gender issues that he encountered in Kenya. Patrick also works for the Curriculum, Evaluation and Management (CEM) Centre in Durham, carrying out evaluations of educational initiatives.

Elizabeth Carruthers is head teacher of Redcliffe Children's Centre in Bristol. She has taught for many years in primary schools and nurseries including three years in the USA. She is co-author of the book *Children's Mathematics* and co-founder of the Children's Mathematics Network. Elizabeth has written articles on mathematics for a variety of academic journals and books. Her research interests include the pedagogy of children's mathematical graphics and research on Children's Centres.

Dondu Durmaz is from Turkey, where she graduated in educational psychology and worked six years in primary, secondary and high schools. She then focused on early years education, particularly on mathematical development in this stage, and took a full scholarship award to do a Masters Degree and PhD in early years education at the University of Warwick under the supervision of Professor Carol Aubrey. Her PhD is entitled 'Policies for early years mathematics in Foundation Stage', and explores the policy-to-practice context of early years mathematics. After her PhD she returned to Turkey to work at Akdeniz University, Antalya.

Sue Gifford is principal lecturer in mathematics education at Roehampton University. She has worked in a variety of London schools, and has published books and articles on children's own recordings of mathematics, early years mathematics education and, more recently, dyscalculia. Her research interests currently include the prevention of mathematics difficulties.

Eddie Gray is reader (Emeritus) of the University of Warwick. He has 20 years of teaching experience in primary and secondary schools – five as a head teacher – and has taught on BA(QTS), PGCE ITT courses, and BSc and Graduate programmes. One-time director of the Mathematics Education Research Centre at Warwick, his research interest, focusing on the cognitive reasons for success and failure in mathematics, spans the spectrum of mathematics learning from pre-school to undergraduate level. The chapter within this text, partially the outcome of a fruitful partnership with Professor David Tall, profits from his observations of children's mathematical learning and the knowledge acquired through the supervision of numerous PhD students, several of whom were practising teachers.

Rose Griffiths is senior lecturer in education at the University of Leicester. Starting as a teacher with a particular interest in working with children who find maths difficult, Rose has taught in primary, secondary and special schools, and worked with young children and their parents and carers, including Sure Start. Her publications include many books for children, parents and teachers. Rose's research interests are in counting and early arithmetic, raising the achievement of looked-after children and childhood bereavement.

Tony Harries is the director of the Initial Teacher Training Division at the School of Education in Durham University, and is a senior lecturer in mathematics education. His main area of research at present is in exploring the role of computer-based environments in the learning of early mathematics. Before coming to Durham nine years ago, he worked at Bath Spa University College, was head of mathematics at a large Bristol comprehensive school, and worked in the development of primary education in Bangladesh. At present, he is also involved in a curriculum development project for teacher trainees in southern Africa.

Steven Higgins is professor of education at Durham University. He has undertaken a number of research projects in primary schools investigating the impact of information and communications technology on children's learning of mathematics, including a study of the impact of interactive whiteboards for the Primary National Strategy. A former primary school teacher, he has a particular interest in how children's thinking and reasoning develops. He has investigated practical approaches to support thinking in classrooms with teachers and the development of pupils' learning skills and confidence in their ability to learn associated with these teaching strategies.

Effie Maclellan is professor of education at the University of Strathclyde. She is also a chartered psychologist and chartered scientist. Before coming to Strathclyde, she worked for more than 20 years as a class teacher and a head teacher in mainstream primary education and in special education. She teaches about, carries out research in, and offers consultancies in, learning, teaching and assessment. In all of this she is excited by use-inspired basic scholarship: combining the quest for fundamental understanding (what is normally thought of as basic research) with a concern for practical usefulness (what is normally thought of as applied research).

Penny Munn is a developmental psychologist and reader in education at Strathclyde University. Her research in numeracy began with investigations into pre-schoolers' conceptions of counting. Her current work is focused on mathematics recovery as a framework for developing the primary maths curriculum, and on teachers' understanding of children's conceptions of number.

Jennifer Suggate worked for over 10 years in the School of Education at Durham University, contributing to the mathematics part of the primary PGCE course. She has now been working on developing computer programs for primary mathematics for over 20 years. Such programs should allow children to interact with animated visual representations of number and the operations on them. Fertile discussion can be provoked by considering carefully different representations of the same numbers and operations. Although now retired, she is still interested in developing new programs and ideas for using them in the primary classroom.

Ian Thompson taught in schools and higher education for 38 years. Observations of his own young children struggling to make sense of number concepts provided the stimulus for his research into children's idiosyncratic mental and written calculation strategies. To date, he has published over 100 articles, book chapters and conference papers, and has edited two other books for the Open University Press: *Issues in teaching numeracy in primary schools* (1999) and *Enhancing primary mathematics teaching* (2003). He was a member of the Advisory Group for the National Numeracy Project, and was seconded to the project for two years. He is currently visiting professor at Edge Hill University, Ormskirk, Lancashire.

John Threlfall lectures in primary mathematics at the University of Leeds, where he is involved in the preparation of primary teachers, teaches on higher degree courses and supervises doctoral study. His main research interest is in children's cognition, especially calculation strategies and mathematical problem-solving, and he has been involved in a number of related projects, including developing classroom materials for the World Class Arena for gifted and talented pupils. He is currently director of the University of Leeds School of Education Assessment and Evaluation Unit.

Kate Tucker is a nursery teacher and head of Foundation and Key Stage 1 at Two Moors Primary School, Tiverton, Devon. She has written widely on early years mathematics and Foundation Stage practice. For several years, she has trained teachers in these areas as part of her work for Devon Education Services. She occasionally teaches on the mathematics module for the Early Childhood Studies BEd students at the University of Plymouth.

Maulfry Worthington has taught throughout the 3–8 year age range for over 26 years. She has lectured in higher education on primary mathematics and on early years courses and was a national numeracy consultant. Maulfry's research interests include children's thinking, play and semiotics, with a focus on children's graphicacy and their early written mathematics. She has many publications including *Children's Mathematics: Making Marks, Making Meaning* (Sage Publications, 2006) which she co-authored. Currently engaged in research for her doctorate at the Free University, Amsterdam, Maulfry is conducting a longitudinal, ethnographic study into children's meaning-making in imaginative play and its relationship with children's mathematical graphics.

Bob Wright is associate professor in mathematics education at Southern Cross University in New South Wales, Australia, and is an internationally recognized leader in understanding and assessing young children's numerical knowledge and strategies. He is the first author of three books related to early number assessment and instruction, and has published many articles and papers in this field. His work in the last 15 years includes the development of the Mathematics Recovery Programme, which has been implemented widely in the USA, the UK, Ireland and elsewhere. Bob is currently leading a project funded by the Australian Research Council focusing on intervention in the number learning of low-attaining 8- to 10-year-olds.

Editor's preface

The first edition of this book arose out of my own increasing unease with the structure of the number curriculum for young children as recommended in various official publications and as exemplified in the myriad commercial mathematics schemes on the market in the mid-1990s. The original book comprised four sections sandwiched between a Prologue and an Epilogue. The Prologue set the scene for the book, looking in particular at two areas: the subject of mathematics itself and the discipline of educational psychology.

In the early twentieth century, mathematicians had begun to reconceptualize their subject in an attempt to put it on firm logical foundations. New branches of the subject had been developed, and more refined and powerful problem-solving techniques had gradually replaced established standard methods of working. These developments affected the way in which mathematics came to be taught at university, at secondary school and later, at primary school. This interest in mathematical precision and rigour was reflected in a particularly influential primary mathematics scheme that appeared in 1964 – the Nuffield *Mathematics 5 to 13 Project* – and in a later offshoot, the *Mathematics for Schools* scheme (or 'Fletcher maths' as it became familiarly known).

Another major influence on the primary mathematics curriculum at that time was the work of Jean Piaget. In reality, Piaget wrote very little about the teaching of mathematics, but nevertheless his theories were to have a profound influence on the thinking of many of those involved in mathematical education. Among the many important ideas contained in his writing, it is probably the concept of conservation that had the greatest impact on the approach to teaching early number. Children are said to 'conserve' number if they are aware that when two collections have been shown to be equivalent, either by one-to-one correspondence or by counting, this equivalence is not destroyed by the rearrangement of one of the sets. Piaget proposed that children generally do not develop this awareness before the age of six or seven, and concluded that they had to grasp the principle of conservation of quantity before they could develop the concept of number.

This emphasis on the importance of conservation led to recommendations by mathematics educators for the delaying of number work until children could conserve number, by which time they would be in a state of 'readiness' for learning. This led, in turn, to the introduction of what became known as the 'pre-number curriculum', involving sorting, ordering and matching activities for children to engage with before they progressed to tackling work that involved actual numbers. These 'sorting, ordering and matching activities' became an intrinsic part of every new mathematics scheme that was written in the period between the Nuffield Project in 1964 and the National Numeracy Strategy in 1999.

So, the Prologue presented a personal interpretation of the reasons for the structure of the primary mathematics curriculum as it appeared in 1996, and concluded with the question 'Is there an alternative approach? . . .'. The next four sections of the book, focusing mainly on the importance of counting and mental calculation strategies, set out to show convincingly that there was indeed 'an alternative approach'. At the end of the book the Epilogue began with a detailed critique of the 'sorting, ordering and matching activities' pre-number curriculum before proceeding to consider the implications for the teaching of early number of the views expressed in the 13 chapters in the body of the text.

Major changes in the primary mathematics over the last decade – some of which are discussed in Chapter 1 – have contributed to a revised structure for the second edition of the book; it contains eight new chapters, six completely rewritten chapters and two updated chapters. It is loosely structured into seven sections, dealing in turn with the background and context for the teaching of early number; the early stages of number acquisition; the place of counting in number development; extending counting to calculating; representation and calculation; assessing young children's progress in number; and a proposal for a mathematics pedagogy for the early years. The chapters are generally short and succinct with a limited list of references, except for the introductory chapter which sets the scene, and the final chapter which looks to the future. All the chapters are self-contained and are written to be read as free-standing units, although many contain cross-references to other parts of the book where specific ideas are dealt with in a different manner.

The following information gives details of the ages of children starting school in England and Wales and in Scotland. It is included to help readers who work in a different education system from those operating in the UK.

| School year | | Age on entry |
England and Wales	Scotland	USA and Australia
Early Years Foundation Stage		0
Reception (now subsumed in FS)	Primary 1	4
Year 1 (Y1)	Primary 2	Kindergarten	5
Year 2 (Y2)	Primary 3	Grade 1	6
Year 3 (Y3)	Primary 4	Grade 2	7
Year 4 (Y4)	Primary 5	Grade 3	8
Year 5 (Y5)	Primary 6	Grade 4	9
Year 6 (Y6)	Primary 7	Grade 5	10

SECTION 1
Setting the scene for teaching and learning early number

This section, comprising just one chapter, in effect constitutes an introduction to the remaining chapters in the book which focus more specifically on the teaching and learning of *early number*. In their chapter, Carol Aubrey and Dondu Durmaz begin by discussing the report of the Williams review panel, before providing a fascinating overview of developments in the teaching of early mathematics that took place during the period of time between the appearance of the first and second editions of this book, that is 1997–2008. The authors review some of the evidence that has been gathered by researchers about the effects of the National Numeracy Strategy (NNS) on children's mathematical development, and focus in particular on such questions as:

- Has children's attainment in numeracy improved since the time before the introduction of the NNS?
- How and to what extent has numeracy teaching changed?
- Why have such changes occurred?

They then describe projects in which they have been personally involved over several years. One longitudinal study focused on the mathematical perform-ance of a cohort of 300 children just completing their primary education, who had experienced the first five years of the English NNS. The authors had been interested to find out whether:

- early achievement was likely to be a major determinant of subsequent success in the context of the NNS;
- it was the case for all children or particular areas of gain (or loss) for particular groups of children;
- it was likely that their performance was related in any way to the NNS teaching received.

A larger sample from the European arm of the project involved children from

Flemish-speaking Belgium, Germany, Greece, Slovenia and the Netherlands. Taking account of the vastly different social, cultural and educational experiences of children in different parts of Europe, the comparative findings were not what they expected.

The next study to be described was a qualitative investigation involving Reception teachers that explored the classroom context and processes of the early mathematics curriculum and the nature of early learning experiences. The following questions were addressed:

- what were Reception teachers views about the implementation of the mathematics in Reception classes?
- what sorts of mathematical experiences were offered to young children of 4 to 5 years in Reception classes?
- how did teachers plan and deliver the mathematics curriculum for 4- to 5-year-olds?

First of all, the authors carried out a small survey of 32 Reception class teachers, and then three case study Reception teachers were followed across the year, employing semi-structured observations, target child observations and analysis of teachers' planning. These three case studies are then discussed, and the chapter finishes with the authors linking the research findings discussed in their chapter to issues arising from the report of the Williams review panel.

1 Still not getting it right from the start?

Carol Aubrey and Dondu Durmaz

Introduction

In July 2007 the Secretary of State for Education called for an examination of the available evidence, including international best practice, to make recommendations for teaching mathematics in early years settings and primary schools by a review panel led by Sir Peter Williams. The review was intended to build on the recent renewal of the Primary Framework for Mathematics (DfES 2006) and the Early Years Foundation Stage Curriculum (DfES 2007). The review was concerned with identifying 'what was the most effective pedagogy of mathematics teaching in primary schools and early settings . . . in helping children to progress in their learning' (DCSF 2008: 2).

It was noted that since the introduction of the National Numeracy Strategy (NNS) in 1999, and its associated Primary Frameworks, attainment of Level 4 and above at Key Stage 2 had risen from 59 per cent to over 77 per cent by 2006 and that further ambitious targets had been set. At 10 years since its inception it was appropriate to review what new strategies were needed to make sure that attainment continued to rise. Recognizing the need to provide children with experiences appropriate to each stage of their development, the review emphasized the crucial role of effective early years mathematical pedagogy in supporting children in learning new skills; developing their understanding of concepts and process; and using, consolidating and refining skills and understanding (DCSF 2008: 34). It was acknowledged that mathematics was perhaps the most demanding subject in its need for in-depth subject knowledge, even at primary level. In early years settings, it was important that practitioners working with young children should have a genuine understanding of mathematical concepts and language as they guided children's thinking and play through exploration of shape, space, pattern and problem-solving (see Tucker, Chapter 3). It was stressed that central to effective mathematical pedagogy in the early years was 'fostering children's natural interest in numeracy, problem solving, reasoning, shapes and measures.' (DCSF 2008: 34).

The purpose of this chapter is to examine some of that evidence more forensically in order to reassess what 'effective pedagogy of mathematics teaching in early years might be' (DCSF 2008: 2) and how, if at all, it is to be sustained.

Context

Prior to the introduction of the NNS, the English National Curriculum for mathematics (DfEE/QCA 1999) had placed more emphasis on mathematical applications and less on written calculation. By contrast, the focus in the *Framework for Teaching Mathematics from Reception to Year 6* (DfEE 1999) was on arithmetic skills: numbers and the number system, calculations and solving word problems. As is well known, the daily mathematics lesson was broken down into three elements, lasting between 45 and 60 minutes with:

- oral work and mental calculation using whole class teaching;
- main lesson for new topics and consolidating previous work;
- a plenary session to draw together what had been learned.

Sample planning sheets in the *Framework* specified topics to be taught each week throughout the year for each Year Group, including Reception (for 5-year-olds), through to Year 6 (for 11-year-olds), though it was anticipated that work would be differentiated for different groups during the main section of the lesson. Advice in the *Framework* stated that there should be a 'high proportion of work with the whole class' (DfEE 1999: 15). An intention of the Labour Government was to improve national standards of primary numeracy as the Third International Mathematics and Science Study (TIMSS) (Harris et al. 1997) had shown England (and the rest of the UK) to have scored below the international average, with relatively low scores in written arithmetic but very good scores for practical problem-solving. A significant influence was Chris Woodhead, then Chief Inspector, and the review of international research that he commissioned (Reynolds and Farrell 1996). This review drew attention to the way effective teaching structures learning tasks on the basis of what children have in common and tried, so far as possible, to bring all children in a class along together, thereby reducing the wide range of attainment and the long attainment 'tail' that had been a common feature of English primary classes. This paved the way for the National Literacy and Numeracy Projects, launched by the previous Conservative Government. Also important was the much publicized introduction of whole-class, Swiss-style mathematics by Sig Prais of the National Institute for Social and Economic Research in the London Borough of Barking and Dagenham, though this does not appear to have ever been subjected to a proper evaluation.

It is not easy to draw conclusions about the impact of the NNS on pupil learning. In 1998, 59 per cent of pupils reached the expected Level 4, while by 2004, 74 per cent of children reached this level, just short of the target of 75 per cent. However, as noted by the international external evaluation team (Earl et al. 2003: 3), much of the increase occurred prior to the introduction of the NNS in 1999, and 'some head teachers and teachers expressed doubt ... about whether increase in test scores actually represented comparable increases in pupil learning'. Presumably the cause was pressure to improve national test performance and test preparation. While there was reported to be considerable evidence of improved teaching since the introduction of the Strategies, evidence of deep changes in teaching practice was 'mixed' (Earl et al. 2003: 5–6) and there was still 'considerable disparity across teachers and schools', in terms of subject knowledge, skill and pedagogical understanding of the Strategy. Moreover, throughout the four years of the evaluation, concerns had been expressed about teacher overload, pressure for acquiescence and undue stress that might result in 'a culture of compliance'.

In the midst of what Alexander (2004) described as 'pedagogical prescription', the government published *Excellence and Enjoyment: A Strategy for Primary Schools* (DfES 2003:16) that attempted to incorporate the Literacy and Numeracy Strategies and in which it claimed that teachers had the freedom to decide how to teach

> ... the National Literacy and Numeracy Strategies, though they are supported strongly, are not statutory ... the Office for Standards in Education (OFSTED) will recognise and welcome good practice ... Our aim is to encourage all schools to ... take control of their curriculum and to be innovative.

Indeed, there is some evidence to suggest that OFSTED was looking beyond basic structures and timing to a greater flexibility in interpreting teaching methods (OFSTED 2002).

Meanwhile, a range of studies found that while teaching methods and classroom organization had changed, at the deeper level of classroom discourse, pupil–teacher interaction was still dominated by closed questions, emphasizing recall rather than speculation and problem-solving, with short answers for which teachers did not provide diagnostic feedback. The pace of lessons was perceived as leaving little time for consolidation and too little opportunity for formative assessment.

Kyriacou and Goulding (2004) reviewed the ways that teachers' approach to the daily mathematics lesson impacted on pupils' confidence and competence in early mathematics, through an in-depth analysis of 18 studies. Results showed that the daily lesson had been well received by teachers and there was some evidence that this had enhanced pupil confidence and competence. A closer examination revealed, however, that intentions to promote higher-quality dialogue, discussion and strategic thinking had not been realized and what had been achieved was closer to increased use of 'traditional whole class teaching with pace' that might be creating problems for lower-attaining pupils. In fact, overall gains might reflect a closer match between teaching and assessment, rather than increased understanding of mathematics. The conclusion was that there was a need for in-service training to strengthen teachers' subject knowledge and their understanding and use of interactive teaching in order that they could better exploit the opportunities to enhance pupils' understanding that arose in the course of teaching.

Research from the five-year longitudinal Leverhulme Numeracy Research Programme of teaching and attainment conducted at King's College London from 1997 to 2002 concluded that the NNS had had at most a small effect on attainment in most areas of numeracy (Brown et al. 2003). The Nuffield Year 4 Project (Askew and Brown 2004) set out to investigate aspects of the impact of the NNS in primary schools, drawing upon data collected for the Leverhulme Research Programme. This comprised large-scale outcome data from two cohorts of Year 4 pupils from 35 schools two years before the introduction of the NNS (1997/8) and two years after (2001/2), plus teacher questionnaire, observation and interview data, also before and after the introduction of the NNS. In the second phase, a small set of five schools in four local authorities were revisited and interviews were carried out with Year 4 teachers, head teachers and/or mathematics co-ordinators, singly or as a group.

An average gain in pupils' results for a numeracy test of about 3 per cent – just over two months' development – was found. Two-thirds of schools had higher test scores and in only half of those cases that had a decline was this more than 2 per cent. In terms of attainment in different groups, variation had *increased* rather than decreased, as had been anticipated by the first director of the NNS, with the introduction of more whole-class teaching. Slightly greater improvements were made within the middle 50 per cent of pupils, with small improvements being made within the top 10 per cent and a small decline within the lowest 10 per cent.

Teachers themselves expressed doubts about the lower attainers' ability to participate satisfactorily in whole-class teaching and felt that their needs were not being fully met. Boys appeared to have benefited more than girls from the introduction of NNS and were over-represented in the top 10 per cent of pupils. In general, improvement in pupils' facility on items related to numbers and the number system and place value, all areas of emphasis in the NNS, whereas changes in some basic skills, such as knowledge of multiplication facts, division, ratio and proportion had not occurred.

Furthermore, observation and interview data suggested that low-attaining pupils derived least benefit from whole-class teaching with the lesson topic not always matching their areas of greatest need. Analysis of post-NNS lessons showed more opportunities to explain mental methods but little evidence of pupils discussing and evaluating different methods as applied to different calculations. One reason for this related to the objectives-driven nature of lessons that allowed little room for alternatives. Another was teachers' view that different methods suited different children and their ways of working. As noted by Askew and Brown (2004), informed interpretation of objectives in the Framework and a move to more strategic ways of working were challenging for teachers to understand and implement. Evidence of 'deep' change as noted by the evaluation team was hard to identify (Earl et al. 2003). In the meantime, teachers interpreted objectives in terms of existing understandings, rather than changed understanding.

The review of research evidence provided has, of necessity, been brief and focused on such searching questions as: has children's attainment in numeracy improved?; how and to what extent has numeracy teaching changed?; why have such changes occurred?

Background

A study carried out by the author and colleagues focused on the mathematical performance of a cohort of 300 children just completing their primary education, who had experienced the first five years of the English NNS. These children were tracked from age 5 to 6 years with follow-up, national standardized assessment tasks (SATs) at ages 7 and 11. The National Curriculum set standards of achievement ranging from Levels 1 to 8 to provide information on how pupils were progressing. At 7 years they were expected to reach Level 2 and at 11 years Level 4. These pupils received the NNS from Year 1 (age 6) to Year 6 (age 11) but missed the Foundation Stage for 3- to 5-year-olds that advocated a flexible introduction to the NNS through a play-based pedagogy in Reception class (for 5-year-olds). We had been interested to find out whether:

- early achievement was likely to be a major determinant of subsequent success in the context of the NNS;
- it was the case for all children or whether there were particular areas of gain (or loss) for particular groups of children;
- it was likely that their performance was related in any way to the NNS teaching received.

An earlier phase of the study had described these pupils' early numeracy development within three testing cycles, at the mid-point and towards the end of Reception year, at 5 years and again at the mid-point of Year 1 at nearly 6 years. It was thus a limited longitudinal design in which a number of other European countries took part. Assessment was carried out using the Utrecht Early Numeracy Test (ENT). This comprised eight sub-tests, five items in each, including comparison, classification, correspondence, seriation, counting, calculation and practical problem-solving. Broadly, one set of sub-tests related to the understanding of relations in shape, size, quantity and order, while a second set of sub-tests related to counting and basic arithmetic.

The larger sample from the European arm of the project involved 18,000 children from England, Flemish-speaking Belgium, Germany, Greece, Slovenia and the Netherlands. Taking account of the vastly different social, cultural and educational experiences of children in different parts of Europe, the finding that differences between countries were negligible was not what we expected. Bearing in mind that English pupils were in formal schooling throughout the testing cycle, Belgium, German, Greek and Dutch children from the mid-point, and Slovene children not at all, this result was even more baffling. Sex differences were also negligible. The relationship between age and test score was complex, with cohort advancement three times as great between the second and third test cycles, when most children were at school, than between the first and second cycles.

It is tempting to assume that numerical attainment can be represented in a single assessment instrument that is adequate in representing different school and pre-school curricula and opportunities to learn at home and in school. Moreover, there are differences in curriculum content of the pre-school and school curriculum and the age at which pre-school education ends and formal education begins. The parental role and contribution of the broader socio-cultural contexts are likely to have influenced early learning experiences too. Further qualitative research would be needed in order to map out the nature of these. At the time, it was concluded that changes in terms of curriculum goals and pedagogical practices associated with our own policy-makers' drive to raise attainments, judged in international terms, might not have had the desired effect.

A comparison with the international data set suggested a trajectory for English pupils different from that found elsewhere in Europe, with more of a bias towards arithmetic sub-tests than their European counterparts who started school later and thus experienced for longer, a broader, holistic pre-school programme. Findings also suggested the need for young English pupils to have a broad and balanced early mathematics curriculum with appropriate emphasis being placed on practical problem-solving.

Meanwhile, by the end of Key Stage 1 and again at the end of Key Stage 2 at the endpoint of primary school, children in our English sample with higher mathematical knowledge at 6 years tended to have higher SAT scores at 7 years and 11 years. For the schools and pupils concerned, nothing much happened to disturb the predictive value of mathematical tests taken at around the ages of 5 and 6 years. By the third cycle of ENT, the numerical score was more closely associated than the total score with Key Stage 2 SAT performance. Overall, at Key Stage 1, the data were consistent with the view that the final ENT score was a reasonably good predictor of performance in SATs (see Aubrey and Godfrey 2003).

In general, there appeared to be some consistency in children's performance in mathematics. Children were making some real progress through time in terms of mathematical development and slower progress during the early years was unlikely to be compensated for by faster progress later on. Age-adjusted scores suggested that children who just failed to reach the national Key Stage 2 target of Level 4 and were assigned to Level 3 had on average progressed steadily through the three ENT tests, attaining just below average for their ages. Those who achieved the target on average started off at the appropriate score for their age and made average progress. Those who reached Level 5 at Key Stage 2 on average started higher and made more progress. Children making almost no progress up to the age of 7 years and classified in Key Stage SATs as 'N' were distinguished less by their low starting scores, than by rapid decline during the earliest years of schooling.

Applying a discriminant analysis to each of the eight individual test scores in each cycle of testing at Key Stage 1 indicated that the best prediction of Key Stage 1 SAT levels was achieved by a combination of a relational topic score with a numerical score, together with the general number knowledge topic score. The results for a similar discriminant analysis at Key Stage 2 indicated that general number knowledge remained important but otherwise the topics involved were different.

Children who brought into their Reception year numerical and relational knowledge did appear to be advantaged in terms of their mathematical progress through primary school. Numerical attainment increased in importance across the primary years. While it was beyond the scope of the analysis to speculate about the relationship of this finding to the emphasis on numeracy in the English mathematics curriculum, it was clear that general number knowledge, involving practical problem-solving, remained important across primary schooling. This was noteworthy, given the Brown et al. (2003) finding that English children's scores for word problem-solving may have declined with the introduction of the NNS and its emphasis on numerical calculation.

The findings suggest the importance of a balanced pre-school education between 3 and 5 years. They also suggest that Reception class teachers (for 5-year-olds) will need to monitor their pupils systematically from the beginning of the year, identifying and coaching those with fewer mathematical skills in order to reduce inequality. Without active intervention, it is likely that children with little mathematical knowledge at the beginning of formal schooling will remain low achievers throughout their primary years and, probably, beyond. What this study clearly demonstrates is that the decline starts early on and low attainers simply continue to slip further behind.

It seems reasonable to suppose that pupils' attainments had been influenced by the changes to the English curriculum brought in by the NNS. Furthermore, it would appear that the NNS advantages some pupils more than others, with low attainers being least advantaged. This may well be related to the fast pace of whole-classroom teaching and learning and a curriculum that leaves too little time for consolidation, and too little opportunity for formative assessment that leads to adaptation to the individual needs of learners (Askew and Brown 2004).

We now have a renewed *Primary Framework for Literacy and Mathematics* (DfES 2006) organized into strands (with seven for mathematics). These relate directly to the Curriculum Orders for mathematics at Key Stages 1 and 2 with the Foundation Stage elements mirroring the relevant sections of the Early Learning Goals of the Early Years Foundation Stage (EYFS) (DfES 2007). The EYFS was statutory from September 2008. Problem-solving, reasoning and numeracy is one of the EYFS's six areas of learning and development that are interrelated and must match the development and age of the learner. This area involves children in reasoning and numeracy in a broad range of contexts in which they can 'explore, enjoy, learn and practise', 'making connections, recognising relationships, working with numbers, shapes, space and measures' in learning experiences that 'provide balance between practitioner-led and child-initiated learning' (DfES 2007: 61). Interestingly, while the renewed Primary Framework is intended to 'bring an increased sense of drive and momentum to literacy and mathematics and a clearer set of outcomes to support practitioners in planning for progression and attainment of all children' (DfES 2006: 2), there is also insistence on personalized learning and securing intervention for those children who need it. As noted by Alexander (2004), the deep irony is that the whole-class interactive teaching of the Strategies was intended to exploit commonalities of the group in order to benefit the individuals.

Earlier it was suggested that it was necessary to carry out a qualitative investigation that explored the classroom context and processes of the early mathematics curriculum and the nature of early learning experiences in an attempt to account for the wide variation in attainment that was found in our quantitative study. A number of questions sprang to mind:

- What were Reception teachers views about implementation of the mathematics in Reception classes?
- What sorts of mathematical experiences were offered to young children of 4 to 5 years in Reception classes?
- How did teachers plan and deliver the mathematics curriculum for 4- to 5-year-olds?

To address these questions, a small survey of 32 Reception class teachers was carried out and then three case-study Reception teachers were followed across the year, employing semi-structured observations, target-child observations and analysis of teachers' planning.

Learning and teaching mathematics

Traditionally, research on young children's early mathematical development excludes the context of learning as a source of knowledge. Observations of Reception class practice, it was thought, would take account of the extent to which mathematics is a socially and culturally defined activity and examine the extent to which practitioners helped young children to bring their everyday understanding into the classroom. Perhaps the years of the NNS have served to remind us not to lose sight of *how* children learn mathematics as the focus of attention has switched to *what* they know.

Many studies over the past two decades have described the nature of number learning in the home. Wynn (1998), for example, generated a substantial body of evidence to support her view that human infants come to the world already equipped with the ability to represent and manipulate very small quantities across a range of different kinds of entities perceived through visual or auditory modalities and, hence, determine the numerical relationship between different amounts. Her notion of an 'accumulator' as a model for this inborn mechanism that amounted to pre-verbal counting was dismissed by Sophian (1998), however, who argued in favour of a perception processing or 'subitizing' model that may better account for the rapid enumeration of small arrays of objects that is a mark of young children's early counting (see Threlfall, Chapter 5 and Wright, Chapter 14).

Children's early awareness of the three 'how-to-count' principles of Gallistel and Gelman (1992): the one-to-one correspondence principle, the stable-order of counting principle and the cardinality principle are evoked in different ways by many chapters in this book (see, for example, Maclellan, Chapter 6). Suffice it to say that a number of studies have described the nature of number learning of young children with their carers in the home, documenting age-related changes in the kinds of counting toddlers used as they mapped number words either singly, in conversation, or as part of routine expressions and jingles to play activities with a parent (see Griffiths, Chapter 4), or recording children's mathematical experiences at home and pre-school and adult-mediated number experiences that included reciting to 20, counting in one-to-one correspondence to ten, recognizing small quantities and occasionally recognizing digits.

This is not so very different from what is required of young children in the Early Learning Goals. However, despite the fact that they are bathed in language, communication and literacy experiences throughout their day, the relative infrequency of such mathematical occurrences has been noted by Aubrey et al. (2000) in the home. Gifford (see Chapter 16) has provided humorous accounts of the way young children subvert the best intentions of educators to engage them in mathematical tasks by incorporating these activities in their own games.

Meanwhile, Aubrey (1997) uncovered the mathematical competence that young children actually brought into Reception classes in simple calculations for real problem-solving, while the curriculum emphasizing play and teacher-led work often focused on areas in which children were already competent. When the NNS came along with its emphasis on number knowledge, Hughes et al. (2000) demonstrated how young children in Key Stage 1 had difficulty outside school in using and applying knowledge to novel problems. Key points to notice are that homes and pre-school settings have varied in the mathematical experiences they have provided and in the quality of adult mediation of these tasks. We do know that adult conversations about number are important to very young children and that their existing competence could often be better deployed. A recognition of the importance of encouraging children to apply their numerical knowledge to real problems continues to need emphasis.

Reception class mathematical experiences and curriculum delivery

Meanwhile, if effective mathematics pedagogy in the early years is fostering children's natural interest in numeracy, problem-solving, reasoning, shapes and measures (DCSF 2008: 34), what do these early years practitioners actually do? No claim of exceptionality is made for the 32 Reception class teachers who took part in the survey. They worked in a range of urban, rural and mixed settings with children from a variety of social and cultural groups.

Observations of three practitioners took place across the Reception class year. Just one of these mathematics lessons in term three for each practitioner was video-taped by the researcher for analysis in this chapter. All three practitioners were very experienced and had been teaching for a number of years in schools that were regularly used by students in training for teaching.

Practitioner A taught in an inner-city school with a very socially and culturally mixed intake, the majority of whom had English as an Additional Language (EAL). The Reception intake was taught literacy and numeracy flexibly during the morning in small groups with two practitioners and two bilingual nursery assistants, rotating these four intensive small groups for maximum input. Hence, it was estimated that not more than 5 per cent of the classroom time was spent in whole-class mathematics teaching. The practitioner expressed satisfaction with the FS curriculum, reported daily opportunities for children to engage in informal exploration of numeracy and up to 10 hours a week for spontaneous activities that children had either initiated or chosen for themselves.

On the day of the video-taped lesson, Practitioner A carried out a three-part lesson for the small group that aimed for children to say and use number names in order, in familiar contexts, count reliably up to 10 and 20, recognize numerals 1 to 9, use language like 'more' or 'less', find one more than a number from 1 to 10, and begin to combine two groups of objects.

In the first part of the lesson, children counted the register group, their small group, as well as their heads, noses, mouths, feet and hands, thus beginning to count in twos, and the teacher recorded this. Practitioner A then introduced 'one more than' with dice configurations recorded on a flip chart and the solution demonstrated by children with number keys. In the main part of the lesson, she rolled two large dice in order to continue with the theme 'one more than' with a series of small numbers and recorded this in a similar way. This activity also allowed her to demonstrate that there were 'lots of ways of making numbers' (e.g. six with five and one, four and two, or three and three). Children then moved on to a workbook activity that enabled them to record 'one more than', with numbers one to six represented by dice and numerals, the teacher demonstrating with her big die. She then proceeded to monitor and support children to complete the activity. A short review section at the end recapped the main parts of the lesson.

Practitioner B worked at a semi-rural primary school in a class with predominantly white lower-middle-class children. She too expressed satisfaction with the FS, reported daily opportunities for children to engage in informal exploration of numeracy and up to 10 hours a week for spontaneous activities that children had either initiated or chosen for themselves. She reported integrating the six areas of learning across the timetable in term one and teaching with a mixture of areas of learning, in distinct blocks and in an integrated manner, in terms two and three. She reported teaching a whole-class mathematics lesson for about 40 minutes to 1 hour, daily.

For the observed lesson, she aimed to use language such as 'circle' or 'bigger' to describe the shape and size of solids and flat shapes. Children carried out activities that identified shapes according to concrete examples and according to their properties. In the first part of the three-part lesson, children observed and talked about two-dimensional and three-dimensional shapes (circles, rectangles and triangles; cubes, cylinders, spheres and triangular prisms) that Practitioner B presented and then described. Solid shapes were passed round in a bag with selected children touching and describing a shape to their friends, whose job it was to identify the shape in terms of properties reported. In the main part of the lesson, children built with large and small block shapes, inside and outside, printed with sponge shapes, drew and traced round shapes or made Play-Doh shapes, using solid shape models. A short review provided a recap of the two- and three-dimensional shapes and their properties.

The third practitioner, Practitioner C, worked in a rural context, in a small village with a middle-class intake. She reported teaching the FS areas of learning as a mixture of distinct blocks and integrated across the timetable, over the year. It was reported that up to 15 hours a week were allocated for children to engage in spontaneous activities that they had either initiated or chosen for themselves. Over the year, whole-class work was reported to increase from 6 per cent (terms one and two) to 10 per cent in term three. The elements of the NNS were reported to be implemented flexibly in the first two terms, with the daily maths lesson being introduced in term three.

In the lesson observed, Practitioner C aimed to introduce simple measurement of time and the 'o'clock' time through clock faces, as well as time as a sequence of events across a day. In the first part of the three-part lesson, the teacher demonstrated 'o'clock' time with a clock face and then children worked in pairs with their own clock faces. In the second part of the lesson, children worked in groups. One pair of children demonstrated 'o'clock' time with their own clock faces matched to models presented on cards, while other groups played a number of time games (time bingo and clock face puzzles that involved rolling a die in order to determine which piece of puzzle was added), or they drew numerals on a clock face that was cut out and had moving fingers attached by an adult. The third part of the lesson reviewed time as 'o'clock' and discussed sequences of time through the day.

Conclusion

Effective mathematics pedagogy in the early years is intended to foster children's natural interest in numeracy, problem-solving, reasoning, shapes and measures (DCFS 2008: 34). In fact we found that young English children between the ages of 4 and 5 had been inducted into a three-part numeracy lesson that had covered most of the Early Learning Goals of the FS. They counted everyday objects, recognized and wrote numerals and used language of measure, shape and space. They were beginning to combine two groups of objects to relate to addition. They were counting and recognizing dots arranged in random arrays and domino patterns to exploit, through a range of classroom games, inside and outside. A broad range of contexts and game-like formats were being presented to young children in which they could explore, enjoy, learn, practise and talk about their developing understanding as well as record it formally. These were the important 'foundations for later mathematical learning' (DCSF 2008: 40) being laid in English classrooms. All this was taking place at a time when few other children in Europe have started formal schooling and for which our larger limited longitudinal study could, in practice, find little benefit. But the whole-class teaching contexts that were being introduced before children were even 5 years of age are precisely those that research has shown accentuate initial variations in mathematical attainment rather than decrease them.

Given the likelihood of small improvements being made within the top 10 per cent and a small decline within the lowest 10 per cent, it is worth noting that these Reception class children included both highly privileged and high-achieving children as well as more disadvantaged children with EAL and statemented children with special educational needs. In the circumstances, it is hardly surprising that early achievement was likely to be a major determinant of later success or that particular areas of gain (and loss) were equally likely for particular groups of children. Indeed, their performance *was* likely to be related to the high-quality early teaching experiences they received. Whether or not this amounts to 'international best practice' however is another matter as it is beyond the scope of this chapter to pursue in more detail the nature of the pre-school curriculum and opportunities to learn in the home and through formal education that exist in other countries.

References

Alexander, R.J. (2004) Still no pedagogy? Principle, pragmatism and compliance in primary education, *Cambridge Journal of Education*, 34(1): 7–33.

Askew, M. and Brown, M. (2004) The Impact of the National Numeracy Strategy on mathematics attainment and learning in Year 4. Paper presented at the International Congress of Mathematics Education, Copenhagen, July.

Aubrey, C. (1997) *Mathematics Teaching in the Early Years: An Investigation of Teachers' Subject Knowledge*. London: Falmer Press.

Aubrey, C. and Godfrey, R. (2003) The development of children's early numeracy through Key Stage 1, *British Educational Research Journal*, 29(6): 821–40.

Aubrey, C., Godfrey, R. and Godfrey, J. (2000) Children's early numeracy experiences in the home, *Primary Practice*, 26: 36–42.

Brown, M., Askew, M., Millett, A. and Rhodes, V. (2003) The key role of educational research in the development and evaluation of the National Numeracy Strategy, *British Educational Research Journal*, 29(5): 655–72.

DCSF (Department for Children, Schools and Families) (2008) *Independent Review of Mathematics Teaching in Early Years Settings and Primary Schools* www.publications.teachernet.gov.uk/eOrderingDownload/Williams%20 Mathematics.pdf (accessed August 2008).

DfEE (Department for Education and Employment) (1999) *The National Numeracy Strategy: Framework for Teaching Mathematics from Reception to Year 6*. London: DfEE.

DfEE/QCA (Department for Education and Employment/Qualifications and

Curriculum Authority) (1999) *National Curriculum: Handbook for Primary Teachers in England*. London: DfEE/QCA.

DfES (Department for Education and Skills) (2003) *Excellence and Enjoyment: A Strategy for Primary Schools*. London: DfES.

DfES (Department for Education and Skills) (2006) *Primary Framework for Literacy and Mathematics*. Norwich: DfES.

DfES (Department for Education and Skills) (2007) *Practice Guidance for the Early Years Foundation Stage*. Nottingham: DfES www.publications.teachernet. gov.uk/eOrderingDownload/eyfs_guide12_07.pdf (accessed 31 March 2008).

Earl, L., Watson, N., Leithwood, K. and Fullan, M. (2003) *Watching and Learning 3: Final Report of the External Evaluation of England's National Literacy and Numeracy Strategies*. Toronto: Ontario Institute for Studies in Education.

Gallistel, C. and Gelman, R. (1992) Preverbal and verbal counting and computation, *Cognition*, 44: 43–74.

Harris, S., Keys, W. and Fernandes, C. (1997) *Third International Mathematics and Science Study: Second National Report Part 1*. Slough: NFER.

Hughes, M., Desforges, C. and Mitchell, C. (2000) *Numeracy and Beyond*. Milton Keynes: Open University Press.

Kyriacou, C. and Goulding, M. (2004) *A Systematic Review of the Impact of the Daily Mathematics Lesson in Enhancing Pupil Confidence and Competence in Early Mathematics*. London: DfES/EPPI-Centre: Institute of Education.

OFSTED (2002) *The Curriculum in Successful Primary Schools*. London: OFSTED.

Reynolds, D. and Farrell, S. (1996) *Worlds Apart? A Review of International Surveys of Educational Achievement Involving England*. London: Her Majesty's Stationery Office (HMSO).

Sophian, C. (1998) A developmental perspective on children's counting, in C. Donlan (ed.) *The Development of Mathematical Skills*. Hove: Psychology Press.

Wynn, K. (1998) Numerical competence in infants, in C. Donlan (ed.) *The Development of Mathematical Skills*. Hove: Psychology Press.

SECTION 2
The early stages of number acquisition

In between the publication of the first and second editions of this book, primary schools experienced a period of massive change; they became very different establishments from what they were in the mid-1990s. The introduction of the National Numeracy Project (NNP) in 1996; its development from a 'project' for a few into a 'strategy' for all in 1999; and its transmogrification into the Primary National Strategy (PNS) in 2003 all contributed to the creation of unprecedented changes in the organization and content of mathematics teaching in primary schools. The National Numeracy Strategy *Framework for Teaching Mathematics from Reception to Year 6* shows the extent to which the NNS had been influenced by the plethora of research findings on the importance of counting: as an activity in its own right; as an important constituent of children's mental calculation methods; and as a significant contributor to the development of a child's general number sense. For example, the *Supplement of Examples: Reception* included in the 1999 Framework has a number section that is firmly based on many of the research findings reported in the first edition of this book (probably because the editor actually wrote the first draft of this section of the *Framework!*).

In this, the second section of this book, the three authors write about pre-school or 'early school' numeracy issues. In 2007, government initiatives that had been focusing on services and support for young children and their families culminated in the creation of the Early Years Foundation Stage, an initiative that was concerned with setting the standards for the learning development and care for children from birth to five.

In Chapter 2, Penny Munn argues that it is important to probe children's subjectivity – ascertaining their own view of the world – in order to gather more information about what seems to be a deficit in young children's number logic. Pre-school children appear to have little or no understanding of the adult purpose of counting, which is to find out how many things there are in a collection. Penny argues that early counting is largely an imitative social practice rather than an activity carried out with awareness, and suggests that teachers should assess children's beliefs about counting before involving them in number operations or comparison of quantities. In primary school, children's counting becomes a psycholinguistic tool for the development of their number knowledge. The extent to which they are allowed to use this tool will depend on the teacher's knowledge and beliefs. If counting is seen merely as a skill to be assessed, then teachers will lose the depth and creativity that their mathematics teaching might have had.

In Chapter 3, Kate Tucker argues against the use of prescriptive and unimaginative methods of teaching early years mathematics, specifically the use of commercial worksheets, and recommends replacing the worksheet ethos with a much more creative and playful approach. She provides a brief outline of some significant theories of play and discusses how the process of making connections binds play and creativity. Indeed, some of the key processes integral to play and creativity are the same processes essential for mathematical thinking. Kate argues that if practitioners and teachers promote playful and creative contexts for mathematics teaching, they will also be encouraging their children to develop good mathematical thinking; to have a positive view of the subject; and to perceive themselves as capable mathematicians. She goes on to give some practical examples of how to establish a learning environment that will promote a playful approach to mathematics, both in terms of focused teaching sessions and children's own independent mathematical activity, and she includes some examples of recorded work stimulated by play. Most importantly, children need to engage in play, talk about their play and know that their mathematical play is valued. Not only will this impact positively on their mathematical understanding and development, it will also act to raise the profile of play as a feature of good mathematics teaching.

Rose Griffiths (Chapter 4) looks at the contribution made by family members to children's early learning about counting, and discusses the ways in which children develop their understanding of counting in everyday situations. She describes a research project where children's counting practices at home were filmed, and explores the variety of contexts in which children's skills were extended as they counted toys, apples, fingers and toes, stairs and how many times they swung on a swing. Families are able to provide children with frequent, meaningful and enjoyable opportunities to count over a long period, often only for a few minutes at a time but with a high level of individual attention, in a way that is more difficult to manage in an educational setting. The challenge for practitioners is: to value what families achieve; to use good ideas from home where appropriate in school settings; and to provide support and advice to families, including helping parents and carers to share good ideas from common family practice.

2 Children's beliefs about counting

Penny Munn

Introduction

Teachers of young children will be familiar with the traditional view of early number abilities exemplified by the following excerpt:

> One has only to imagine the difficulties of a child who does not understand conservation. Suppose that such a child counts a bowl of oranges and decides that there are six there, and then someone spreads the oranges out into an extended row. If the child thinks that there are more oranges than before, it follows that the child does not really know what the word 'six' really means.
>
> (Nuñes and Bryant 1996: 6)

This example of the traditional view assumes a basic incompetence in children that lies at the heart of many discussions of what children know (or can learn) about number in the infant school. In recent decades, developmental psychology has moved away from the notion that 'incompetent' children gradually learn to think and act like adults. In the 1960s, the discovery of infants' early abilities to make sense of the world and to influence their carers led to a revision of assumptions about young children's incompetence. A focus on children's abilities rather than their inabilities led to the emergence of a quite different picture of their development. Studies such as those by Donaldson (1978) and her colleagues illustrated how the very experiments designed to illuminate childish thinking can actually produce incompetence in children. An emphasis on naturalistic observation rather than experiment has shown competent children managing their social worlds and honing their intellectual skills on the daily challenges these worlds present (Richards and Light 1986; Dunn 1988). These changes in developmental psychological theory presented a challenge to the Piagetian orthodoxy.

Research into children's number knowledge has followed a similar pattern.

The belief that young children have no understanding of the nature of number has given way to acknowledgement of early competence. Large research programmes have demonstrated young children's ability to deal with the logic of counting, addition and subtraction. Gelman and Gallistel's (1978) seminal studies (see Maclellan, Chapter 6) have shown that 3- and 4-year-olds recognize the principles of counting provided the quantities that they are dealing with are very small (i.e. no more than four). Their findings stimulated large-scale research studies into the developing understanding of number in young children (for a review, see Bryant 1995).

Researchers allege that very young children are competent with number, yet simple observation shows that children miss the most obvious implications of number logic until they are older. How is this contradiction to be resolved? In this chapter, I plan to show how attending to children's subjectivity – to their own view of the world – casts a wholly different light on what looks like a deficit in logic. Anyone's behaviour (whether adult or child) can be misrepresented as illogical if we omit any reference to their personal view, to their beliefs about the world, or to the state of their knowledge. I aim to show that children's behaviour with number can be explained by their beliefs and knowledge about the adult world, and that there is little need to hypothesize any inherent deficit in their ability to think and learn. I also aim to articulate the implication of this view that counting is not an attainment to be checked off a list of basic skills, but a psycholinguistic tool for continued learning in number.

Instead of reviewing the evidence for the 'deficit' view (far too long a task for a chapter such as this), I shall describe just three sources of evidence for deficits in children's early number logic. The first of these purports to show the lack of organizing principles underlying children's counting activity:

1   Young children may sometimes look very proficient at counting, but their performance breaks down when they are asked to count objects in random arrangements or circles. Under these conditions they usually forget where they began counting and count some objects twice.

The second, number conservation, forms the cornerstone of assumptions that children are not competent with number:

2   When asked to judge the similarity of two rows of objects, children rarely count both rows and compare the results to arrive at their judgement. They judge the rows on their visual properties. Consequently, when one row is squashed up in comparison to the other and the children are asked whether they are the same or different, they invariably say that the shorter row contains fewer objects.

The third seems to show that children do not really understand the function of counting because they do not use it spontaneously:

3   Three- and four-year-old children asked to judge the relative quantities in two rows of counters tend to judge by sight. They usually fail to count the rows unless they are specifically prompted to do so by the question 'how many?'.

Considering such overwhelming evidence, how is it possible to assert that young children *really* have an understanding of number? Note that the three examples rest on observations of *external* aspects of the children's behaviour, with only inferences about their beliefs and knowledge states. It is the implicit comparison in these observations with 'rational' behaviour that creates the impression of a deficit in children's thinking, which exists more in our minds than in the child's. Our own actions in counting and estimating are automatic and we know immediately what the 'right' response is. It is easy to conclude that small children have a logical deficit that prevents them from seeing the solution that seems so obvious to us.

How can we distance ourselves from our own very egocentric thinking about children's abilities? First, we should consider number knowledge, not as we experience it ourselves, but as it develops in young children from around 2 years of age. Second, we should include children's subjectivity – their beliefs and knowledge states – in our accounts of their development. Fuson (1988) has written a very detailed account of the development of number concepts and her broad outline of early developments is as follows.

Pre-school children
- Children learn to say the number word sequence. Initially, they imitate the string of words. They are also learning the appropriate contexts for counting.
- Children begin to co-ordinate pointing, objects and number words (see Threlfall, Chapter 5). They count things as an activity in itself.
- Children integrate counting and cardinality: they begin to use their counting to address questions of 'how many?' when they are asked this question (see Maclellan, Chapter 6).

School-age children
- Children begin to count from any point in the chain, not just the beginning (one, two, etc.). This helps 'counting-on' strategies to develop.

- Number words in themselves become countable items for children. This gives them a flexible means of solving addition and subtraction.

For pre-schoolers, in particular, this is not a *single* development in number understanding, but multiple overlapping developments in verbal, motor and cognitive activities that become integrated with each other over time. We know very clearly how children's *actions* towards number change over time. How then do their beliefs change, and what is the relation between their actions and their beliefs? I shall use a longitudinal study of Scottish pre-schoolers and a series of intervention studies of Australian schoolchildren to address these questions.

Beliefs about counting

Before formal instruction in number begins

I shall use the framework of the pre-school number development that Fuson (1988) has outlined to describe some changes in pre-schoolers' counting and beliefs about counting. The data come from a study of Scottish children I followed through the final year of nursery and into the first term of primary school. The children were 51 months old on average when I first visited them in nursery and were 64 months old on average at the final visit, when they were in Primary 1. They attended eight nurseries in the Glasgow area and comprised 25 girls and 31 boys, all but one having English as their first language. I talked to them individually about number and reading at each of four visits, asking them whether they could count and read, and playing a series of games designed to illuminate their understanding of number (see Munn 1994). Three of the questions I asked were: 'Do you count at home? What do you count? Why do you count?' – questions that elicited a description of the children's understanding of counting and their beliefs about this activity.

The children's responses to the questions 'What do you count?' and 'Why do you count?' showed that it was very rare for them to understand the adult purpose of counting before they went to school. After school entry, some children seemed to have gained a little understanding, but it was uncommon to have a child respond to the 'Why?' question by saying 'To know how many'. This was true even for those children who were quite competent at the counting involved in giving nine or ten blocks. They could count in all three senses: saying the words, linking the words with the objects, and linking the last word in the sequence with the amount (see Threlfall, Chapter 5). Yet only one of the children at the pre-school visits responded to the 'Why?' question by replying 'To know the many'. The rest of the children showed by their responses that they were perplexed by the notion of counting as a quantifying activity. One little girl at the first visit (age 48 months) responded to the question 'What do you count at home?' by saying, 'But counting's just saying the words, isn't it?'.

Despite the nature of the children's beliefs about counting, they all said that they *could* count, showing that they believed that to count was to say the words in the correct order. It was only at the visit after school entry (average age 64 months) that some of the children began to say confidently that they counted 'to know how many things they had'. They also began to quote contexts in which they themselves might want to tally objects (in the following, *C* = child, *I* = interviewer):

> C: My mum's pennies – just her pennies.
> I: Why does she count her pennies?
> C: Because she needs to know how many she needs to buy things.
> I: Anything else that you count when you are at home?
> C: Just my teddies and my pens.
> I: Why do you count your teddies and your pens?
> C: To see how many I have got so that I know how many colours I need.

Not all the children were this sophisticated on school entry. There were three categories of reply to the 'What?' question and four categories of reply to the 'Why?' question. When asked *why* they counted at home, children gave answers that fell into one of the following four categories (apart from 'uncodeable' responses, such as conversation switches and obscure reference):

Category 1: Counting to please the self

These responses contained reasons not really connected with counting, or simple assertions of desires:

> Because I want to.
> 'Cos I do.
> So people can sit in them (i.e. the chairs that this child counted).

Category 2: Counting to conform to others' expectations

This group of responses contained reasons that were related to other people's desires for their activity:

> My cousin tells me to.
> Because my mummy and daddy want me to.

Category 3: Counting in order to learn

This group of responses contained explicit references to learning:

'Cos so I can know my numbers.
To learn all my numbers.

Category 4: Counting to know how many there are

It was only this type of response that contained any direct reference to quantification, to knowing how many things there were once one had counted:

To know how many toys there are.

Five of the 56 children gave category 4 responses as a reason for counting. Seven of the children gave category 3 responses and two of the children gave category 2 responses. The remainder were either uncodeable or gave category 1 responses. This distribution of responses suggests that it takes children quite a long time to replace counting as an activity in itself with counting as an activity related to quantification. Those children who said that they counted to learn seemed to be very aware of the role that numbers and counting played in school. They still saw the activity of counting as an end in itself, but as a school activity rather than the play activity it had previously been. After they had started school, the children were more willing to answer the question 'What do you count?', but the variety of responses indicated that children still held beliefs about counting that were at variance with adult beliefs about counting as verbal quantification.

Why was it that these children, who could count and who had number concepts, had such diverse beliefs about the purpose of counting? There is no single feature of their thinking that will explain this. Pre-school children's understanding of other people's mental activity is typically undeveloped. Children's experience of counting games with adults is often simply playful. In playful joint counting the quantitative goal may be absent or may not be made explicit. This, together with young children's natural focus on physical action rather than mental aspects of activity, serves to obscure adult intentions when counting for rather a long time. Children are also dependent on adults for most things and for this reason they have no real need to tally objects, keep score or keep count. Quite the opposite – count words are more likely to have a playful purpose, to be part of a game such as hide-and-seek, or a playful routine with adults or older children. Games of 'How high can I count?' or routines embedded in daily life, such as ritual counting of steps or other landmarks, very rarely have quantification as a central feature.

The diversity of children's beliefs about counting can in itself account for their apparent numerical incompetence – their tendency to count on past the beginning of a circle of objects, to speak as though items change in number when the shape of an array changes, their failure to count spontaneously to solve a quantitative problem. These features of children's lives, and the beliefs consequent on them, may be sufficient in themselves to explain the nature of young children's engagement with the number system. Once children begin to develop quantitative numerical goals for themselves, they will start to generate the logical properties that we automatically associate with number.

There are very clear differences between the pre-school children's actions on the one hand and their beliefs on the other. Although children's counting ability is often extensive and accurate, they have remarkably little sense of the adult definition of counting in the early years. They seem to believe that counting has a playful purpose and they don't really connect it with quantification. There is a clear disjunction between the children's counting behaviour and their beliefs about counting. This indicates that, although the children may implicitly follow some of the principles of counting, early counting is essentially an imitative social practice rather than an activity done with awareness. The point at which their activity begins to change from social practice to self-aware cognitive activity is a point of social transition. For some of the children school entry seems to trigger this change in beliefs about counting; a transition that causes both changes in experience and a transformation in identity.

After formal instruction in number has begun

The early primary stages

In the primary school, children's beliefs about and representations of their own counting processes form a crucial part of their subjective experiences of number. This experience is the source and engine of their intellectual development, and is what we should consider if we are to understand the processes of change during their journey into number understanding. This section of the chapter extends the discussion to include information on subsequent studies of older children's subjective thoughts and experiences of counting; however, these necessarily involve more structured interview methods. As children grow older they rapidly absorb our attitudes towards number and calculation, and learn to keep their innermost thoughts, beliefs and strategies to themselves. A well-designed and sensitively administered interview can provide evidence of their thoughts and beliefs, but I have not included a detailed description of interview methods here. The interested reader can consult the references to discover details of interview design and administration.

During the first two years of primary school, most British children will develop an understanding of number that allows them to move on to using a count-on strategy and to an initial understanding of addition and subtraction. This means moving on from a 'sequence' notion of number to mathematical concepts of numbers – 5 becomes the number that contains 4 and is contained within 6, as well as the number that comes after 4 and before 6. At the same time, children are usually constructing the number word sequence beyond 30, and are beginning to work out the pattern of decade numbers. I say 'constructing' here quite deliberately, because there is a lot of evidence that young children do not rote learn the number sequence. They actively develop and test out hypotheses about the sequence; remember short strings that they learn to repeat in different contexts; and use analogical reasoning of patterns experienced during counting activities to develop their construction of the number word sequence.

The evidence for this active construction lies in the very common patterns of errors seen in English-speaking children. All teachers (and parents) will be familiar with the example of 'twenty ten' as a number commonly generated to fill the space after 29 before children have learned the decade rule, but there are many examples of what I would call 'clever mistakes', that is, mistakes that are evidence of the child's thinking processes in operation. Further examples typical of children learning to count in English are:

> Omission of the decade numbers (e.g. 58, 59, 61 . . . 68, 69, 71 . . .)
> Insertion of incorrect decade number (e.g. 28, 29, 40, 41 . . . 49, 40)
> Confusion of 'teen' and 'ty' endings (e.g. 11, 12, 30, 40, 50, 60 . . .)
> Jumps of a decade or more (e.g. 28, 29, 49, 40, 41)
>
> (Martland 2004)

At first sight, these look like simple errors, but close observation reveals that children listen to themselves counting, and by a process of self-auditing, self-correction and analogical reasoning they separate out the irregularities, learn the less frequent sequence of the '-ty' words, and construct for themselves the repeating decade pattern to 100. When they get to 100 they intuit accurately that the sequence continues from 1 again, and can confidently count 101, 102, 103, 104, 105, 106, 107, 108, 109, without having to have the sequence modelled for them and without having to learn it by imitation. It is at this point, however, that a puzzling error often occurs. Often children at this stage will get to 109, pause, think, and then say triumphantly 'Two hundred!' or (more rarely) 'One thousand!' or 'One million!'. Why would children be clever enough to work out for themselves that the sequence after 100 starts again at 1, and then get stuck on something that they have known for a very long time – the number after 9? Insight into a possible reason for this common pattern comes from a very reflective 6-year-old, who thought aloud while being asked to count in places he had not been before, as illustrated by the following excerpt from the transcript of the video-taped interview:

> Interviewer: (encouraging child to count higher and higher)
> Child: I can count ever so high. I've never been up this high before . . . 89, 90 . . . 99, 100.
> I: What comes next?
> C: (thinks) 101, 102, 103, 104, 105, 106, 107, 108, 109.
> I: What comes next?
> C: I don't know.
> I: Can you work it out?

C: I don't know. It seems as though it should be 10 but it can't be 10 because we're up ever so high now, past a hundred, and 10 is right back at the beginning. It must be 200 next.

In this remarkably articulate response, this child shows clearly that he is not only bringing his reasoning and pattern recognition skills to this problem, but also his beliefs about where '10' belongs in the pantheon of numbers. At this stage of constructing his representation, he cannot believe that 10 has a role 'up among the hundreds', a number place he has never visited before, so he selects a more obvious candidate – the next 'hundred' along in the sequence. His response shows that he is aware of the way the 'hundreds' sequence is ordered, even if he is not yet clear about its precise location in the sequence. The interplay between these two aspects of children's representations of the number word sequence – ordering and location – is a theme that we will revisit in the next section when we consider later developments of the representation of the sequence.

At this stage of development, children are often still counting by ones when they use the number word sequence to solve arithmetical problems. At the early primary stages, this is entirely appropriate as children will be unable to use the structure of the sequence reliably until they have a semantically based representation of it. However, the count-by-ones strategy can be a tender trap for children who become proficient in its use. It can offer the certainty of a correct answer (particularly if props such as number lines are readily available) but the strategy itself does not give children the subjective experiences required to develop a semantically based representation of the sequence.

Children need this kind of representation in order to develop more advanced calculation strategies. At this point, if they explore and play with their representation of the number word sequence they often make more errors than if they had played safe and stuck with their count-by-ones strategies. These are further examples of 'clever mistakes' since they involve further exploration of the count sequence and a search for pattern and order that will be integrated into the semantic representation of the number word sequence. However, if children are made to feel stupid for making clever mistakes then they may well give up the intellectual search and opt for safe strategies that bring them teacher approval. At this stage, a learning environment that encourages risk-taking and intellectual search is far more conducive to good early number development than one which emphasizes getting the right answer and remembering number bonds correctly.

The later primary stages

After children have moved on from the early stages of informal learning, their beliefs about counting play a central role in the way they direct their own learning. At this later age, however, the psychology of their learning is slightly more complicated than at earlier ages. By the time children are working to construct the complexities of the number word sequence beyond 100, the learning context has usually moved away from the group counting aloud that characterizes initial number learning. The children's strategies for solving problems with counting have in most cases moved beyond the simple count-by-ones strategies common in the early primary stages, and exploration of the higher ranges of the number sequence now takes place with a lot of skipping of detail. This aspect of group number learning may in itself cause a barrier for slower developing children, who typically get stuck with the count-by-ones strategies. They are in danger of developing a representation of the number sequence that is purely verbal, and that does not have the same semantic underpinnings found in faster developing children. So, for instance, they may be able to recite the decade sequence but will struggle with more complex problems such as counting forward by tens from 73 or backward by tens from 173 (see Ellemor-Collins and Wright 2007a; Ellemor-Collins et al. 2007b).

For this kind of problem, a semantically based representation of the number sequence that embodies aspects of both ordering and location is required. At this stage, children have usually been taught about place value and will typically use the information in written representations of number to aid their thinking (see Thompson, Chapter 11). Their conceptual understanding of multi-digit addition and subtraction, for instance, is very much based on the way their representation of the number word sequence has developed, and on the informal counting strategies that are embodied in their sequence at the semantic level. At this level of arithmetic, sequence-based (jump) strategies develop from informal counting strategies and are associated with fewer errors. By contrast, collections-based (split) strategies can be prone to error as the physically based 'place' that gives meaning to individual numerals can easily slip from children's memory while they are engaged with the problem (see Figure 2.1).

In normally-attaining children, a balanced use of these strategies is evident, with the strategy being chosen according to context (problem type, task demand, social situation, etc.). However, low-attaining children often do not develop the sequence-based strategies that emerge from thinking about whole numbers. This is a shame, as the use of the whole first number provides both number sense and continuity with early number strategies. Instead, they often use the collections-based strategies that use place to give mathematical meaning to individual numerals. By so doing, they not only leave themselves open to frequent errors, but also restrict their subjective experiences of working with number. In terms of this subjective experience, if they treat the numerals as single-digit numbers with added place rules, then they are experiencing only the numbers from 1 to 9. This impoverished experience will have a predictable effect on the development of their semantic representation of the number word sequence. By contrast, children who often use the 'jump' strategy are having many subjective experiences of numbers beyond 10, and these experiences will add to the development of their semantic representation of the

23 + 16	
Jump (sequence based) strategies	Split (collections based) strategy
23 + 10 = 33; 33 + 6 = 39	20 + 10 = 30; 3 + 6 = 9; 30 + 9 = 39
23 + 6 = 29; 29 + 10 = 39	

45 + 19 = 64	
Jump (sequence based) strategies	Split (collections based) strategy
45 + 10 = 55; 55 + 5 = 60; 60 + 4 = 64	40 + 10 = 50; 5 + 9 = 14; 50 + 10 + 4 = 64
45 + 9 = 54; 54 + 10 = 64	

Figure 2.1   'Jump' (sequence-based) and 'split' (collections-based) strategies.

number sequence. Developing a semantic representation of the number sequence to underpin sequence-based strategies is therefore very important for low-attaining children. They will find it difficult to integrate sequence-based and collections-based strategies while they are not actively developing a semantically based number word representation.

There are two broad aspects to the representation of the number sequence beyond 100 – the ordering of the numbers with respect to each other and their location with respect to the structure of number: the repeating pattern of ones, tens, hundreds and thousands. Rapid ordering calls on judgements of relative size, and relies on an integration of ones, tens, hundreds and thousands in the counting sequence. Rapid location, by contrast, is dependent on a child's sense of the structure of the number line – the repeating and intercalated pattern of ones, tens, hundreds and thousands. A child with a good sense of this structure will, for example, be able to decide quickly that 98 is very close to 100, and locate 98 accurately on a number line. A child without such a sense of sequence will quickly identify that 98 is more than 95, but may not be so accurate in locating the number precisely on an empty number line ranging from 1 to 100 (see Wright et al. 2006 for examples).

While there are many aspects of children's knowledge of number that can be changed at this stage through teaching, the issue of belief about counting is still central. The child who believes that counting is the only mathematical tool available to solve number problems will be disadvantaged. The child who can use counting as an optional tool, and who can strategically deploy a range of tools, will be in a much stronger position to develop more complex ideas as the maths curriculum unfolds.

Implications for teaching and learning

Before formal instruction in number begins

It would be a mistake to regard the early stage of understanding as a stage which should be left behind as soon as possible, to be replaced as quickly as possible with 'correct' notions of number. Pressure on learning in the early stages is likely to result in a dip in ability as children move towards more complex mathematical thinking later in their primary career. At the early stages, children need to develop their thinking in a leisurely fashion rather than be locked into 'correct' mathematical concepts that are unsuited to their thinking. There are indirect links between the primitive 'sequence' thinking about number and the later-appearing sequential number representation. It should be apparent by now that a properly constructed, semantically based representation of the number word sequence is a foundation that will support children's development for a number of years. An investment of time, patience and creative maths teaching in the early years will pay off three or four years later as children embark on the mathematical thinking that begins to be required of them in the upper primary school. The concept that is central to such teaching is that of counting as being the child's tool for learning number rather than just as a skill to be acquired.

The approach suggested here contrasts strongly with methods that train children in counting and number. Rather than providing positive reinforcement for counting, an effective early years approach rests on the insight that children's beliefs are central to their intellectual development. In the early years four activities can lead young children into quantitative counting: monitoring beliefs; taking children's counting seriously; talking about goals when counting; and stimulating the development of children's numerical goals. The aim of these strategies is to manage children's beliefs so that they naturally move towards quantitative counting.

1 Assess children's beliefs about counting before working on addition, subtraction or comparison of quantities.   One of the main features of young children's behaviour with number is that they do not count where it would be useful for them to do so. The argument presented in this chapter is that this is related to their belief that counting is playful rather than quantitative. Since any sort of comparison, addition or subtraction will involve counting, it makes sense to check whether children believe there is a relation between counting and quantification before commencing any activities with a numerical goal. If children do not have this belief then the activity's presentation can be modified accordingly.

2 Take young children's counting seriously.   Counting without quantification is not necessarily meaningless, and is certainly not meaningless to small children. The purely verbal counting seen in young children has received particularly bad publicity because it has been seen as a trap for the unwary teacher who might otherwise attribute far too much number knowledge to young children. However, it would do very little harm to loosen the criteria for what counts as using number. Young children's counting often has a social rather than a numerical goal. For instance, children may recite the number sequence to imitate an admired family member, to show that they can count, or to take part in a well-established ritual. It is important not to negate non-numerical counting, as it can provide a point of contact with a child's social being. Adults also have count sequences with a purely social goal. Take, for example, the teacher who says, 'I want quiet please! One, two, three, four, five!' This is every bit as much a social and ritual use of the number sequence as the young child's counting. So, too, is much of the adult's counting that takes place in the home as a means of informal teaching. Such counting provides a framework for the development of properly numerical counting and as such it should be gently encouraged. Conversations with children about 'big' numbers also have a social rather than a purely numerical goal. As with counting, these should be encouraged.

3 Make the purpose of counting explicit for children. We often assume that our purposes and goals are clear to others so much so that it is often a surprise to discover that children do not understand why we are doing quite simple things. If activities with counting are presented in contexts where adult goals can be mused on out loud, then children will have more chance of grasping the mental aspect of the activity that they see. Dramatic activities in which the characters 'think out loud' in everyday contexts are good for providing children with explicit knowledge of other people's goals, and most nursery teachers are adept at using storybooks and puppets in such a broadly educational way.

4 Stimulate children to develop their own numerical goals. Much of young children's failure to count is related to the lack of numerical goals embedded in their lives. They rarely compare, tally to enumerate, or form an intention to check, and so quantitative counting simply does not form part of their behavioural repertoire. As children mature, they may adopt some of their parents' goals – particularly in relation to money – or they may develop goals of their own related to sharing or to getting things just right. A numerical agenda that comes from the child's own life will be a more powerful stimulator of counting than any adult-imposed goal. One little boy told me that he usually counted the yoghurts in the fridge when he got home from school, because every day his mother pretended that she had eaten some of them while he had been away. This kind of game is much more effective as a number lesson than helping to lay the table, because it engages the child's personal wants and needs. It illustrates the way in which helping children to develop their own numerical goals can be radically different from imposing an adult numerical goal.

After formal instruction in number has begun

There are two key strategies that should underpin formal instruction in number, and these take into account the way in which number development can best be supported over the long term. Both strategies assume that children's maths ability is a part of their social identity rather than a decontextualized skill that they 'possess'. The first strategy is simply to make sure that children are engaged at an appropriate level. Maths is not learned by repetition and memorization, but by deep thinking. The second strategy is to value mistakes as learning opportunities and create an environment in which children find intellectual risk-taking to be enjoyable and rewarded.

In the infant and early primary years, most children are developing their representations of the number sequence. They are also beginning to move beyond the count-by-ones strategies that are linked to a relatively unstructured representation of the number word sequence. At this stage, children need to be encouraged to experience and think about the numbers beyond 30. The teacher should find ways of engaging children with their maths work at a challenging level; if they find it an unpleasant endurance trial, then something is wrong. The teacher should take the time to understand what children are saying and allow children to take risks in their search for number patterns and interesting strategies. 'Mistakes' should be carefully considered and the teacher should create a classroom environment that helps children to view their own and others' errors as interesting discussion points rather than as embarrassing evidence of stupidity (see Thompson, Chapter 15). Such a classroom will allow children's intrinsic motivation to guide their learning and release early maths from the constraints of searching for and memorizing the 'right' answer.

Given ideal learning conditions in the early years, children will develop a well-structured, semantically based representation of the number sequence and will find maths challenging and interesting, even though they may still have problems and misunderstandings. Without a strong early foundation children whose development has halted at the count-by-ones stage, or who have a poorly structured representation of the number sequence (these two things are often linked) will struggle with maths, and teachers will find it hard to help them. Even if such children can pass tests, they will find it hard to memorize facts that they cannot understand intuitively, and they will often use inappropriate strategies. Procedurally learned strategies are unlikely to extend learning experiences for such children and can make maths difficult and unpleasant for them. Interested and caring teachers can use a range of teaching methods to help low-attaining children develop sequence-based strategies. These teachers may also use current research output to understand the thinking that determines low-attaining children's strategy use, and to provide suitable experiences that will extend their learning. Teaching strategies based on such understanding can also be used to include low-attaining children in whole-class activity, so that their mathematical experiences can be extended by discussion.

At all stages, teachers can benefit from an increased awareness of the ways in which children use counting to develop their ideas about number. The potential to use counting as a learning tool means that children's beliefs about counting play a key role in their learning. If children believe that learning in maths is about memorizing procedures and guessing the right answer, then they are unlikely to develop a deep understanding of number. Sometimes it is clever for children to make mistakes and sometimes a clever response by the teacher to mistakes can help to make the children's subjective experiences the object of a classroom maths discussion. Such classroom environments will help children advance to higher levels of understanding in mathematics.

References

Bryant, P. (1995) Children and arithmetic, *Journal of Child Psychology and Psychiatry*, 36(1): 3–32.

Donaldson, M. (1978) *Children's Minds*. London: Fontana.

Dunn, J. (1988) *The Beginnings of Social Understanding*. Oxford: Blackwell.

Ellemor-Collins, D. and Wright, R.J. (2007a) Assessing pupil knowledge of the sequential structure of numbers, *Educational and Child Psychology*, 24(2): 54–63.

Ellemor-Collins, D., Wright, R.J. and Lewis, G. (2007b) Documenting the knowledge of low-attaining 3rd- and 4th-graders: Robyn's and Bel's sequential structure and multidigit addition and subtraction, in J. Watson and K. Beswick (eds) *Proceedings of the 30th Annual Conference of the Mathematics Education Research Group of Australasia*, Vol. I, pp. 265–74, Sydney: MERGA.

Fuson, K.C. (1988) *Children's Counting and Concepts of Number*. New York: Springer-Verlag.

Gelman, R. and Gallistel, C.R. (1978) *The Child's Understanding of Number*. Cambridge, MA: Harvard University Press.

Martland, J.R. (2004) Non-standard responses in the utterance of the Forward Number Word Sequences and Number Word After tasks in the range 1 to 112. Paper presented at the NCTM Research Pre-session, San Antonio, Texas.

Munn, P. (1994) The early development of literacy and numeracy skills, *European Early Childhood Education Research Journal*, 2(1): 5–18.

Nuñes, T. and Bryant, P. (1996) *Children Doing Mathematics*. Oxford: Blackwell.

Richards, M. and Light, P. (eds) (1986) *Children of Social Worlds*. Oxford: Blackwell.

Wright, R.J., Stanger, G., Stafford, A. and Martland, J. (2006) *Teaching Number in the Classroom with 4- to 8-year-olds*. London: Sage Publishing.

3   Mathematics through play

Kate Tucker

Introduction

The education of our primary school children is very much target driven, with undoubted pressure on children to achieve good results in their Standard Assessment Tasks. As a result of this, bookshops are awash with Key Stage revision guides and brightly coloured mathematics booklets aimed at early years children. Many of these publications 'teach' mathematics by posing closed questions while at the same time demanding that children respond by colouring in and filling in boxes. This gives a clear message to parents and children alike that it is the product, and not the process, that is important in the doing of mathematics. Traditionally, this 'right or wrong' approach is how mathematics teaching has been perceived. It is less well associated with play. The importance of the role of play in the development of mathematical skills and concepts is clearly expressed in the Primary National Strategy's *Primary Framework for Literacy and Mathematics* (DfES 2006: 4), where we are informed that 'The development of mathematical understanding should include the use of stories, songs, games and imaginative play'.

Young children in the home meet mathematical concepts every day and operate in rich mathematical contexts even before they set eyes on a maths worksheet. One of the most powerful, self-motivating contexts for mathematics in the home and in the child-care setting is play. It is play that can provide meaningful links between those fundamental early experiences and statutory schooling. Undoubtedly, play is enjoyable for young children owing to the freedom it facilitates; the sense of ownership it affords and the self-esteem it promotes. It is through play that children can repeat, rehearse and refine skills, displaying what they know and understand, and can practise what they are coming to terms with.

Research and play

There is a wealth of research concerned with the notion of play – some aspects of which have directly influenced the teaching of mathematics. One of the most well known is that of Piaget whose constructivist theory suggests that active learning, first-hand experience and motivation are catalysts for cognitive development. He sees learning as developing through clearly defined ages and stages, where there is a continuum from functional play, through symbolic play, to play with rules. Piaget's theories, now well critiqued, have nevertheless influenced teachers in the past (see Munn, Chapter 2).

While Piaget's research focuses on the development of the child in social isolation, the work of Vygotsky (1978) emphasizes the significance of social interaction and the use of language. The social interaction of children with their peers and adults, through which, he argues, children create meaning from shared experience, is crucial to his social constructivist theory. Learning, he contends, occurs in the 'zone of proximal development', which represents the difference between what the child knows and what the child can learn with the assistance of a 'more knowledgeable other'. Play with others, therefore, can provide these 'zones' because of the meaningful and motivating contexts in which they occur.

Bruner (1991) regarded play as a vehicle for socialization and saw the practitioner as someone who could support the child's learning by providing a 'scaffold'. The influence of his 'spiral curriculum', where children revisit play materials and activities over time, using them differently at each encounter as their stage in development dictates, can be seen in the mathematics section of the Primary National Strategy's *Primary Framework for Literacy and Mathematics* (DfES 2006).

Smilansky and Shefatya (1990) also concerned themselves with play and the social context. They defined socio-dramatic play as play that requires interaction, communication and co-operation, and which allows children to test out ideas and concepts, unlike dramatic play, where a child might play alone and not have these opportunities. They argued that socio-dramatic play could be enhanced by the support of a sensitive adult who could work alongside the children in role, thus offering 'play tutoring'. Such role play acts to draw together experiences and knowledge, thereby enabling the child to make meaningful links between these facets. The provision of a shop, café or office in the early years classroom is therefore validated, in that these are the very contexts in which specific mathematical concepts, such as counting and the use of money, can be explored meaningfully.

The *Statutory Framework for the Early Years Foundation Stage* (DfES 2007: 11) fully endorses play when it stipulates that: 'All the areas (the six covered by the early learning goals) must be delivered through planned, purposeful play, with a balance of adult-led and child-initiated activities'. However, there is often a feeling in schools that managers demand that play should have specific learning outcomes in order for it to be validated. Play is often seen as out of kilter with target-setting and the demands of a challenging curriculum. However, not only is teaching and learning through play advocated in this early years initiative, it is argued that it improves the quality of learning and raises standards if the provision is well planned and evaluated. Indeed, play has several important functions in mathematical development as it promotes an understanding of the cultural role of mathematics along with the varied activities in which it has a significant part. Lewis (1996) suggests that during play children might be at any time engaged in:

- making decisions;
- imagining;
- reasoning;
- predicting;
- planning;
- experimenting with strategies;
- recording.

These processes, integral to play, are also essential for mathematical thinking.

Play and creativity

Creativity is a key component of young children's learning. Fawcett (2002) acknowledges that creativity comprises four main aspects: imagination, purpose, originality and value, and presents her own definition of creativity in young children. She argues that children are likely to be creative when they:

- show curiosity;
- use ideas and experiences;
- make new connections through play;
- evaluate the process.

The notion of making connections between experiences, and making connections between aspects of mathematics itself, is fundamental to the mathematical development of young children. When children encounter a new experience they are better placed to understand and make meaning of it if it can be linked to previous meaningful experiences. Haylock and Cockburn (2003) argue that in order to understand the mathematical concepts of number and number operations, for example, children must build up a network of connections between four types of mathematical experience: manipulating concrete objects, symbols, language and pictures.

Play situations can provide the very context in which mathematical vocabulary and symbols can be introduced and in which the child can practise their use without fear of failure but with a sense of ownership. The child is therefore more likely to understand these mathematical ideas more easily at a later stage because of the meaningful connections that have been made. If we interpret 'pictures' as an arrangement that a young child might make with small-world objects or blocks, and 'symbols' as their own mathematical marks, then play contexts could be extremely meaningful in the learning of mathematics (see Carruthers and Worthington, Chapter 10). Play not only acts to increase connections between experiences and separate pieces of mathematical knowledge, but it also widens children's perception of mathematics and helps create a positive attitude to the subject (Holton et al. 2001).

Creativity and making connections between different experiences are significant features in the *Statutory Framework for the Early Years Foundation Stage* (DfES 2007). This document states that none of its six areas of learning and development should be delivered in isolation, but that they are equally important and are interdependent in terms of balanced child development. Similarly, in its description of the educational programme of creative development, it makes specific reference to the importance of links with mathematics, along with other learning areas. This at once highlights the significance of making connections between experiences, and crucially, illustrates that creativity extends well beyond the paintbrush and dressing-up box into the world of mathematics, design and technology.

The *Primary Framework for Literacy and Mathematics* (DfES 2006) outlines how its effective implementation will be characterized by making teaching and learning vivid and real, and acknowledges the importance of making links between experiences, curriculum areas and areas of learning. Surely then this implies that the process of play and the provision of playful context is a necessary element of mathematics education. While the *Framework* acknowledges that the three-part daily mathematics lesson still has a place within a range of teaching strategies, it also encourages pedagogical choice and flexibility in order to ensure that the teaching style is appropriate for the children being taught. If teachers and practitioners, therefore, deem that their children will learn mathematics through play, and research suggests that the children will, then its provision is fully endorsed.

Children will be creative when they are involved in good quality play; when there is the opportunity for them to pursue their ideas; and when they are given time to review and evaluate their experience. They benefit greatly from practitioner- and child-initiated play, and indeed a balance of both is most effective (DfES 2007). Play will take place during practitioner-intensive activity, where the practitioner works with a group of children addressing a specific learning objective, and also during independent activities. This is summarized in Figure 3.1 'Mathematical activity'.

It would be considered good practice and in accordance with both the *Statutory Framework for the Early Years Foundation Stage* (DfES 2007) and the *Primary Framework for Literacy and Mathematics* (DfES 2006) to ensure that mathematics is taught in a meaningful and stimulating context, whether teaching Foundation Stage or Year 2 children. This might be achieved by linking all areas of the learning environment, both inside and outside the school, by a common theme or by the children's interest. If the children are enjoying their observations of minibeasts and springtime, for example, it would be much more meaningful for them if the learning contexts were linked. This might involve: small worlds containing toy minibeasts and plant pots; play-tray 'ponds' with coloured water, toy pond creatures and fishing nets; and seed catalogues that could be made in the graphics area. Focused teaching sessions could also use the very same resources to help solve some related mathematical problem. The skill of the practitioner is to 'advertise' mathematical ideas or problems to be pursued independently in the learning environment while the practitioner engages in focused teaching of smaller groups and observes independent play. Of course, some children will develop their own line of enquiry and play when they are engaged independently, but if the environment is well planned, with varied and interesting resources to count, it is highly likely that the environment will be buzzing with maths talk and exploration.

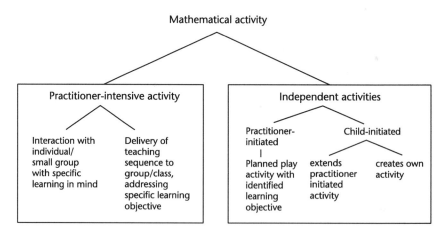

Figure 3.1 Mathematical activity.[1]

The mathematical learning environment

The *Primary Framework for Literacy and Mathematics* (DfES 2006: 4) states that 'The development of mathematical understanding should include the use of stories, songs, games and imaginative play'. The learning environment has a very significant role to play in a child's learning. While the physical environment needs to be planned carefully to ensure a rich context for mathematical exploration, the emotional environment should maintain an ethos that promotes and values independent mathematical play. If the learning environment is mathematical, then mathematics happens (Worthington and Carruthers 2003). Practitioners need to audit their provision of learning contexts, such as play-trays, small-world play, malleable material area, and so on, to ensure that they present mathematical possibilities, and motivate and challenge the young learner. There are many diverse and varied ways in which these learning contexts can become imaginative and creative environments for mathematical play and which offer meaningful links with other areas of learning and curriculum (Tucker 2005). A few suggestions follow.

Play-trays

Play-trays offer young children fantastic opportunities to explore varied, fluid media and provide strong links between mathematics and science. By providing children with peat, cocoa-pods, pea gravel, corn, pasta and rice, among other things, they can explore pouring, emptying and filling sacks, plant pots and other related containers. This provides children not only with opportunities to explore capacity, to count and investigate number, but also to explore the texture and properties of different media. With imagination, green water, with the inclusion of toy animals, can become a pond with creatures to catch in nets. This opens all sorts of mathematical possibilities such as counting creatures in ones, twos, fives, tens and exploring mathematical operations.

Small worlds

This specific type of role play allows children to engage in imaginary play on a miniature scale and it provides excellent links with geography. These play contexts encourage the use of purposeful positional and spatial language as the children move and place the small-world objects with the purpose of acting out their narrative. Children can create their worlds with twigs, leaves, unit blocks, toy vehicles and animals, once again opening up opportunities for counting, ordering, and making repeating patterns.

Role play

The key to successful role play is the provision of time, space and open-ended resources. The key to successful mathematical role play is to allow children the freedom to explore mathematical vocabulary and re-enact mathematically rich situations. Role play rich in mathematics is not dependent on having a cash till, price tags and coins. It is more likely to depend on the practitioner's frequent modelling of mathematical vocabulary, written numerals and standard symbols, and on explanations of methods for calculation in meaningful contexts, both in play and during everyday routines. Good role-play areas do not have to look like theatrical sets to be successful, but they do need to facilitate children's own selection of resources to count and to use as tokens. They need resources with which they can write meaningful mathematical graphics in order to make meaningful connections with other experiences, develop their narrative, and practise and refine their skills.

Graphics area

This area provides a seamless link with literacy. It is here that children can make their own menus, shopping lists, cards, price tags and explore the number system by making their own number lines. Good-quality mathematical activity in the graphics area demands a rich supply of writing materials and both numbered and empty number lines. As with role play, it also relies on 'more knowledgeable others' modelling the use of mathematics in this context.

Light box and mirror box

These learning contexts provide good links with science and art. With the right type of objects, such as coloured acetate, shiny buttons and 'jewels' and coloured perspex shapes, the context provides children with opportunities to create and discuss simple repeating patterns, count, order for size and shape and explore symmetry and properties of shapes.

Display

Displays of recorded work following a practitioner-intensive activity have little, if any, impact on the mathematical culture in the learning environment. The most successful displays are those that are interactive. These can be either 2D or 3D and involve children in daily discussion about, for example, what has changed from the previous day, the meaning of the information it displays, or the repeating pattern it presents. Children can also be given ownership of the display space where they are free to exhibit their own mathematical graphics, whether it be their own independent mathematical investigation, number lines made in the graphics area, or mathematical graphics made during role play. This can be a powerful means of supporting the child's self-esteem, enabling them to perceive themselves as competent mathematicians, and also acts to raise the profile of play and independent mathematical activity.

Using number, counting and play

Children learn to count by developing and practising skills through their involvement in a wide range of experiences during which they use the language of number and comparison. The role of the practitioner is to provide many interesting objects for children to engage with, both like and unlike, to give them the opportunity to practise and refine their counting skills.

Counting collections

Children are often drawn to baskets and boxes of coloured glass beads, buttons and 'jewels' to feel, explore and count. Children themselves can collect natural materials such as acorns, conkers, pine cones and shells, all of which are ideal for counting and which provide obvious links with geography and science. Large counting collections enable children to readily explore the equivalence of number and to count in twos, fives and tens. Strategic placing of such counting collections in the learning environment encourages children to count chosen objects spontaneously for the sheer delight of handling and exploring different attractive materials. It also enables them to select materials freely for their use in their role play or other independent mathematical activity.

Number lines

There has in the past been a tendency to over-emphasize the cardinal nature of number at the expense of meaningful exploration of its ordinal nature (Haylock and Cockburn 2003). The use of number lines in the teaching of mathematics is crucial if children are to have a real understanding of the number system and go on to use and apply number with confidence and competence. Children's use of number lines in their play and in self-initiated mathematical investigations can be both extensive and impressive if they are accustomed to seeing them used in meaningful mathematical activity (Worthington and Carruthers 2003).

There are many different manifestations of number lines and it is useful if children see and use a variety: numbered and empty; large enough to jump along; small enough to hold; fixed or permanent; and easily transportable

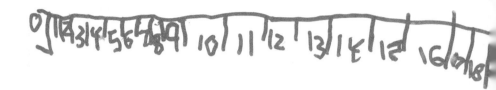

Figure 3.2   Number line made by a Reception child following playful activity.

from one place to another in the learning environment. Figure 3.2 shows a number line made independently by a Reception child in the graphics area. This followed his participation in a counting game with his practitioner during which children jumped from zero to ten along a large floor number line. The child then developed his own play along the number line with some of his peers, experimenting with some of the ideas they had seen in the focused teaching session. It was these experiences in a playful context that motivated him to make his own number line independently in the graphics area. It also gave his practitioner the opportunity to assess the full extent of his mathematical understanding.

Mathematical operations

From early Foundation Stage children can explore and experiment with different structures of the four mathematical operations: addition, subtraction, multiplication and division. Sometimes there is an over-emphasis on some structures to the exclusion of others (Haylock and Cockburn 2003), such as the combination of collections as an addition structure and take-away as subtraction. Indeed, division and multiplication are not readily explored in the early years.

Figure 3.3 shows the mathematical graphics of a nursery child who spontaneously recorded her 'maths story' after small-world play. The child had developed her play with some woodland toys and introduced pine cones as 'food'. She had shared out six cones between a mole, owl and snake. In her later discussion with her practitioner she explained that it was 'fair' that each animal had the same number. Without such discussion, her graphics would have been difficult to interpret, and worse still, their mathematical significance might have been misunderstood or overlooked. The quality of her play,

Figure 3.3 Nursery child's pictorial recording of her small world play.

her use of language and the freedom she had to select her writing materials and talk to her practitioner revealed her clear mathematical thinking. The *Independent Review of Mathematics Teaching in Early Years Settings and Primary Schools* argues that:

> Early years settings should ensure that sufficient time is given to mathematical discussion around practical activities such as play with vehicles outside, cooking, shopping and constructing. To be effective,

mathematical learning for children in this age group needs to be predominantly social in nature and rooted in these play activities.

(DCSF 2008: 36)

Figure 3.4 illustrates some recorded work of a Year 2 child following his
small-world play. His teacher had provided a play-tray with small logs, pine
cones and 14 toy minibeasts, with the learning intention that the children
would use the minibeasts to explore repeated addition as a form of multiplication. During the child's playful investigation, he explored how the minibeasts
could travel along the logs in different ways, developing a narrative around his
actions. His investigation in a playful context enabled him to create meaningful images by placing the minibeasts in twos, and it promoted the use of
associated mathematical language. His subsequent picture illustrates the
connections he made between experience, image and symbols.

Implications for teaching and learning

Undoubtedly, it is the _process_ of play that is important. Mathematical play
provides a non-threatening context where incorrect answers are not perceived
as mistakes but as solutions that might lead to a better understanding of
the aspect of mathematics to which they relate (Holton et al. 2001). Play is

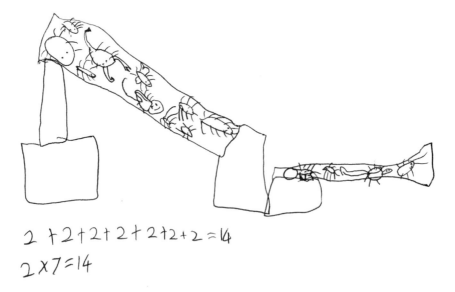

$$2 + 2 + 2 + 2 + 2 + 2 + 2 = 14$$
$$2 \times 7 = 14$$

Figure 3.4   Mathematical recording of a Year 2 child's small world exploration of repeated
addition.

explicitly endorsed in the *Statutory Framework for the Early Years Foundation Stage* (DfES 2007) and in the *Primary Framework for Literacy and Mathematics* (DfES 2006: 103). The latter argues that 'Play underpins all development and learning for young children'. Teachers and practitioners should therefore feel encouraged to work to create a culture in which children feel confident to try, take risks, operate independently and ultimately develop mathematical self-esteem. In order to facilitate this, changes may well be needed in class management.

Practitioners in the Foundation Stage need to ensure a balance of child- and practitioner-initiated play, but teachers throughout the primary school need to provide an informed balance of focused teaching and independent mathematical activity in a playful context. This has implications for the management of time during the lesson. Making provision for children to talk about what they are doing in the learning environment is crucial (Fisher 2002). Children need time to talk about their mathematical play, to review and evaluate it, and teachers need to listen. If teachers and practitioners can plan for time during which they can listen to children, they can scaffold learning by asking open questions; model mathematical language; clarify any misconceptions the child might have; and help prepare the way ahead for further play. This will also act to enhance the profile of mathematical play itself. Perhaps in the early years and throughout primary school, we as teachers and practitioners should have the courage to abandon the worksheet and embrace the process of play, thus raising its profile as an integral feature of good mathematics teaching.

References

Bruner, J. (1991) The nature and uses of immaturity, in M. Woodhead, R. Carr and P. Light (eds) *Becoming a Person*. London: Routledge/Open University Press.

DCSF (Department for Children, Schools and Families) (2008) *Independent Review of Mathematics Teaching in Early Years Settings and Primary Schools* www.publications.teachernet.gov.uk/eOrderingDownload/Williams%20Mathematics. pdf (accessed June 2008).

DfES (Department for Education and Skills) (2006) *Primary Framework for Literacy and Mathematics*. Norwich: DfES.

DfES (Department for Education and Skills) (2007) *Statutory Framework for the Early Years Foundation Stage*. London: Department for Education and Skills.

Fawcett, M. (2002) Creativity in the early years: children as 'authors and inventors' (a non-paginated discussion paper insert), *Early Education* (38).

Fisher, J. (2002) *Starting from the Child*. Milton Keynes: Open University Press.

Haylock, D. and Cockburn, A. (2003) *Understanding Mathematics in the Lower Primary Years*. London: Paul Chapman Publishing.

Holton, D., Ahmed, A., Williams, H. and Hill, C. (2001) On the importance of mathematical play, *International Journal of Mathematical Education in Science and Technology*, 32(3): 401–15.

Lewis, A. (1996) *Discovering Mathematics with 4- to 7-Year Olds*. London: Hodder & Stoughton.

Smilansky, S. and Shefatya, L. (1990) *Facilitating Play: A Medium for Promoting Cognitive, Socioemotional and Academic Development in Young Children*. Gaithersburg, MD: Psychological and Educational Publications.

Tucker, K. (2005) *Mathematics Through Play in the Early Years: Activities and Ideas*. London: Paul Chapman Publishing.

Vygotsky, L.S. (1978) *Mind in Society*, translated and edited by M. Cole, V. John-Steiner, S. Scribner and E. Souberman, Cambridge, MA: Harvard University Press.

Worthington, M. and Carruthers, E. (2003) *Children's Mathematics: Making Marks, Making Meaning*. London: Paul Chapman Publishing.

Note

1   Figure 3.1 is a modified version of a diagram appearing in Kate Tucker's *Mathematics Through Play in the Early Years: Activities and Ideas*, published by Paul Chapman Publishing in 2005.

4   The family counts

Rose Griffiths

Introduction

When I first started teaching in the 1970s, there were two local primary schools which had painted lines in front of the school entrance, showing parents the limit beyond which they were not allowed to go. Talking to your child's class teacher was not encouraged, and woe betide any parent who dared to ask a question or, worse still, make a suggestion! Fortunately, nowadays there is general agreement that parents and families play a major part in children's educational experience, and that educational settings should work in partnership with them (Desforges and Abouchar 2003; Muschamp et al. 2007). There is perhaps less agreement about *how* families do or should contribute to their children's educational achievements, and still some challenges facing educational settings who might like to build on 'home knowledge' for school, but find it difficult to do so.

Central government in England is clear about the need for meaningful partnership. The Department for Children Schools and Families stated in the Children's Plan: 'Parents' support for their children's learning is an essential foundation for achievement' (DCSF 2007: 53) and 'Partnership with parents is a unifying theme of this Children's Plan. Our vision of 21st century children's services is that they should engage parents in all aspects of their children's development, and that children's services should be shaped by parents' views and command parents' confidence' (DCSF 2007: 57). The Primary National Strategy had previously also acknowledged the appropriateness of working with parents, especially for young children: 'Home-school liaison continues to play a critically important role in children's experiences and the contribution of adults in and out of school has a significant impact on their early education' (DfES 2006: 106). The *Independent Review of Mathematics Teaching in Early Years Settings and Primary Schools* (DCSF 2008: 73) states firmly that: 'It is self-evident that parents are central to their child's life, development and attainment. They cannot be ignored or sidelined but should be a critical element in any practitioner's plans for the education of children'.

Young children counting at home

A project in Leicester aimed to find out more about what parents and carers did at home with their children to help them learn to count by filming them engaged in counting activities. A selection of these film clips would later be used to produce a DVD for parents, carers and practitioners, called *Getting Children Counting*.[1]

We began by asking parents from two Sure Start areas to have our film crew (two women) visit them for a morning or afternoon. (Sure Start centres aimed to provide integrated services for families with young children in some of the most economically disadvantaged areas of England.) Our 12 families each had a child aged two, three or four. Parents were asked to show us anything they did that helped their child learn to count. The adults concerned were able to discuss the activities they intended to include with a worker who they already knew, for reassurance before filming if they wanted. We emphasized that we did not want them to try new activities, as we did not want the children to be asked to do anything unfamiliar or stressful. Our hope was to capture a picture of common counting practices among the families.

The film from each family provided between 15 and 75 minutes of footage to watch, mostly filmed in the children's own homes. The counting activities from each family were listed with an account of what the focus child did: between 3 and 13 activities per child, making 94 'activity clips' altogether. In seven families, another child (usually a younger brother or sister) was evident as well, watching their older sibling and sometimes joining in.

Features of learning to count

Maclellan discusses the complex process of learning to count in Chapter 6. One issue we considered when we began this project was whether we needed to include some indication of this complexity in our DVD for parents and carers. We wanted the selection of clips we chose (and the voiceover on the film) to do three things:

1   to reassure people, by showing them some familiar counting activities and ways of responding to children, and to confirm that these were useful;
2   to raise people's interest in *how* children learn to count (and in what happens as they are learning);

3   to offer new suggestions or advice to extend the support that parents and carers could offer their children.

Giving too much information about counting contexts and principles in the DVD might be intimidating, however; for example, we might want to show that learning the number names is important, but it is not *all* there is to learn. Importantly, though, the film clips and our discussion with parents raised questions for practitioners. What counting do parents and carers commonly do with their children? What aspects of home practice are especially valuable? What do parents want to know to support their child's learning? And how can practitioners build on the work done at home, to make our work in educational settings more effective?

Learning the counting sequence

Learning the number words, in the right order, was given a high priority by nine of our twelve families. Children often practised the counting sequence in spare moments as an incidental activity, for example, when they were walking to the shops, or while their mother or father was preparing vegetables or changing a baby. This was practice where the focus was just on the counting words – not trying to find out how many of something there were. Sometimes children were asked to show a visiting adult how far they could count: 'Show nanna you can count to twenty now'. All the counting was forwards; none of our families had practised counting backwards, and one parent said 'It's never occurred to me that it might help'. The ability to count both forwards and backwards, and to start at any point in the sequence and carry on, may give children more success and confidence in early arithmetic, for example, when exploring the links between addition and subtraction (see Anghileri 2000 and Wright, Chapter 14). Counting backwards seems to be a useful activity to suggest to parents and carers, perhaps especially with children who have become confident 'forwards counters' up to about 10.

Counting in any language

Five of our families were multilingual, and their children were learning the number names in two languages. All the children seemed happy to swap from one language to another, but parents in one family asked whether they should practise only in English until their child started school. This is a question I have been asked by many teachers, too. As already mentioned, learning the number names is only one aspect of learning to count, and the principles of one-to-one correspondence and cardinality, for example, develop irrespective of which language is used, so we responded that families (and teachers) can help by practising in any language in which they feel comfortable (see

Chapter 6 for Maclellan's outline of Gelman and Gallistel's five 'counting principles').

Counting objects

The largest number of the children's counting activities were ones where they were trying to find a total: how many cars, teddies or apples they had. Learning the number names might still be a focus, but they were also guided to learn about one-to-one correspondence. Most parents showed their children how to put things in a line or, more commonly, to move them out of the way as they counted them. Counting objects in pictures in a book can be more difficult, as you cannot move things out of the way, but this activity did give one parent the chance to comment to her child that it was hard to do, and to say 'Can you remember which ones we've counted already?', making explicit the fact that this was important. All but one of the parents modelled counting by pointing to one thing at a time as they counted, and corrected children if they didn't do this: 'No, try again! Go slower!'

Ten of the twelve children counted toys, including cars, dolls, skittles, plastic cups and saucers, animals and bricks. All these items were things that the children played with regularly and which they enjoyed using. They were interested in knowing how many of each toy they had, or in some examples were checking to see if any were missing. This level of motivation seems important; we want children to care how many things there are, so that they will try to count accurately. Counting their own fingers or toes (or their sibling's or parent's) was a warm and personal activity which children obviously enjoyed. Rahma, aged 3, whispered, 'It's tickly' as her big sister counted her plaits, and wanted her to count them again. This is an aspect of counting practice that has a particular place in a family setting.

Stephanie (aged 3) tried to get her mum to take off her shoes so that she could count her toes, but her mother refused, not wanting other people to see her feet. 'No, not on film. You can do it another time.' Five of the twelve families showed that they used songs and rhymes about counting, but one further adult said she did sing with her child, but was too shy to do so on camera. We realized that other counting activities were also under-represented in the film clips. For example, conversation with parents revealed a higher incidence of children being involved with counting toothbrushes, pennies, DVDs, items of clothing, and so on, than was shown to the film crew. One parent said 'I didn't think of that (counting tee shirts as she pegged them on the line) as helping my little boy learn to count – it's something I would do anyway, even if he wasn't here.' These examples of adults counting for their own interest or purposes are valuable to children, but were undervalued by the adults concerned.

Six of the children regularly played at stacking bricks or stacking beakers, and counting them. A discussion with a group of parents suggested several reasons for their popularity. Many children in this age group enjoy stacking things up and knocking them down, and counting the number of bricks or beakers as they build; 'Seems a natural thing to do', said one parent. Another said 'Stacking beakers are quite cheap. They are sold as educational, aren't they? I've bought some with numbers on, so my little girl can learn her numbers.' Two parents mentioned that their health visitors had asked their children to stack three or four wooden bricks on top of each other as part of their developmental check at age 3, and one said, 'So I knew it was a good thing to do.'

Putting things right

When you are learning to count, it is helpful if someone checks your counting for you, at least some of the time, to show you how to improve. The film clips showed a general tendency for parents to correct quickly, often by saying the right number straight after their child, or by suggesting they start again. In every case, it seemed that going wrong and having it pointed out to you was an expected, matter-of-fact part of the activity. This detailed individual coaching was evident in all our families.

Occasionally, a parent would leave an error unchallenged. For example, one parent reported that her son Jaden (aged 2) had had a book with pictures of trucks for over a year, and he still enjoyed counting the wheels. He counted seven wheels (when there were actually eight), but his mother did not correct him. Instead, she said gently, 'Seven wheels you've counted'. His enthusiasm for the book would no doubt provide her with another opportunity to count all the wheels later on. Sometimes, when children made mistakes, adults made the task easier (e.g. by offering to point to each item, to help the child count them one at a time) before they tried counting again. There was always praise when a child finished; a completed sequence of counting often ended with mutual clapping, and saying, 'Hooray', 'Clever girl!' or something similar.

Counting actions

Counting actions or events seemed more common at home than I have seen in educational settings. Perhaps it is partly because of the time, space and individual attention it can take to count as a child hops, skips, swings, demonstrates 'karate kicks' or bounces on a space hopper. For many children, counting actions seemed to provide a useful context for counting to higher numbers than counting objects. For example, Achayla, aged 4, only counted to a maximum of five with toys or household objects (because that is all there were), but counted confidently to twenty when she was hopping. When she was on the swing in the garden, she extended her counting using her own version of the counting sequence: '37, 38, 39, 50, 51, 52, 53, 54, 55, 56, 57, 58, 59, 30, 31 . . .'

Counting large groups of objects has particular challenges, as Ginsburg comments:

> Young preschoolers achieve sufficient mastery . . . to enumerate small sets with considerable success. But they make mistakes when enumerating larger sets, mainly because they are not skilled at considering things once and once only. This is difficult for them since they lack a systematic plan for keeping track of things and hence rely only on rote memory, which soon becomes overburdened.
>
> (Ginsburg 1989: 43)

Perhaps counting actions has a particular role to play when children are beginning to count using bigger numbers, as a string of actions can be carried out so that you can only count one at a time. For example, Stella (aged 2) counted with her mum and her mum's partner, as they threw a balloon from one to another around the three of them. The adults waited till Stella had shouted the number of the throw before they passed the balloon again, so Stella did not have to worry about what she had counted and what she had not; she could concentrate on getting the next number right. Her face and her voice showed how much she enjoyed this activity, and how pleased she was as the numbers went higher and higher. This level of intense enjoyment was often evident in children's counting with their family members.

Counting actions or counting objects?

Sometimes it was difficult to decide whether to categorize an activity as counting actions or objects. One child was drawing snails, and counted the little swirly flourish with her crayon as she drew each one: 'One, two, three, four'. Then she counted finished snails. It was clear in the latter case that she was counting the drawings, but it seemed more appropriate to describe her initial counting as counting her own actions. Perhaps it does not matter what category is used; but the activity of counting while you draw, and then counting your drawings, seemed to have more potential for learning than just counting items on a picture. Counting sandcastles as you make them, and then when they are all finished, would give similar advantages. Each extra object drawn or made also gives a clear picture of what 'one more' looks like.

Counting as you go up or down stairs provided another example where the object (each stair) and action (stepping) could be considered separately. If the activity is seen as counting the stairs, then Jamie and his mother got the wrong answer every time they went up or down, because they did not count a stair when they paused to talk about what they could see through the banisters. Although there are eleven stairs, they counted nine or ten. However, if the activity is seen as counting their own stepping actions *when they pay attention to them* they are very successful.

Call and response

When going up the stairs, Jamie's mum said the number first, and he copied each time, counting out loud from one to nine. Later on, when they counted from one to nine again while coming down, Jamie counted first and his mum responded, correcting when needed:

> Jamie: Eight
> Mum: Eight
> Jamie: Seven
> Mum: No, nine!
> Jamie: Nine

This pattern of a parent leading by saying one number at a time for the child to repeat, 'call and response' style, and later giving the child the opportunity to lead and the parent (or other adult) to follow, was evident in the counting that Rahma (aged 3) did with her teenage sister, counting both in English then in Somali. Ahmet followed a similar pattern when looking at written numbers and saying the numbers out loud in Turkish, and then later in English. The value of frequent, repetitive, short periods of individual attention at home was clear in film clips of three of the children. For example, Asma's initial counting 'One, two, three, six' needed five repeats of a 'call and response' sequence with her mother, before Asma remembered (or perhaps acknowledged?) that it should be 'One, two, three, four'.

Changes in children's focus of attention

Hewitt (2000) has raised the issue of whether sometimes an adult assumes a child is making mistakes, when actually the child has begun to concentrate on something different. He describes playing a game with Danya, aged 13 months, where he hid a small stacking beaker under one of two larger ones while she watched, and she then uncovered the hidden cup.

> As we played this game I made verbal reactions. If there was a cup underneath I said *Yyyeeesss!* with a big smile on my face. If not, I would say *Ohhhhhh!* . . . I realised that Danya was no longer interested in playing the game that I was playing, [as she seemed to be deliberately making mistakes], instead she had moved on to something else she wanted to learn about – my verbal and facial expressions and

their significance. After all, she knew where the small cup was, so why stay with something where there was little left to learn?

(Hewitt 2000: 5)

Similar situations, where a child seemed to 'move on' to a new activity, arose among our 12 children. For example, Stella had started to count a large pile of pennies by picking them up one at a time, saying the next number, and then putting the penny into the jar. In an earlier activity, she had counted groups of objects accurately to numbers bigger than 10, but the pile of coins contained many more than she had previously been able to count. After she had put just five coins into the jar singly, Stella changed tactics. She started to take bigger and bigger handfuls of coins, dropping a whole handful into the jar at once, but still counting forward one number at a time. One interpretation is that Stella does not realize that you need to count things one at a time, with one number for one thing. Another possibility is that she is counting handfuls, or perhaps counting the action of putting a handful into the jar. But a further possibility is that her focus has changed; she watches her own hand attentively as she is picking up the coins and seems to be concentrating most of all on trying to pick up as many coins as possible in each turn. Perhaps she has reassessed the size of the pile of coins, and decided that it will take too long to put them in singly, so she has implemented a more efficient method. An adult might think the focus of this episode is on counting, while for Stella it may have been filling the jar.

Reading and writing numbers

Our brief to the families had not encompassed reading or writing numerals, but eight of the twelve families felt this was an important aspect of their child's work on counting. Penny Munn's interviews with children aged 4 and over showed children themselves associating counting with reading and writing numbers (see Munn, Chapter 2). Five of our children aged 2 or 3 had started to recognize written numbers, and one 2-year-old could find numbers one to ten without difficulty.

The difference between numbers and letters formed an interesting discussion between Achayla (aged 4) and her mother. When asked to write a number 4, 'because that's your number, your special number', Achayla wrote a letter A (for Achayla). Child and mother then spent some time sorting magnetic numbers and letters, deciding which ones were numbers.

Not unexpectedly, the older children were more likely to have started writing than the younger ones. One parent asked about the 'correct way' to write numerals one to nine in English, as her own schooling had been in Gujerati, using a different script. (This is not to say that all parents schooled in

English would use a standard way of writing numbers.) Kenner's observations of children aged 6 teaching each other to write numbers in Chinese and English, or Arabic and English, show a high level of interest in using different scripts (Kenner 2004), with children using methods they had been taught in community-run Saturday schools. However, one parent who had himself learned Gujerati numbers as a child at Saturday school said he felt this use of alternative scripts for numbers was changing: 'Even when we're writing in Gujerati now, I use the English (International) numbers, and so do the newspapers.' The pervasiveness of the numerals 1, 2, 3 . . . on calculator keys, TV controls, phones and on many other pieces of electronic equipment may indeed have made them truly international.

Learning at home

The ways in which home and educational settings support children's learning are undoubtedly different, and, of course, vary from one family to another as they do from one setting to another. Our 12 families were all working class, living in areas that are in the lowest 10 per cent nationally for economic and social indicators. The counting activities they showed us varied from one family to another, but all were keen to help their children. Research that compared the contribution of home with that of nursery or school to young children's learning (e.g. Tizard and Hughes 2002) has previously shown that both middle-class and working-class families can provide educational experiences of a rich and varied nature, the importance of which may be underestimated by professional educators and by parents themselves. The EPPE (Effective Pre-School and Primary Education) Project also concluded that:

> Although parents' social class and levels of education were related to child outcomes the quality of home environment was more important. The home learning environment is only moderately associated with social class. What parents do is more important than who they are.
>
> (Sylva et al. 2005: 12)

Even though the sample of families involved in the project described in this chapter was very small, we were able to see some common patterns. The families were all interested in how to help their children to learn to count; they enjoyed seeing the progress the children made; and they often noticed common features in children's learning about numbers, both from their friends' children and their own other children. For example, 3-year-old Rahma's teenage sister noticed her making up bigger numbers as she counted: '60 31' as the next number after 11 or 12, and she recalled another sibling doing a similar thing when he was younger. The families were pleased to have confirmation that the things they were doing were useful, and were receptive to suggestions about other activities they could try.

The children's learning at home was personalized in a way that is not possible in many other settings. Activities were characterized by a high level of individual attention (including when a sibling joined in or watched) from a person with whom the child had a strong emotional bond, often shown through physical closeness and concentrated eye contact. As other authors have reported (Gregory et al. 2004) the support offered to a child at home may involve a wide community of adults and other children, all with an interest in the child doing well.

There was considerable evidence of children directing their own learning. We were told that many activities (which might take only a few minutes to do) were repeated over and over again as the adult responded to the child's interest over a period of weeks, until the child tired of an activity or moved on to something more ambitious. The objects and actions being counted were ones in which the child had an interest, so there was a purposefulness about their counting. The children often initiated activities, or continued to work on activities after their adult had stopped – sometimes taking on the role of the adult with a younger sibling.

Implications for teaching and learning

Parents, carers and other family members all contribute to children's learning at home. If we want to maximize the impact of home learning, perhaps we should concentrate on celebrating what happens already, and sharing ideas with families, based on things that other families do successfully (while acknowledging that different children and adults enjoy different activities). We need to consider parents' 'frequently asked questions' in the light of family activity, not just trying to get parents to replicate what happens at school or nursery. This does not preclude us from suggesting a useful focus for new activity (e.g. practising counting backwards); it just means that instead of 'What would I like parents to do?' we should ask 'What would parents like to do?'.

Changing patterns of parenting and child care are a challenge. More children live in complex family arrangements, with shared care (e.g. between separated parents) being more common, and practitioners may sometimes be uncertain about how best to work in partnership with families. But the children in our families were not slow to suggest things they wanted to do at home. Perhaps practitioners could sometimes take greater advantage of this by discussing possible 'homework' with children, and encouraging them to play a more central role in school to home liaison.

The Home School Knowledge Exchange Project (Winter et al. 2004) investigated children's learning at home and at school, and commented that activities which involve communicating from school to home are easier to initiate than those which go from home to school. Looking at the practice of parents and family members who are successfully helping young children to learn at home can provide ideas for our nurseries and classrooms. For me, one starting point I would like to explore when young children are learning to count is how we could do more counting of actions not just objects.

Note

1   The DVD can be purchased from the Association of Teachers of Mathematics www.atm.org.uk/buyonline/products/exs003.html (accessed 31 March 2008).

References

Anghileri, J. (2000) *Teaching Number Sense*. London: Continuum.

DCSF (Department for Children, Schools and Families) (2007) *The Children's Plan: Building Brighter Futures*. Norwich: Her Majesty's Stationery Office.

DCSF (Department for Children, Schools and Families) (2008) *Independent Review of Mathematics Teaching in Early Years Settings and Primary Schools* www.publications.teachernet.gov.uk/eOrderingDownload/ Williams%20Mathematics.pdf: (accessed June 2008).

DfES (Department for Education and Skills) (2006) *Primary Framework for Literacy and Mathematics*. Norwich: DfES.

Desforges, C. with Abouchaar, A. (2003) *The Impact of Parental Involvement, Parental Support and Family Education on Pupil Achievement and Adjustment: A Review of the Literature* (Research Report 433). London: DfES.

Ginsburg, H.P. (1989) *Children's Arithmetic: How they Learn it and How you Teach it*, 2nd edn. Austin, TX: Pro-Ed.

Gregory, E., Long, S. and Volk, D. (eds) (2004) *Many Pathways to Literacy: Young Children Learning with Siblings, Grandparents, Peers and Communities*. London: RoutledgeFalmer.

Hewitt, D. (2000) The first two years, *Mathematics Teaching*, 173: 4–11.

Kenner, C. (2004) Community school pupils reinterpret their knowledge of Chinese and Arabic for primary school peers, in E. Gregory, S. Long and D. Volk (eds) *Many Pathways to Literacy: Young Children Learning with Siblings, Grandparents, Peers and Communities*. London: RoutledgeFalmer.

Muschamp, Y., Wikely, F., Ridge, T. and Balarin, M. (2007) *Parenting, Caring and Educating* (Primary Review Research Survey 7/1). Cambridge: University of Cambridge Faculty of Education.

Sylva, K., Melhuish, E., Sammons, P., Siraj-Blatchford, I. and Taggart, B. (2005) The effects of pre-school on children at age 7. Paper presented to the British Educational Research Association Annual Conference, Glamorgan, 14–17 September.

Tizard, B. and Hughes, M. (2002) *Young Children Learning*, 2nd edn. Oxford: Blackwell.

Winter, J., Salway, L., Yee, W.C. and Hughes, M. (2004) Linking home and school mathematics: the home school knowledge exchange project, *Research in Mathematics Education*, 6: 59–75.

SECTION 3
The place of counting in number development

This section comprises three chapters that together make a strong case for substantial emphasis to be placed on counting in the number curriculum of young children. The authors provide a detailed analysis of what is involved in the apparently simple skill of counting; they discuss the early research that underpinned the corresponding section in the first edition; and they also examine more recent research – either their own or that of others. For example, John Threlfall (Chapter 5) reports recent research that takes a closer look at counting as a skill that supports different purposes. He explores three different aspects of the development of counting: as a sequence of numbers; as a sequence of numbers when matched with objects; and as a sequence of numbers that is used to establish cardinal value. In each case there are steps that young children seem to go through en route to arriving at fluent performance, and it is proposed that familiarity with these can aid teachers in shaping supportive provision.

In Chapter 6, Effie Maclellan argues that children's understanding of number is rooted in counting. However, what people understand by counting varies. On the one hand there is a view that counting is being able to recite and apply the number–name sequence to objects and actions. On the other hand there is the view that counting also means having grasped the cardinal property of number. This means that some children will understand counting as an enactive process carried out on concrete objects while others will implicitly recognize that counting can take place in the absence of immediately available countable objects. A sound grasp of counting involves procedural competence (e.g. successfully determining that there are seven items in an array), conceptual competence (understanding why a procedure works) and utilization competence (using procedures in appropriate contexts and in ways that are most adaptive to achieving the arithmetical goal). The research evidence points to a developmental progression towards integrating cardinality with counting, when the child recognizes that counting is the appropriate means of quantification. This progression can be pedagogically supported, involving teachers in the extremely important twin tasks of understanding stages of development in counting and deliberately inducing progression.

Focusing on the interpretations that can be made of arithmetical symbols, Eddie Gray (Chapter 7) uses illustrative examples to show how children's interpretations of arithmetical expressions either emphasize numerical concepts and relationships or trigger an arithmetical procedure. Using counting and its compression, the distinction between thinking about arithmetic and doing arithmetic is considered with reference to the terms 'process' and 'procedure', and the role of a 'procept' – a symbol that ambiguously represents both a process and a concept. He argues that children who compress counting procedures into known and derived facts develop a powerful tool that supports success. Arithmetic is easier for those who know facts and use them flexibly than it is for those who have to carry out lengthy, often intricate, counting procedures on a regular basis. He concludes that we need to help all children to see number as a flexible entity that evokes either a mental object to be manipulated or a counting process to be carried out, and suggests that such flexibility is only achieved at its highest level if supported by known knowledge that can be used to derive unknown knowledge in a meaningful way – compressing knowledge into sophisticated thinkable concepts is the key to increasingly powerful thinking.

5 Development in oral counting, enumeration and counting for cardinality

John Threlfall

Introduction

During the first period of their lives, from almost as soon as they can understand spoken language, young children are exposed to number words in different contexts, in which the number words are used in different ways and have different meanings (Fuson and Hall 1983). In some contexts, number words are used as names, for example on buses, on houses, as telephone numbers, and so on; in other contexts they are used to indicate numerical quantity (three of these, four of those); in yet others they are used to indicate quantity as measured amounts (lengths, weights, ages); they are also used sometimes to indicate position (although position is also indicated using the special words 'first', 'second', 'third', and so on); and in many contexts number words are used in counting.

This chapter explores the development of children's use of number words in counting contexts. It will be seen that there are three variants of counting in different contexts, and that, while these are deeply interrelated, it is possible to consider each separately in relation to how they develop in young children.

The counting contexts

When counting in what Fuson and Hall (1983) call the *sequence* context, there is no reference to objects. Rather, the intention is merely to recite the number words, in order, as a 'string'. Contexts in which this happens for young children include some nursery rhymes (one, two, buckle my shoe; one, two, three, four, Mary at the cottage door), or the game so often played with parents and carers: 'How far can you count?'. In this chapter, this kind of counting will be referred to as 'oral counting'. There are also counting contexts in which number words are applied to objects, but without any intention to say how many objects there are. In this form of counting, which in this chapter will be referred to as enumeration, the known number string is matched to objects as the number words are said, with one object for each number word. A common context in which this occurs is counting as stairs are climbed.

A third form of counting occurs in Fuson and Hall's (1983) *cardinal* contexts, in which number words are used to refer to numerical quantity. Children can arrive at cardinality without counting, by 'subitizing' – the recognition of the size of small collections 'at a glance' (see Aubrey, Chapter 1), but the intention of counting in a cardinal context is to use counting to establish how many objects there are, and it needs to be understood that the number word arrived at by the count describes the cardinality (numerical quantity) of the set of objects which has been counted. As Fuson (1988) reports, in order for children's counting to be used to determine the size of a collection, there has to be a shift from the count to the numerical meaning. In this chapter, this kind of counting will be called counting for cardinality.

It can be seen that counting in these three contexts has different purposes, and so 'counting' can be separated into at least three forms of behaviour – oral counting, enumeration and counting for cardinality. Of course, counting for cardinality depends on successful enumeration, which in turn depends on being able to recite the number string correctly. However, both oral counting and enumeration can and do occur without an association with cardinality, and in oral counting there is not even any involvement of objects. Each of the three will now be considered in more detail.

Oral counting

Oral counting can be defined as the ability to produce in speech a correctly ordered string of numbers. For the smallest numbers, this is just a matter of memory, but later in the sequence recognition of the patterns that occur within tens and hundreds, and so on, is involved in all children's skill in oral counting. Fuson (1992) claims that in the early 'memorized' part, when young children are asked to recite the number sequence, they typically produce a string of number words in the correct order which occur on every occasion, together with a sequence of numbers following that which is the same on each occasion but which is incorrect; for example, number names in the correct order but with some missed out, and then further number words which change on each vocalization. For example, a child may on one occasion say: 'One, two, three, four, five, seven, eight, ten, twelve, thirteen, twenty', and then on another occasion say: 'One, two, three, four, five, seven, eight, ten, thirteen, eighteen, twelve'. Over time, the numbers in the 'stable correct order' part increase.

As the known numbers extend into the later teens and beyond, most children use linguistic structure to develop oral counting in preference to merely remembering what comes next. For example, children soon learn the pattern within each decade of X-ty-one, X-ty-two, X-ty-three, and so on, but it is common at that time for children's counting to involve pauses as the decades are 'bridged', as they try to think of the next '-ty' word.

Early development in oral counting was one focus of a study by Bruce (2000), in which children attending one of six contrasting early years settings in west Yorkshire were given a series of simple number tasks (see Bruce and Threlfall 2004; Threlfall and Bruce 2005). The mean age of the children in the sample of 50 girls and 43 boys was 4 years 4 months, with a range of ages from 3 years 6 months to 4 years 10 months. For the oral counting task, the children were asked to count as far as they could, starting at one. No equipment was provided other than a small teddy bear to which the child was speaking. If the child stopped at any point, she was asked, 'Can you go any further?' The results are shown in Table 5.1.

As Table 5.1 shows, there is a general improvement with age, the median value of the successful count for the youngest group being 9; that for the middle age group 11; and that for the oldest group 14. A pattern can be seen in these results, which indicates that children under aged 4 are largely engaged with learning the number sequence under 10, with those from 4 years to 4 years 6 months grappling with 10, 11 and 12, and those over 4 years 6 months going through the teens and beyond. Nevertheless, within all of the age groups there are some children who did not count past 5 and others who did count past 20.

Table 5.1 'Stop points' in oral counting (*n* = 93)

'Stop point' of count	Number of children	Number of children aged 3y 6m–4y 0m	Number of children aged 4y 1m–4y 6m	Number of children aged 4y 7m–4y 10m
1, 2 or 3	4	2	0	2
4 or 5	10	6	1	3
6, 7 or 8	9	3	2	4
9	8	3	3	2
10	8	2	5	1
11	11	1	6	4
12 or 13	5	1	4	0
14	8	0	3	5
15, 16, 17 or 18	4	2	1	1
19	4	0	2	2
20	4	0	0	4
Past 20	18*	3	4	11

Note: * Of these 18 children, 5 stopped at a decade change point such as 29 or 39, while the other 13 children stopped at some other point, such as 28 or 37.

The relatively high incidence of 14 as a 'stop point' in this study may reflect a particular difficulty with '15' within the otherwise straightforward sequence from 14 to 19. While 14, 16, 17, 18 and 19 follow a linguistic pattern of adding 'teen' to the respective single-digit number, 15 is not 'fiveteen'. The children who stop at 14 are perhaps unsure about 15 and, therefore, either stop completely at 14, or jump to 16, continuing the pattern 'correctly'.

How the counting goes wrong

At the end of a correct string, 50 of the children in the Bruce (2000) study (54 per cent of the sample) just stopped, with a few adding a comment such as 'That's all I know'. The remaining 43 children continued with numbers that were incorrect, but in different ways:

1   The addition of just one further number following a correct string, often two greater; for example, 'five' followed by 'seven' or 'fourteen' followed by 'sixteen'.
2   The continuation of the string in the correct order, but with some numbers omitted, usually missing out just one or two numbers, for example, '. . . eleven, twelve, thirteen, sixteen, seventeen, eighteen . . .'.
3   A move into a repeating loop of numbers, most often the repetition of two numbers, for example, repeating 'four' followed by 'six' a number of times.
4   A return to parts of the string already produced, for example, saying the number string to 28, then returning to 20 and stopping finally at 27.
5   An idiosyncratic continuation of the number string, for example '. . . thirteen, fourteen, fifteen, fourteen, thirty, twenty-one, twenty-eight, thirty, thirty-four'.

These different kinds of error did not show any significant pattern in relation to age, with examples of each type made by children from all three of the age groups identified in Table 5.1. The results in this study contrast a little with Fuson's (1992) proposal that the typical structure of counting strings among the age group is a correct string followed by an incorrect section that is the same on each occasion, and then a string that varies.

Enumeration

Enumeration is when the number names 'are said in an entity situation and each number word refers to an entity' (Fuson 1988: 10). This can occur without the 'cardinality' purpose of saying how many 'entities' there are. A child is enumerating when, for example, she places some toys in a row, and counts along the row, perhaps patting each one on the head, and saying one number word as each one is touched.

Fuson (1988) describes the kinds of error that can occur in enumeration, which include counting some objects twice, missing some objects out, or just not keeping the verbal 'count' on a one-to-one relationship with the objects. Enumeration also involves some kind of method of referring to the objects, and Fuson (1988: 85) describes a development 'from touching to pointing near objects to pointing from a distance to using eye fixation'. She describes this as a 'progressive internalisation' which occurs across the age range 3 years 6 months to 6 years. This development was explored through a further task in the study by Bruce (2000). In the enumeration task, each child in the sample was asked to count along a line of equally spaced identical blocks (30 blocks in total).

Table 5.2 shows the number of children who were successful up to different stop points, and the methods used. Almost every child consistently operated in one of three ways: they pointed to each block; they touched each block; or they tracked across the blocks by eye. Table 5.2 suggests that pointing at the blocks, but not actually touching them, was the preferred method of enumeration for the majority of the children in the study, although there was no significant difference in success rates between the children who pointed and those who touched. However, the children who used visual means to keep track were less successful.

Analysis of methods used at different ages shows no statistically significant differences, but age was found to be significantly related to success (Kendall's tau = .338, $p < .001$). The incidence of keeping track of the objects

Table 5.2 Numbers of children correctly enumerating to different 'stop points', and the methods employed ($n = 87*$)

Method of keeping track	Number of blocks correctly enumerated						
	4–6	7–9	10–14	15–19	20–29	30	Total
Touching	6	6	10	5	4	2	33
Pointing	11	7	10	5	6	5	44
By eye	4	1	3	2	0	0	10
Total	21	14	23	12	10	7	**87**
Cumulative total (% of	87	66	52	29	17	7	
cohort, $n = 93$)	(93.5)	(71.0)	(55.9)	(31.2)	(18.3)	(7.5)	

Note: *Six children did not make a clear response, simply saying a few numbers, or just not responding. They are not included in the table except in relation to the percentages in the cumulative totals.

'by eye only' in this study was surprising, since it had been previously reported only about older children (Fuson 1988). Its use by children in this study might suggest that some young children in English schools are utilizing surprisingly sophisticated cognitive and visualizing skills, except, of course, that these children were less successful. It may be that the children adopted this approach because they were keen to emulate older children and adults, who they had noticed do not tend to touch or point when counting, or perhaps their parents and teachers had actively encouraged these more 'advanced' skills.

Counting for cardinality

Some young children are able to count to 10 in the sense of reciting the number string, and may even be able to enumerate across a set of objects, yet have no idea that this can be used to say how many objects there are. They lack an understanding of the relationship between counting and cardinality (Fuson 1988). Cardinality is a complex concept that takes time to develop (Bermejo et al. 2004) and its relationship to counting is equally complex.

For example, Sophian (1995) reports that, at ages 3 and 4, more children are inclined to count to solve questions of the form 'how many' about a set of objects, than count in response to questions of the form 'give me x objects' when there is a larger set of objects available, and Fluck and Henderson (1996) report that young children are more successful on 'how many' tasks, than on 'give me x objects' tasks. These results may be explained by the findings of Sophian (1995) and Fuson (1988) that some young children learn to respond to 'how many' questions by the activity of enumeration and then giving the last word in the count as the answer, without actually having an appreciation of such counting as a means of determining cardinality. Bermejo et al. (2004), for example, have shown that when children are asked to count along some objects starting at a larger number than one, they still give the last number word in their sequence as a response to the question of how many objects there are (see Maclellan, Chapter 6). In this way 'last word responding' can create an illusion of competence, and Sophian (1995) argues that realizing that counting can help them to solve 'give me x objects' problems requires a more developed understanding of the relationship between counting and cardinality.

For this reason, in the Bruce (2000) study, a 'give me x objects' task was preferred to a 'how many' task to explore counting for cardinality. Each child was asked to make collections of a specified size, by giving 'teddy' progressively larger quantities of identical plastic blocks. The blocks were set out close together in a large group, and the child was asked to select, in turn, 2, 3, 5, 8, 10 and 17 blocks. The task was stopped if the child failed on consecutive attempts. Table 5.3 shows the outcomes of this task. In the table, 'grabbing' refers to looking quickly at the blocks, and then picking up blocks in groups (see Munn, Chapter 2). Any attempt at one-to-one counting of blocks was classified as 'counting'.

If children who 'grabbed' had an understanding of cardinality, and the question as a request for it, then grabbing might be supposed to be based on subitizing – the recognition of quantity by visual perception. However, it should also be recognized that some children in the sample would not have understood what the task was asking of them beyond being asked to give teddy 'some' blocks, and these children too would be 'grabbers', who may on occasion have been successful by chance.

It can be seen from Table 5.3 that, of the children who were successful for each of the quantities, more counted than grabbed the blocks, and there is a statistically significant association between method and success (Kendall's tau = .489, $p < .001$), with the most successful individuals being those who grabbed small quantities (up to three, say), but counted larger quantities, and the least successful being those who grabbed all quantities. None of the children who persisted with grabbing was successful for quantities greater than five. The use of subitizing, reliable in producing two and three blocks by grabbing, could not be sustained far when the quantity increased.

In this study, more children used serial counting to successfully produce requested subsets of two and three objects than used grabbing, with even the youngest children just as likely to count as to grab. This conflicts with the findings of Fluck and Henderson (1996) in which 85 per cent of an equivalent age group were 'grabbers', and may reflect raised levels of encouragement of counting for cardinality in the early years settings of the Bruce study.

Table 5.3 Success rates in selecting quantities of blocks, and method used ($n = 93$)

Quantity requested	Total number of successful children	Method used			
		Counting		Grabbing	
		Number	Mean age	Number	Mean age
2	88 (94.6%)	54	4y 5m	34	4y 7m
3	75 (80.6%)	45*	4y 4m	28*	4y 6m
5	52 (55.9%)	39	4y 5m	13	4y 7m
8	25 (26.9%)	25	4y 6m	0	–
10	16 (17.2%)	16	4y 6m	0	–
17	5 (5.4%)	5	4y 7m	0	–

Note: *Two children (not included) picked up the blocks one at a time, but did not seem to use a one-to-one counting process.

A sequence towards counting for cardinality

From further examination of the methods used by children in this study, and their relative success, Bruce and Threlfall (2004) postulate a developmental sequence in the responses of young children to 'give me x objects' tasks, which reflects in part the emergence of counting for cardinality:

1   The child recognizes a request for quantity, but cannot respond to the value of the quantity, and just grabs the same amount each time.
2   The child knows that different number words imply different quantities, but is unsure about the values, and so offers 'handfuls' of different sizes.
3   The child estimates by subitizing, and grabs roughly correct quantities.
4   The child counts out blocks, but does not appreciate the activity as a means of determining quantity (merely emulating adult behaviour).
5   The child counts out small quantities successfully, but, recognizing his or her own limitations, reverts to grabbing for larger quantities.
6   The child counts everything successfully.
7   The child subitizes small quantities, because it is easier, and counts larger quantities, because it is necessary.

Implications for teaching and learning

The results from different studies about counting vary in terms of what seems to occur at what age, and in what sequence, so the implications for teaching and learning may be said to vary as well. For example, the Bruce (2000) study, which has been widely reported above, gave results that may have arisen at least in part from the context of the study, which was of children in an urban area of England, and differences between this study and others may reflect differences in the social background and culture of the participants. Differences may also arise from how teachers or parents in different countries or regions model counting to children and encourage them in different ways. It may be noted in this respect that oral counting and enumeration in particular have an entirely social purpose from the child's point of view. Children do not say the number names in order, or match them to objects, to serve their own purposes. They do these things to fit in to a specific 'community of practice', or, looked at another way, to please the teacher or parent. As a result, one might suppose that there is a particularly strong cultural influence in these areas of skill. If this is the case, research may not be as generalizable as may be hoped, and local research is necessary to delineate the variations that occur as a result of local practices, in order to formulate appropriate guidance to practitioners in different contexts.

So, for example, where a point in what follows arises from the Bruce (2000) study, it may be more applicable to English urban contexts than to others.

Oral counting

1   A relatively large number of children in the Bruce (2000) study struggled to recite the number string in English to 10. This suggests an overestimation in the literature of the oral counting abilities of many children within this age range, and learning to memorize the number sequence in early years settings might for many children require a considerable investment of time and resources.

2   The challenge of counting in English through the irregular 'teens' suggests a need for teachers to combine work on linguistic patterns with memorization exercises (see Thompson, Chapter 15).

3   The 'organic' growth in oral counting indicated by the typical counting strings identified by Fuson (1992), in which there is an 'experimental' sequence following the well-established part, seems from the Bruce (2000) study not to be universal, with many children just reciting what they are sure about. Teachers may need to give more attention to encouraging children to proceed past 'safe' points, as it gives more to work with in developing oral counting.

4   The different ways in which children go wrong in oral counting, such as continuing a string but with some numbers omitted, moving into a repeating loop or returning to earlier parts of the string, can be used to inform emphases in teaching. For example, if a puppet is used to model counting behaviour, and sometimes makes the kind of error in counting that corresponds to the type made by the children being worked with, this can enable the children to recognize the mistake, and to correct it in their own counting.

Enumeration

5   The importance of enumeration as a sub-skill seems to be under-emphasized in current curriculum guidance, and the ways in which children go wrong, such as counting some objects twice, missing some objects out, and getting out of step, could again helpfully be modelled by an error-prone puppet (see Thompson, Chapter 15).

6   Teachers need to be aware that some children may employ 'use of eyes only' prematurely as a method for enumerating objects, possibly as a result of encouragement by other adults. The relative lack of success of this approach, indicated by findings in the Bruce (2000) study, raises a dilemma for teachers. It may be felt that 'eyes only' – a sophisticated strategy often used by older children and adults – should be

encouraged. However, the relative lack of success achieved by young children when employing this method suggests a need to move them 'back' to pointing or touching, which would probably improve performance. The interiorization of counting actions is a development that can be accelerated only to a degree.

Counting for cardinality

7   It seems from the Bruce (2000) study that many young children count for cardinality even when very small quantities are involved, seeming to have lost faith in subitizing for identifying the size of very small collections, and yet the study also suggests that the most successful approach to determining cardinality is to use subitizing for small quantities and counting for larger quantities. Although the evidence from that study is slight, it may be for the best if teachers do not discourage small quantity subitizing by insisting that all quantities are counted, but concentrate instead on raising children's awareness of the limits to its reliability.

8   The detailed developmental sequence in responses to the 'give me x objects' tasks that is described earlier could be used to support the teaching of early number through raising awareness of what may have preceded and what may follow the current approach used by the child, so that appropriate input and intervention can be shaped to enable the child to move forward. However, the sequence is not suggested as a teaching model, and certainly does not propose 'stages' through which children should be progressively taught. The difference between a helpful awareness and a somewhat similar prescription for action is crucial in actually bringing about learning, since the latter is only effective when one can be sure that children change in a predictable sequential manner. This does not seem to be the case in the development of counting, whether that be oral counting, enumeration or counting for cardinality.

Acknowledgement

This chapter is largely based on research carried out by Bob Bruce. Thanks are due to him, and to the staff and children at the early years settings who took part in the study.

References

Bermejo, V., Morales, S. and deOsuna, J.G. (2004) Supporting children's development of cardinality understanding, *Learning and Instruction*, 14: 381–98.

Bruce, R. (2000) Factors within pre-school educational establishments that affect the number attainment of the young child. Unpublished EdD thesis, University of Leeds.

Bruce, R.A. and Threlfall, J. (2004) One, two, three and counting, *Educational Studies in Mathematics*, 55: 3–26.

Fluck, M. and Henderson, L. (1996) Counting and cardinality in English nursery pupils, *British Journal of Educational Psychology*, 66: 501–17.

Fuson, K.C. (1988) *Children's Counting and Concepts of Number*. New York: Springer-Verlag.

Fuson, K.C. (1992) Relationships between counting and cardinality from age 2 to age 8, in J. Bideaud, C. Melijac and J-P. Fisher (eds) *Pathways to Number: Children's Developing Numerical Abilities*. Hillsdale, NJ: Lawrence Erlbaum Associates.

Fuson, K.C. and Hall, J.W. (1983) The acquisition of early number word meanings: a conceptual analysis and review, in H.P. Ginsburg (ed.) *The Development of Mathematical Thinking*. New York: Academic Press.

Sophian, C. (1995), *Children's Numbers*. Madison, WI: Brown and Benchmark.

Threlfall, J. and Bruce, B. (2005) 'Just' counting: young children's oral counting and enumeration, *European Early Childhood Education Research Journal*, 13(2): 63–78.

6 Counting: what it is and why it matters

Effie Maclellan

Introduction

Counting is a considerable cognitive achievement (Sophian 1998) and significant in the development of the abstract knowledge that constitutes number. A sound grasp of counting involves the mastery and interplay of procedural competence, conceptual competence and utilization competence (Gelman and Meck 1986; Hiebert and Lefevre 1986). Procedural competence is the ability to perform a task, for example, successfully determining that there are seven items in an array. Conceptual competence is the understanding of *why* a procedure works, with connections being made by the child between procedures and their abstract underpinnings (Hiebert and Lefevre 1986), while utilization competence is linking conceptual and procedural competence through the use of procedures in appropriate contexts and in ways that are most adaptive to achieve the arithmetical goal, such as enumerating a set of objects.

The integration of these competences is not necessarily easy (Gray et al. 2000) as some children cling to counting as an enactive process carried out on concrete objects while others become increasingly less dependent on concrete materials to support them, implicitly recognizing that *figural* representations of perceptual material where the child 'sees' the items and can therefore count in the absence of immediately available countables; *motor acts*, such as pointing, nodding and grasping, which typically accompany the counting process; and finally the *utterance of a number word* can substitute for perceptual items. When the child no longer needs any material to create countable items and does not consider it necessary to use any counting process, counting has become a wholly abstract activity. Gray et al. (2000) characterize this distinction between the process of counting and the object of counting as the proceptual divide, with those who have achieved proceptual thinking having a cognitive advantage because they can link procedures and concepts (see Gray, Chapter 7). While there is no real argument about the complex constitution of counting, there is debate as to the relationship of its elements (Rittle-Johnson et al. 2001), a debate which becomes important if we accept that overall mathematical competence depends on the integration of procedural, conceptual and utilization competence as Gelman and Meck (1986) and Hiebert and Lefevre (1986) maintain.

The debate

Piaget dismissed counting as being of little value. He maintained that although young children could recite and even apply the number–name sequence to objects and actions, they nevertheless did not understand the significance of their behaviour because they had not grasped the cardinal property of number (Bryant 1997). Gelman and Gallistel (1978) on the other hand maintained that young children did, to varying degrees, understand what they were doing when counting and that this understanding was grounded in five principles:

1 The one-one principle: the correspondence between count words and objects to assign a distinct counting word to each of the items in the array of countables, and use each tag only once. So in counting a 3-item array, the child who said 1, 2, 2 would not be demonstrating understanding of the one-one principle whereas the child who said 1, 6, 2 would (by dint of giving each item a different name).

2 The stable-order principle: counting in a set order and using that order consistently. Because consistency is the essential property of the stable-order principle some children may use their own idiosyncratic counting lists, reliably. The child who for one 4-item array says 1, 2, 3, 4 but for a subsequent 4-item array says 2, 1, 6, 7 does not have a grasp of the stable-order principle (although does have a grasp of the one-one principle). But the child who repeatedly counts a 4-item array as 1, 3, 2, 6 and starts off more numerous arrays with the same sequence is evidencing knowledge of the stable-order principle. Gelman and Gallistel (1978) found that children who used their own idiosyncratic lists 'were better able to apply the stable-order principle than were children who used conventional lists of number words'. Nevertheless, in the interests of arithmetical communication, it is essential that children do learn the conventional sequence of number words.

3 The cardinal principle: knowing that the final number word in the count represents the numerosity of the set. Being able to assign a distinct number word to each countable and being able to do this consistently is not all that is involved in being able to count. A crucial component is the knowledge that numerosity is a property of all countable entities. In other words, counting is not merely a process in which one engages but it can actually yield a product.

Repeated practice in counting any given numerosity (always assuming that the one-one principle and the stable-order principle are being honoured) will terminate in the appropriate number word. When the child recognizes that this final number word has special significance in that it is not only the last count word but that it also represents the numerosity of the set, the child has grasped the cardinal principle.

Gelman and Gallistel (1978) view these three principles as the 'how-to-count' principles since they specify the way to execute a count. The remaining two are 'what-to-count' principles which define, to the child, what can be counted.

4 The abstraction principle: counting does not necessarily depend on the classification of objects on the basis of their perceptual properties such as colour and size. Counting can be applied to any array or collection of entities, whether these are physical or non-physical, heterogeneous or homogeneous. There has been, historically, the view from developmental theorists that children first classify objects according to perceptual properties such as colour or shape and only later classify according to abstract properties such as number or function. This perception of how children learn to classify seems to have been understood as meaning that children could only count objects which were perceptually similar. Gelman and Gallistel (1978) argue that while children may well place restrictions on what is or can be counted, they do not limit themselves to counting collections of identical objects and are perfectly willing to count collections of miscellaneous and heterogeneous objects and refer to them as 'things'.

5 The order-irrelevance principle: the awareness that number names are arbitrary and temporary designations rather than inherent properties of the countable items. As long as all the items in the array are counted and as long as each is counted only once, it matters not whether the counting is effected from left to right, from right to left or from somewhere in the middle as long as all the items in the array are counted and as long as each is counted only once. The child's understanding that the order of counting is irrelevant is thought to signify some awareness that number names are arbitrary and temporary designations rather than inherent properties of the countable items.

Although for both Piaget and Gelman and Gallistel (1978), cardinality is the essential feature of counting, Piaget characterized it as recognizing equivalent numerosity of different sets while Gelman and Gallistel (1978) made a cognitively less demanding requirement of identifying the last number counted as representing the set's numerosity. They believed that if children recognized the importance of the last number counted, they necessarily understood that in counting a set, its cardinality became increasingly larger with each successive item tagged. Bryant (1997) disputes this. Consistent with this distinction, Bermejo et al. (2004) maintain that counting and cardinality are not the same and that while counting is *one* means of evidencing cardinality (as indeed are subitizing and estimating), counting is a procedure for quantification while cardinality is the understanding that a set's numerosity is represented by a number word. Bermejo et al. (2004) illustrate the issue through comparing use of an erroneous/idiosyncratic count sequence (asking for a set of five items to be counted starting at 'three') with the request to determine the set's numerosity. So, counting the set of five items starting at 'three' produces an outcome of 'seven'. If the child can determine that there are indeed five items and not seven in the set, such a child understands cardinality (regardless of whatever the last number counted may turn out to be).

Although counting and cardinality are different entities, Bermejo et al. (2004) maintain that there is a developmental progression towards integrating cardinality with counting when the child recognizes that counting is the appropriate means of quantification. So the child who, requested by the teacher to give a sweet to every child in the group/class, counts the number of children and then counts out an equivalent number of sweets from the tin is integrating cardinality with counting, to utilize procedural and conceptual knowledge. Other evidence for the difference between counting and cardinality is cited by Bryant (1997) and Sophian (1998), suggesting that not only do some children have no idea that counting is an appropriate procedure to follow but that others choose not to count when asked to 'give me four bricks' and instead grab a handful. The recognition that counting is the situationally appropriate procedure to adopt to achieve an objective appears to develop with age (Sophian 1998) but can also be pedagogically supported through deliberately inducing contradictory evidence in counting tasks (Bermejo et al. 2004).

The relationship between procedural and conceptual knowledge of counting

The distinction between procedural and conceptual knowledge is not always obvious (Hiebert and Lefevre 1986), but one now agreed way of determining conceptual understanding is to observe the child judging the validity of another's procedures (Freeman et al. 2000; LeFevre et al. 2006). Children who themselves count a set of objects correctly are credited with procedural knowledge while those who can detect errors in the counting of others are credited with having conceptual knowledge of counting. In a large study (LeFevre et al. 2006) Canadian pre-school and early primary children were asked to judge an animated frog's counting: when a correct count was executed; when there was a violation of the correspondence between count words and objects (so that an incorrect cardinality resulted); and when the order irrelevance principle was tested (with the effect of a correct cardinality achieved through an unusual ordering of the items). Resulting scores were characterized as low (below the 25th percentile within their grade), average (between the 25th and 75th percentiles) and high (above the 75th percentile). Children identified correct counts at adult levels of performance, averaging 97 per cent. Their identification of incorrect cardinalities improved with grade, averaging 74, 83 and 90 per cent across the stage span but their appreciation of the order irrelevance principle appeared to deteriorate, averaging incorrect counts of 46, 42 and 39 per cent, respectively.

While performance for incorrect cardinalities improved with grade for all three skill groups, the improvement was not uniform. Average- and high-skill children reached near ceiling performance in Grade 1, whereas low-skill children took until the end of Grade 2 to reach approximately the same level. In contrast, children in both low- and average-skill groups were more accepting of the order irrelevance principle. High-skill children were more likely to assert that an unusually ordered count resulted in a numerosity error. This finding is counter-intuitive, especially because the high-skill children were better at detecting incorrect counts and were better at actually executing the counting procedure. The overall findings from this study build on previous ones to show few significant correlations between conceptual knowledge and procedural knowledge. Despite good procedural skills, children's understanding was neither complete nor flexible.

Clearly then the emergence of counting in children is complex and a bit messy. It appears to begin in children as young as 2 or 3 years of age but takes a number of years to develop. The child has to learn the culturally determined sequence of numbers and the contextually appropriate use for each. Counting sequences are rote learned initially and children use them for many months before slowly realizing that the highest verbalized number also symbolizes set numerosity. It is at this point teachers need to be aware of two possible consequences: the child may be mechanically following characteristic procedures that have been rote learned; or the child may be respecting a principle that governs procedures (Freeman et al. 2000). Fluck et al. (2005) summarize the situation in the following general terms: although children often become proficient at 'counting' by 3 years and 6 months, they generally do not understand counting as a method of determining quantity much before age 4 and the first signs of a principled understanding of cardinality are not apparent before age 5.

Although procedural knowledge of counting precedes conceptual knowledge (Rittle-Johnson et al. 2001), one must be cautious about concluding this temporal arrangement to be absolute since the discerned direction of acquisition could always be a function of perceived task difficulty rather than of developmental difference in the order of acquisition. A further reason for being cautious is that conceptual knowledge seems to precede the counting-on procedure. Since counting is the means through which the child penetrates addition, it may well be that the relationship between counting and cardinality is more curvilinear as Lefevre et al. (2006) evidenced. However, regardless of the order of acquisition of procedural and conceptual knowledge, it is perhaps somewhat optimistic to assume that most 5-year-olds have principled understanding of cardinality given the widespread evidence for difficulties in the execution of arithmetical procedures and in learning and/or retrieving arithmetic facts from memory which, in turn, contribute to the persistence of immature problem-solving strategies such as verbal or finger counting (Rousselle and Noël 2007). Both the complexity of the relationship between counting and cardinality and the confidence we can have in whether cardinality is established present a pedagogical challenge for teachers.

Implications for teaching and learning

Counting would seem to be the basis of the arithmetical knowledge that the young child constructs. Given the currently dominant view of learning as a socio-psychological, purposeful activity in which the construction of shared meaning is achieved by each individual through discussion and negotiation, it follows that counting may mean different things to different children. Children at the beginning of formal schooling will have variously different competences: they may, or may not, be procedurally skilled in reciting the conventional sequence of number words but in any one class there is likely to be a spectrum of developmental achievement in conceptual understanding. The teacher therefore needs to be sensitive to the procedures that children are using, to what these procedures suggest about the robustness of children's conceptual knowledge and to what it means for the pedagogical practices that the teacher will adopt. Consistent with current constructivist views of learning, it would be important for the teacher to build on what conceptual and procedural resources the child brings, rather than risk devaluing the child's extant competence through a 'one size fits all' approach.

The relationship between counting procedures and their conceptual underpinnings is not straightforward, so teachers need to keep in the forefront the possible confusion between the two different competences of number knowledge. First, they must not be beguiled, as mothers can be (Fluck et al. 2005), and overestimate the child's cardinal understanding on the basis of accurate procedural competence. But, second, they need also to recognize that through counting procedures being applied to structurally similar counting problems, the child is enabled to 'transfer' what is done in one situation to another and thereby derive what is common, which is the conceptual knowledge. This suggests that there should be many opportunities for counting offered in the classroom. These opportunities should allow the practising and perfecting of procedural counting but they should also allow, through situating children in structurally similar counting contexts, the opportunity for abstracting the conceptual knowledge of cardinality. Tasks such as watching out for correct or incorrect counting in relation to one-to-one correspondence, stable order of counting or order irrelevance in counting are considered appropriate ways of making conceptual knowledge explicit (LeFevre et al. 2006). And the intervention to induce cognitive conflict through comparing an erroneous/idiosyncratic count sequence with the request to determine the set's numerosity (Bermejo et al. 2004) has also been found to be developmentally supportive.

The essential nature of counting as a cognitive achievement which requires abstract knowledge raises questions about the use of concrete materials. Although the pedagogical advocacy of concrete materials stemmed from the importance attributed to Piagetian stages in thinking, the work of Gray et al. (2000) and the evidence on which they build suggests that uncritical acceptance of the use of concrete materials could impede rather than support the development of abstract knowledge. This is not to suggest that concrete materials are always inappropriate but Gray et al. (2000) draw attention to a developmental progression from the exclusive use of perceptual items which could be embedded in a range of counting demands. For example, there might be situations when the child had to choose whether to use particular manipulatives or their fingers, followed by a stage when children were challenged to find the answer without even using their fingers!

It is now well documented that concrete materials in the form of manipulatives do not, *of themselves*, convey numerical knowledge and that even although they may help the child to find the procedurally correct answer, their use is not transferred to problem-solving situations that could benefit from modelling manipulatives. Furthermore, the teacher's *requirement* on children to use manipulatives (a practice that can be routinely observed in many infant classrooms) may ignore and/or devalue such tactical or experiential learning that the child has developed informally. If we are unwittingly encouraging dependency by the ready availability of physical entities for counting, we need to consider in which situations and for which children manipulatives are supportive, possibly useful or downright inappropriate.

Once children can count, not only can they make precise quantitative judgements, they are also in the powerful position of being able to penetrate the tasks of addition and subtraction. For children who can neither retrieve the addition and subtraction 'facts' from memory nor derive new 'facts' from an existing repertoire, the only way in which children can find sums of, or differences between, numbers is to count. Clearly, many young children at the start of school will be in this position, but so too will many others who have been at school for a number of years. Indeed, some children will be totally reliant on counting to obtain answers to addition and subtraction operations during the entire period of primary schooling, and while this is not necessarily a practice to be advocated, counting can always be used as a check on other tactics for quantification. Having learned that counting is a meaningful strategy to solve addition and subtraction operations, there is the potential for the counting strategy to become elaborated into different procedures.

Typically, when adding, the child first uses the procedure of counting-all. The child counts out each set of objects (addends), combines the two sets into one new set and then counts the objects in the new set. Extensive and repeated practice of counting objects eventually leads to the ability to use the counting words themselves as objects to count. That children learn that objects do not have to be perceptually present in order to be counted (but can instead be represented by the counting words) is highly significant because this is evidence of the child having some (albeit primitive) knowledge of counting as a mental activity.

A refinement of the counting-all procedure is the counting-on procedure where the child starts counting with the number name which represents the numerosity of one of the arrays to be added. Furthermore, the child may well be efficient and start with the larger array. In using the counting-on procedure the child is both minimizing the amount of counting which has to be done and evidencing an understanding of cardinal meaning. Counting-on emerges from counting-all in some children who are as young as 4 years of age. Given that counting-on represents a qualitative advance in understanding, and given that the available evidence suggests that those children who have learning difficulties in mathematics are 'tied' to the most rudimentary of counting procedures, it would seem to be important to ensure that the procedure of counting-on is part of each child's repertoire (see Wright, Chapter 14).

An early counting procedure for subtraction is to count out the initial quantity (the minuend), remove the specified number of objects from the array (the subtrahend) and then recount what is left. Again, with increased understanding, this can give way to more sophisticated procedures. One such procedure is counting-down where the child initiates a backward counting sequence, starting from the minuend and continuing until each member of the subtrahend has been accounted for. So, in using this procedure for finding the difference between five and two, the child will verbalize '5 . . . 4, 3, 2'. The backward counting sequence contains as many number words as the given smaller quantity and the last name uttered in the sequence is the answer.

A more sophisticated procedure, still, is counting-up. Here the child initiates a forward counting sequence, starting from the subtrahend and ending with the minuend. So, in finding the difference between 5 and 2, the child will verbalize '2 . . . 3, 4, 5'. The number of counting words uttered in the sequence has to be kept track of by the child because it is this number which represents the difference between the initial numerosities. While counting-down corresponds to the most basic way of thinking about subtraction: to the notion of taking away; counting-up is a more sophisticated way of thinking about subtraction. Counting-up interprets subtraction as complementary addition. This (albeit, initially implicit) knowledge of the complementarity of addition and subtraction is powerful arithmetical information and may need to be explicitly taught to children at a sufficiently early stage of their primary education. Without explicit teaching of counting-up, children are essentially 'deprived' of this resource until such times as their understanding of the relationship between numbers allows them to see for themselves that addition and subtraction are inverse operations. The potentially lengthy time taken by children to discover for themselves (as against the shorter time which might be needed for systematic teaching) that counting-up is an appropriate procedure for subtraction operations may well account for the fairly common finding that subtraction is more difficult than addition for young children (see Thompson, Chapter 8).

Conclusion

There is now little doubt that children's understanding of number is rooted in counting. It is also clear that because some version of counting develops from a very early age, children will have very various understandings when they start school: from algorithms for quantifying perceptually available items to conceptual sophistication which can both improve use of procedural knowledge and reduce the number of procedures that need to be learned. This is not to suggest that children will be perfectly proficient in computation. Nor is there any suggestion that children can articulate their knowledge about number. Children will still need the teacher's help, and they will still need structured activities. But the evidence does now suggest that there should be a sharp focus on counting. Since children find counting an intrinsically satisfying activity, teachers are well placed to offer goal-directed opportunities for counting to be practised in the different contexts.

Furthermore, because of the power that counting has in appreciation of addition and subtraction, the different counting procedures need to be accorded their appropriate place. There is nothing to be lost, and indeed much to be gained, from explicit teaching of the counting procedures. The pedagogic issues turn on knowing which procedure a child is habitually using in order to make some judgement as to whether the particular procedure(s) being adopted is/are enabling or hindering the child. Finally, if teachers are to support children in their counting endeavours, it may mean that pedagogic practices which are based on dated and incomplete accounts of number development should be reviewed.

References

Bermejo, V., Morales, S. and Garcia de Osuna, J. (2004) Supporting children's development of cardinality understanding, *Learning and Instruction*, 14: 381–98.

Bryant, P. (1997) Mathematical understanding in the nursery school years, in T. Nuñes & P. Bryant (eds) *Learning and Teaching Mathematics*. Hove: Psychology Press.

Fluck, M., Linnell, M. and Holgate, M. (2005) Does counting count for 3- to 4-year-olds? Parental assumptions about preschool children's understanding of counting and cardinality, *Social Development*, 14(3): 496–513.

Freeman, N., Antonucci, C. and Lewis, C. (2000) Representation of the cardinality principle: early conception of error in a counterfactual test, *Cognition*, 74: 71–89.

Gelman, R. and Gallistel, C. (1978) *The Child's Understanding of Number*. Cambridge: Harvard University Press.

Gelman, R. and Meck, E. (1986) The notion of principle: the case of counting, in J. Hiebert (ed.) *Conceptual and Procedural Knowledge: The Case of Mathematics*. Hillsdale, NJ: Lawrence Erlbaum Associates.

Gray, E., Pitta, D. and Tall, D. (2000) Objects, actions, and images: a perspective on early number development, *The Journal of Mathematical Behavior*, 18(4): 401–13.

Hiebert, J. and Lefevre, P. (1986) Conceptual and procedural knowledge in mathematics: an introductory analysis, in J. Hiebert (ed.) *Conceptual and Procedural Knowledge: The Case of Mathematics*. Hillsdale, NJ: Lawrence Erlbaum Associates.

LeFevre, J., Smith-Chant, B., Fast, L., Skwarchuk, S., Sargla, E., Arnup, J., Penner-Wilger, M., Bisanz, J. and Kamawar, D. (2006) What counts as knowing? The development of conceptual and procedural knowledge of counting from kindergarten through Grade 2, *Journal of Experimental Child Psychology*, 93: 285–303.

Rittle-Johnson, B., Siegler, S. and Alibali, M. (2001) Developing conceptual understanding and procedural skill in mathematics: an iterative process, *Journal of Educational Psychology*, 93(2): 346–62.

Rousselle, L. and Noël, M-P. (2007) Basic numerical skills in children with mathematics learning disabilities: a comparison of symbolic vs. non-symbolic number magnitude processing, *Cognition*, 102: 361–95.

Sophian, C. (1998) A developmental perspective on children's counting, in C. Donlan (ed.) *The Development of Mathematical Skills*. Hove: Psychology Press.

7 Compressing the counting process: strength from the flexible interpretation of symbols

Eddie Gray

Introduction

In most infant classrooms during a mathematics lesson, we can see some form of counting. Children count counters, pencils, shapes, marbles, acorns, toys – anything. If it is countable it is counted. Counting is one of the actions young children participate in using everyday objects from the real world. Objects from this world can be seen. On the one hand, they are manipulated, named and described, providing the initial phases in the development of geometry; on the other, they can be quantified, giving the initial phases in the development of arithmetic.

Geometric growth stems from handling real-world objects. They are seen and manipulated, conceived of visually and holistically as they appear to the senses, and named. It takes time for the regularities of these shapes to be described in a more subtle verbal form, for their properties to be identified and relationships based on those properties to be established. Arithmetic also has a physical counterpart originating in the real world, so it has visual elements but it is possible for these elements to change. Actions on objects of the real world form objects that are part of the arithmetical world. However, whereas perception and manipulation lead to the gradual accommodation of geometric concepts, the formation of numerical concepts is far more subtle. It involves a shift in attention from the objects of the real world to the objects of the arithmetical world – numbers and their symbols.

The part that counting has to play in the shift of attention is the focus of this chapter. We see how actions upon objects of the real world may be steadily compressed to form objects of the arithmetical world. Children who use the underlying strength of these new objects have a source of flexibility and power which provides them with a stepping stone towards further mathematical growth. Those who do *not* become trapped within the complexity of the actions and left bewildered as arithmetic and mathematics generally become ever more complex.

Counting plays a sophisticated and central role in the development of number concepts. But how is this done? If it is so fundamental, why is it that well into Key Stage 2 we may see some children still relying extensively on it to add and subtract – even to establish multiplication facts? Perhaps it seems natural that if so much energy and time is expended upon the development of sound counting skills within Key Stage 1, some children within Key Stage 2 appear to be reluctant to use alternative approaches. The more we work at remembering how to do something, the more we are likely to use the remembered approach; it is perhaps the case that the more we remember how to *do*, paradoxically, the less we may *know*.

'It will help you if you count'

It will prove fruitful to distinguish between the terms 'process' and 'procedure', which will be used extensively in this chapter. The word 'process' is used in a general sense, as in the 'process of counting', the 'process of addition', or the 'process of subtraction'. It need not be something that is currently being carried out in thought or by action; for example, we may speak of the process of addition without actually performing it. Nor is there any implication that the process must be carried out in a unique manner. For instance, the process of addition may be carried out by counting or by some other method. The term 'procedure' is used to describe a specific algorithm for implementing a process. Flexibility in carrying out a process will play a fundamental role in our story. Within simple arithmetic, counting may stimulate the growth of such flexibility but it may also inhibit it. How may such a contradiction arise? What is it about counting that may cause such a paradox?

Try to visualize James. He is a small 5-year-old sitting among a group of similarly aged children carrying out counting activities. His voice carries above the others within the group '. . . five, six, *seven*'. There is silence as he then quietly writes. A closer examination of what he is doing reveals that he was adding 4 and 3 using his fingers to count on from four. Now think of Joseph who is aged 8. He is also trying to work out 4 + 3. He is sitting motionless but his lips are moving and, looking closely, we can see his eyes moving slowly from left to right. The lip movements stop and then start again. His eyes repeat their movement. This happens several times, and each time a little more tension is evident in the deep frown on Joseph's face. Eventually Joseph's teacher interrupts his concentration: 'Use counters or your fingers Joseph. It will be easier'. There is some relief on Joseph's face as he goes for the second option without making it too obvious – he uses his fingers under his desk. Why? He explained later that he '. . . wants to do things like the clever children. They do it in their heads'. Counting on his fingers under the desk helps him to continue his subterfuge: it still looks as if he is doing things like the 'clever children'. The teacher shares his secret. It is almost as if they have entered into a conspiracy: the current difficulty has been sorted out because he has been told how to *do* the sum using an easier approach. On the next combination, however, we begin to see the lips move and the eyes roll. Again his teacher very quietly intervenes and suggests that he should use his fingers: '. . . it will help you understand what you are doing'.

Two children, both counting, but there is a tremendous difference in the quality of this counting over such a spectrum of age. The 5-year-old is experiencing counting as part of a programme of conceptual development which may eventually give him choices. Joseph and children like him are counting because they are unable to do anything else – they have no choice. Faced with a problem such as 4 + 3, they translate it into a counting action. They have had plenty of experience doing this: an addition or subtraction sign means count, albeit a different sort of counting. It can take so long to do the counting and get an answer that such children may not remember the numbers they started with. Once again they have practised a counting procedure. Simple arithmetic is about counting. Joseph did not realize that when the other children were doing things in their heads, they were using methods that are far easier than his. Even when he has difficulty, he is advised to try an approach that is harder than theirs. That this is so was aptly explained by Amanda, who is aged 9:

> I find it easier *not* to do it [simple addition] with my fingers because sometimes I get into a big muddle with them [and] I find it much harder to add up because I am not concentrating on the sum. I am concentrating on getting my fingers right . . . which takes a while. It can take longer to work out the sum than it does to work out the sum in my head.

What insight from a child who herself is having difficulty with arithmetic. She focuses on the two features emerging from elementary arithmetic that could create a dichotomy: being able to *do* and *think* at the same time. Doing the first may get in the way of the second, but within the classroom environment, there can be clear difficulties in making the choice: 'If we don't [use our fingers] the teacher is going to think, "why aren't they using their fingers . . . they are just sitting there thinking" . . . we are meant to be using our fingers because it is easier . . . which it is not' (Amanda, age 9).

The dual face of numbers

Through their experience of a counting procedure, young children learn to associate a counting action with a sequence of number words. The last number word tells them how many things have been counted and, with familiarity, the child can use this number word to stand for countable items (see Maclellan, Chapter 6). So, when counting five objects, the child points to each object in turn and repeats the sequence of number words 'one, two, three, four, five'. The final five tells them that 'five' have been counted. Later when they hear the word 'five' or see the symbol '5', they may associate these things with five countable items.

One of the interesting things about numbers and, no doubt one that we all know but do not make explicit to the children we teach, is that we treat them as if they were real 'things' – 'five is half of ten', 'three and four make seven'. Though there is no need to associate these things with other, real-life, objects to make sense of them, we can do so if we wish.

Early counting experiences associate numbers with things. By doing so it is possible that for the learner the notion of *seven* lines may have qualitatively little difference from the notion of *straight* lines. Of course, there is one difference; the first is the result of an action and is arithmetical, the second the result of perception and is geometrical. However, the word 'seven' and the word 'straight' may be associated with the objects to which they refer: they may be properties of the set of lines. To continue associating numbers with other objects is very limiting. To say 'my sister is *seven*' may have a similar quality to saying 'my sister is *tall*'. The seven is concretized by being associated with real items: the numbers are used as adjectives and associated with other nouns. Real power in arithmetic derives from not only being able to see this but also to see the numbers as nouns (i.e. as 'things'). When we do this we can establish relationships between the 'things' – something even young children after their initial experience with counting can do. They will tell us that the things can be seen differently. Nicky (age 5) looked at the two expressions 2 + 1 and 1 + 2 and said, 'See those two, they are both the same, they're both three'. Paul, his friend, thought he could give all of the numbers that make five. He started by saying, 'Two things together make a number' and he quickly reeled of examples that make five: '. . . two and three, four and one, five and nothing'. He had some trouble with one and four but decided he could do it if he counted.

Within these two examples we see two different but complementary aspects of numerical symbols, whether spoken or written. They refer to countable items and they compress ideas that allow us to see other relationships. Those children that recognize symbolic ambiguity, which either triggers the recreation of the number through a counting process or its use as a thing, have a very powerful tool at their fingertips. Those that do not, like Joseph, are more unfortunate – they only have half of the key available to them. Unfortunately, this is the most difficult half, the half that Joseph does not have!

Compressing counting procedures

Children's growing sophistication in handling counting procedures may be seen as an example of a steady compression which can eventually permit choice between these and the use of number concepts. We can see this by considering the relationship between the addition process and the concept of sum in, for example, the addition of 4 + 3. The most elementary method used to carry out the addition process is to count four objects (1, 2, 3, 4), then to count three objects (1, 2, 3), then to put all the objects together and count the total (1, 2, 3, 4, 5, 6, 7). This succession of three separate counting procedures is called 'count-all'.

The next stage occurs when it is realized that it is not necessary to count a set of four followed by a set of three. One of the numbers, 4 for example, may be seen as a number object and the child can simply *count-on* a further three numbers in the number sequence. The sum of 4 + 3 becomes **4** . . . 5, 6, 7. We may see 'count-on' as another procedure used to carry out the process of addition. It may be spontaneously constructed and 'invented' by children (Baroody and Ginsburg 1986), 'personalized' (Gray 1991), or 'taught' (DfES 2006).

An important aspect of the two counting procedures used to carry out the addition process is the procedural compression signifying a change from lengthy procedures associated with count-all, to the more contracted ones of count-on. However, the move from one to the other is not as simple as it seems. Count-on is a sophisticated double counting process. To calculate 4 + 3 requires not only counting on beyond 4 in the number sequence but also keeping a check that precisely three numbers are being counted. In the infant class, we may see some children using counters and others using fingers. Sometimes the only evidence that a child is counting comes from the close observation that shows a nodding head, moving eyes or moving lips. Joseph tried this but he could not easily keep two numbers in focus at once.

Of course we should not pretend that count-all and count-on are the only classifications which describe the steady compression of counting procedures. Steffe et al. (1983) provide us with a clearer picture of the things children create when they count; they indicate a growing sophistication in the objects used. Children may even change the numbers around, start with the larger 'because it is nearer the answer' and count-on the smaller. Baroody and Ginsburg (1986) see this distinction not only as an important step on the way to learning more formal arithmetic but, they suggest, it also provides an indication of the child's efforts to reduce the number of steps and the time used to carry out the process. Clearly then, it is possible to provide even finer gradations than those that form the focus of this chapter. Recognizing them may provide an insight into the way in which children's thinking is developing. Fixation on any one may provide a longer-term prognosis of the child's achievement in arithmetic and in mathematics as a whole.

It is not our purpose to dwell on the finer details but to provide a coarser analysis which may be useful within the classroom and provide a sense of where such procedures may lead to. It is the notion of 'compression' which helps us do this. Whichever form of classification we use – the coarse one or the finer gradations which give a more detailed picture – we see that with experience children compress lengthier procedures into shorter procedures. The procedure may not only be quicker but it is suggested that its operation also uses up less memory space and makes it more possible to link directly the inputs to the outputs – to *know* the solution.

Linked directly to 7, the sum of $4 + 3$ becomes a 'known fact'. In any isolated incident it is not easy to distinguish whether or not such facts are meaningful or rote learned. The difference may only become apparent when such facts are decomposed and recomposed to give 'derived facts' (see Thompson, Chapter 8). For instance, we may use the fact that $4 + 3 = 7$ to 'derive the fact' that $14 + 3$ is 17. It would even be possible to use another known fact such as $4 + 4$ to derive the sum of $4 + 3$.

By considering the compression of counting procedures we can begin to see more clearly what the experiences we give children may be leading to and, more importantly, what this experience is telling them. Count-all and count-on evoke different processes of counting, while known facts can evoke the concept of sum. Consequently, when young children are presented with elementary number combinations such as $4 + 3$, they can interpret the notation in two qualitatively different ways: as a *process* to *do*, or as an *object* to *think* about. The latter is of course a mental object that arises out of progressive compressions of the former.

The child who has compressed counting procedures into known and derived facts possesses a powerful tool with which to achieve success in arithmetic. If they encounter problems with larger numbers, they are able to use the knowledge they already have. As combinations become more difficult, those who *know* facts and *use* them flexibly find arithmetic far easier than those who have to carry out counting procedures. For such children, subtraction may become just another way of looking at addition; it is relatively easy for the flexible child who can use a related addition fact.

Such flexibility can be seen in stark contrast to the difficulties experienced by children who use counting procedures. These procedures may be successful for simple combinations but they may become extremely difficult for larger numbers. Concrete materials can be used to support (or rather, avoid) the double counting that is so frequently a feature of children's difficulties. Calculating 4 + 3 by count-on requires the counter to not only count beyond 4 in the number sequence but also to keep a check that precisely three numbers are being counted. The use of concrete materials to do this can give the semblance of progress when little progress has actually been achieved and the subtleties of the double counting of the count-on algorithm have not been sufficiently well appreciated to be carried out without physical supports. Joseph's failure without concrete aids and his eventual success with them, albeit with small numbers, aptly illustrate this point.

The child who relies on count-on for addition is much more likely to use its inverse, count-back, for subtraction. This can be horrendously difficult even with some physical support. Consider Jenny who attempted to count-back 13 from 19 keeping a check on the double count by using her fingers: '19, 18, 17, 16, 15, 13 . . . 14, 15 . . . 14, 13, 12 . . .' It is surprising that she arrived at the correct solution. Though she almost immediately recognized her miscount at 15, this caused her some added difficulty: was she counting up or counting back? To overcome such difficulty, we often use a number line to help children count back but this may have a fatal flaw. Counting back on a number line may be no more than an example of single counting, hardly more sophisticated than count-all, and it may not generalize into a flexible form of subtraction.

The numerical procept

The evidence suggests that there are two main interpretations of arithmetical expressions such as 4 + 3. One makes use of numerical concepts and relationships, while the other triggers the use of counting procedures. This leads us to an important feature of arithmetical symbolism. Not only does it provide a sense of what to *do* but also what to *know*.

Now we begin to see what is so special about arithmetical symbolism. It is really so very simple. Numerical symbols do not represent either a process or an object; they represent both at the same time. Consider, as an example, the symbol '5'. It can be written and it can be seen. It can be spoken and it can be heard. The symbol '5' represents the fusion of a number name with a counting process. We can recreate the counting process whenever we see the symbol or hear its name. But we can also use the concept of 'five' without any reference to countable items. Many different processes give rise to the object five. Not only the process of counting 'one . . . two . . . three . . . four . . . five . . .', but also the process of adding four and one, of adding three and two, two and three, of taking three away from eight, or two away from seven, of halving ten, and so on. All these processes give rise to the same object. The symbol '5' represents a considerable amount of information, not least the counting *proc*ess by which it is named and con*cept* or idea by which it is used. Gray and Tall (1994) believed such a fundamental ambiguity deserved its own terminology. This is embraced within the notion of *procept*: a symbol which ambiguously represents both *proc*ess and con*cept*. There are many numerical symbols that evoke either process or concept:

- 3 + 4 is either the process of *addition* of 3 and 4 or the concept of the sum, 7;
- 3/4 can mean (among other interpretations) the process of *division* of 3 by 4 or the concept of the fraction, 3/4;
- 3 × 4 represents the process of *repeated addition* and the concept of the product, 12.

Not all mathematical symbols are procepts but they do occur widely, particularly in arithmetic, algebra and aspects of higher mathematics. We may consider number as a procept: as a process and as a concept, both of which are represented by the same symbol. Children who use count-all recreate the process embedded within each symbol. Children who use count-on may use either the process or the concept: they may treat one number as an object and use the process embedded in the other to increment in ones. Though usually shorter than count-all, count-on remains a counting process which takes place in time. By using it a child may be able to compute the result without necessarily linking input and output in a form that will be remembered as a new fact. Some children – often with a limited array of known facts – may become so efficient in counting, that they use it as a universal method that does not involve them in the risk of attempting to use a limited number of known facts. However, count-on may lead to development of a procept. It can produce a result that is seen both as a counting procedure and a number concept.

The proceptual divide

In the early stages number is widely seen as a counting process. It is only when the child realizes that the number of elements is independent of the way in which the elements are arranged and the order in which they are counted that number can begin to take on its own stable existence as a mental object. During Key Stage 1, most children count at least some of the time, and some children count all the time. Those who count quickly can succeed in the number facts to 10 almost as well, and sometimes better, than those who know or can manipulate number facts. But those who achieve higher levels do so because they begin to see numbers as mental objects to be manipulated (Gray 1994). The more successful may still count, but they do so less and less, and when they do count, they use the technique sparingly in subtle ways (see

Thompson, Chapter 8), and thus are more likely to succeed than those that continue to count on a regular basis. The latter may develop intricate counting techniques using imaginary fingers, parts of the body, selected objects in the room, and so on, to cope with the number facts to 20. But in doing so they give themselves a harder job to do than those who use number facts in a flexible way.

The divergence between those who interpret processes only as procedures and therefore make mathematics harder for themselves, and those that see them as flexible procepts, is called the 'proceptual divide' (Gray and Tall 1994). It is hypothesized that the difference between success and failure lies in the difference between the use of procepts and procedures. Those who use procedures where appropriate and symbols as manipulable objects where appropriate are said to be proceptual thinkers. It is further hypothesized that count-on is one procedure that causes a bifurcation between those who display the ability to think proceptually and those who think in terms of procedures (Gray 1993).

This divide between success and failure is found throughout the mathematics curriculum. At any stage, if the cognitive demands on the individual grow too great, it may be that someone, previously successful, founders. Like Joseph, they may ask 'tell me how to do it', anxiously seeking the security of a procedure rather than the flexibility of procept. From this point on, failure is almost inevitable. It is for this reason that mathematics is known chiefly as a subject in which people fail, fail badly and fail often.

Implications for teaching and learning

If number is seen as a flexible procept, evoking a mental object, or a counting process, whichever is the more fruitful at the time, then children are likely to build up known facts in a meaningful way. Thus the 'fact' that $4 + 3$ is 7 becomes a flexible way of interchanging the notation $4 + 3$ for the number 7. If 4 is taken from 7, then this number triple tells us that the number 3 remains. In this way, seeing addition as a flexible procept leads to subtraction being viewed as another way of formulating addition. Successful children learn how to derive new facts from old in a flexible way.

It helps us to realize that what we need to do is to help all children achieve the flexible form of thinking developed through compressing number processes into concepts. But at its highest level, such flexibility is only achieved if children also know number facts and number tables. The introduction of the National Numeracy Strategy (NNS) (DfEE 1999) and its subsequent update (DfES 2006) make explicit reference to the need for such knowledge by all children. In particular, through its specified objectives for Years 1 to 3, the latter emphasizes the use of known knowledge to 'derive' unknown knowledge thus implicitly acknowledging the importance of numerical flexibility.

Too frequently, however, for some children, counting remains the focus of attention. This can make it very difficult to compress the number processes into an object. As the NNS implies we not only need to provide all children with opportunities to think about the power and flexibility of the symbolism, but for some we need to give opportunities which may help them to make necessary links between combination and output without the use of a lengthy procedure. The ease with which many children now use computers may supply one solution. Of course, the use of a computer will not in itself help children to learn number facts, but it would help them to relate similar problems and observe the patterns. Through the visual display and through appropriate interaction, a child may resolve and see on the display at the same time not only the fact that $4 + 3$ is equal to 7 but also that $3 + 4$ is 7, $2 + 5$ is 7, $9 - 2$ is 7, and so on. Because several combinations can be built and seen in sequence, a child can easily try $13 + 4$, $23 + 4$, and may begin to see a pattern. Such an approach not only provides an alternative representation for the numbers but an alternative way to deal with them. We offer a 'button-pressing' procedure, which permits the child to see a representation, which includes inputs and outputs without lengthy counting procedures militating against their connection. In such a way, we may help the child appreciate the pattern and develop some flexibility to solve harder combinations. Will such a strategy improve all children's ability at arithmetic?

Howat (2006) found that there were failing children (median age 8.5) in arithmetic who were unable to cope with place value because they had not constructed the concept of 'ten' as a thinkable concept that could be ten ones or one ten. Without this knowledge they were overwhelmed by the problem of coping with the arithmetic of two-digit numbers. Their response to any problem was to attempt counting on in ones. Working closely with these children, Howat found that some had cognitive difficulties starting so far back in their development that were deeply ingrained and seemed no longer responsive to her remedial action.

Therefore, in some senses there may be a problem. After all, if some children, because of their lack of success at arithmetic, turn to using procedures while we may want to make them flexible, it may be that the best we can do is to teach them procedures to make them flexible. In other words, we do not make them really flexible at all. Simply giving procedural children more examples to practise may help them in one way; it may make the procedures they use a little faster and perhaps a little more efficient, but in other ways it could be very damaging in that what they do without guidance is to develop their own idiosyncratic methods which, in fact, make the mathematics far harder. We therefore need to combine the practice of those facts which are essential building blocks in the system with the flexible means by which they can be manipulated most easily. This may mean practising number combinations so that they become automatic, but this must not set arithmetic in the context of something which *must* be learned by rote. Those who are successful at arithmetic have more than this. They use the facts they know to build the ones they do not know. They see the arithmetical symbol in a flexible way: it is both a process which enables them to do mathematics and a mental concept which enables them to think about it.

Frequently, it is implied that a child's failure to grasp the underlying nuances of arithmetical symbolism, and later those of other more sophisticated forms of mathematical symbolism, is the result of the inadequacies of teaching. Gray and Tall (2007) suggest differently, indicating that a natural process of abstraction, whereby knowledge is compressed into more sophisticated thinkable concepts, is the key to developing increasingly powerful thinking. For the most able this may occur naturally. Others may be helped through the use of techniques that encourage them to focus on the essential elements for compression into thinkable concepts. But there is no evidence that through such help it can work for *all* children. They conclude by suggesting that until the nature of the required sophistication supporting the compression of complicated phenomena into thinkable concepts is grasped and we are then able to express it in a way that makes sense to teachers and students, arithmetic and mathematics in general will remain for many a world of overbearing difficulty relieved only partially by limited rote learning.

References

Baroody, A.J. and Ginsburg, H.P. (1986) The relationship between initial meaningful and mechanical knowledge of arithmetic, in J. Hiebert (ed.) *Conceptual and Procedural Knowledge: The Case for Mathematics*. Hillsdale, NJ: Lawrence Erlbaum Associates.

DfEE (Department for Education and Employment) (1999) *The National Numeracy Strategy: Framework for Teaching Mathematics from Reception to Year 6*. London: DfEE.

DfES (Department for Education and Skills) (2006) *Primary Framework for Literacy and Mathematics*. Norwich: DfES.

Gray, E.M. (1991) An analysis of diverging approaches to simple arithmetic: preference and its consequences, *Educational Studies in Mathematics*, 22: 551–74.

Gray, E.M. (1993) Count-on: the parting of the ways in simple arithmetic, in I. Hirabayashi, N. Hohda, K. Shigematsu and Fou-Lai Lin (eds) *Proceedings of the XVII International Conference for the Psychology of Mathematics Education*, 1: 204–11. Tsukuba: Programme Committee.

Gray, E.M. (1994) Spectrums of performance in two-digit addition and subtraction, in J.P. Ponte and J.F. Matos (eds) *Proceedings of the XVIII International Conference for the Psychology of Mathematics Education*, 3: 25–32. Lisbon: Programme Committee.

Gray, E.M. and Tall, D.O. (1994) Duality, ambiguity and flexibility: a proceptual view of simple arithmetic, *Journal for Research in Mathematics Education*, 25(2): 116–40.

Gray, E.M. and Tall, D.O. (2007) Abstraction as a natural process of mental compression, *Mathematics Education Research Journal*, 19(2): 23–40.

Howat, H. (2006) Participation in elementary mathematics: an analysis of engagement, attainment and intervention. Unpublished PhD thesis, University of Warwick.

Steffe, L.P., von Glaserfeld, E., Richard, J. and Cobb, P. (1983) *Children's Counting Types: Philosophy, Theory and Application*. New York: Praeger Scientific.

SECTION 4
Extending counting to calculating

The chapters in Sections 2 and 3 focused in the main on the nature of the counting process: its purposes, its constituent parts and its inherent complexities. The two chapters in this section discuss the next stage: the development of informal calculation procedures. The authors consider the extent to which counting plays a part in young children's mental addition, subtraction, multiplication and division strategies. In Chapter 8, Ian Thompson describes the range of mental calculation strategies for addition and subtraction reported by a research project that involved 103 Year 2 and Year 3 children. Using specific examples he relates his findings to the findings of other researchers, focusing particularly on counting strategies and what have become known as 'derived fact strategies'. He then discusses two British research projects concerned with the actual teaching of mental calculation strategies, and concludes with a few suggestions as to how we might proceed in this area.

Julia Anghileri (Chapter 9) explains how children's first experiences of multiplication arise when they make groups containing the same number of objects and realize that they can count the groups rather than the individual items. She uses examples of children's work to illustrate some of the potential language difficulties associated with the vocabulary of multiplication and division. She then charts the progression in multiplication and division skills that are evident in the early years classroom, and identifies links between the counting procedures that children use for solving addition and subtraction problems and those that they develop to solve multiplication and division problems. She suggests that teachers should help children to focus on the diversity of the language associated with equal grouping and sharing activities and on how such language may be related to counting patterns.

8 From counting to deriving number facts

Ian Thompson

Introduction

The idea that young children are capable of deriving unknown number facts from facts that they already know only really gained a hold in the UK in the mid-1990s. This was despite the fact that American writers such as Carpenter and Moser (1984) and Steinberg (1985), as well as British writers like Thompson (1989) and Gray (1991), had written about this phenomenon some time earlier. In 1991, the year of the first Standard Assessment Tasks (SATs) for 7-year-olds, the guidance notes for teachers provided by the School Examinations and Assessment Council included the following advice: 'It is important that you assess each child's ability to add and subtract by using recall of number facts only, *not by counting or computation*' (my italics). The notes spelled out clearly that children should not be using computation in any obvious way to arrive at their answers, and that evidence of attainment could only be shown if the number facts were known by the child and produced spontaneously.

At that time, the appropriate National Curriculum attainment target required that children should 'Know and use addition and subtraction facts up to 10' (or 'to 20' at Level 3). The question that immediately comes to mind is: 'What has happened to the "use" part of the attainment target?'. It seems somewhat perverse that a child who has found 4 + 5 by arguing that 'four and four is eight, so it must be nine' has been penalized – rather than being rewarded – for not only 'knowing' a number fact, but also 'using' it to derive an unknown fact!

Fortunately, attitudes towards mental calculation changed quite quickly over the next few years. The 1995 version of the National Curriculum discussed the necessity for children to be taught to '. . . develop a range of mental methods for finding, from known facts, those that they cannot recall . . .'. This acceptance of mental calculation methods and derived fact strategies was consolidated with the arrival of the National Numeracy Project in 1996, which merged imperceptibly into the National Numeracy Strategy (NNS) in 1999 and then less imperceptibly into the Primary National Strategy (PNS) in 2003. It is important to be aware at this stage that one of the three key principles (later changed to four) on which the NNS was originally based was 'an emphasis on mental calculation' (DfEE 1999: 11). Also, in Recommendation 10 of the *Independent Review of Mathematics Teaching in Early Years Settings and Primary Schools* (DCSF 2008: 60) we are informed that 'This review recommends a renewed focus by practitioners on oral and mental mathematics'. This chapter uses specific examples to illustrate research findings on young children's mental calculation strategies for addition and subtraction before discussing the issue of the teaching of mental calculation.

Research on mental calculation strategies for addition

Several researchers have generated models for describing levels of addition strategies used by young children for solving simple word problems. The model selected for discussion here is that of Carpenter and Moser (1984):

- counting all;
- counting on from the first number;
- counting on from the larger number;
- using known number facts and using derived number facts.

The following examples are taken from those used by 59 children from Year 2 (6- to 7-year-olds) and 44 from Year 3 who were involved in a small-scale research project investigating mental calculation strategies. The children were from three different schools in the Newcastle-upon-Tyne area. Many of the strategies to be discussed were incorporated into the NNS *Framework for Teaching Mathematics from Reception to Year 6* (DfEE 1999). Some reference will be made to where these strategies sit in the aforementioned publication and also in the *Primary Framework for Literacy and Mathematics* (DfES 2006a). Several of the examples illustrate the extent to which some children, even when they have learned more sophisticated calculation strategies, combine these with counting techniques. A wide range of addition strategies was generated by the children in the study, and examples were found of each of the types identified by Carpenter and Moser (1984). These methods are discussed under the following headings: counting-all, counting-on, counting-on-from-larger, near doubles, bridging-up-through-ten and step-counting (see Wright, Chapter 14).

Counting strategies

Counting-all
This is the most basic addition strategy and it develops quite naturally from the early learning goal 'Begin to relate addition to combining two groups of

objects . . .'. The *Practice Guidance for the Early Years Foundation Stage* (DfES 2007: 68) includes the following objective for children between the ages of 40 and 60+ months: 'Find the total number of items in two groups by counting all of them.' Having counted out four blocks to build one house and five blocks to build a bigger one, a child operating at this stage, when asked how many blocks there are altogether, will count all the blocks again beginning at one (see Carruthers and Worthington, Chapter 10).

Counting-on
Jacqueline (finding $5 + 6$):

> 5 . . . 6, 7, 8, 9, 10, 11. It's eleven.

The step from 'counting-all' to 'counting-on' is a big one, although most children appear to manage it by age 7. Jacqueline needs to have reached the 'counting for cardinality' stage discussed by Threlfall (Chapter 5), appreciating that the five describes the numerosity of a particular collection. She also needs to realize that the number sequence is a breakable chain, where oral counting can begin at any point within this chain. In the *Stepping stones* section of the document *Curriculum Guidance for the Foundation Stage* (DfEE/QCA 2000: 77) we read that practitioners should 'Provide experience of reciting number names from starting points other than one . . . to help children "count on" '. If Jacqueline were unable to do this, there is no possibility of her being able to use the 'count-on' strategy (see Gray, Chapter 7). However, activities of this type have, unfortunately, not been included in the *Practice Guidance for the Early Years Foundation Stage* (DfES 2007).

She also needs to appreciate that it is not just objects that can be counted, but that the number words themselves can. To count on Jacqueline recites the number names that are the successors of five, while simultaneously keeping track of how many of them she has spoken; she is effectively carrying out a double count, saying 'Six, seven, eight, nine, ten, eleven', while simultaneously ensuring that she has spoken exactly six words. Any more or fewer would result in an incorrect answer. Another way of appreciating the sophistication of the strategy is to realize that Jacqueline makes a cardinal/ordinal switch followed later by an ordinal/cardinal switch: the cardinal number 5 in $5 + 6$ is transformed into an ordinal number so that the count can be continued to 11; then the ordinal number 11 is converted back to a cardinal quantity to give the answer. And yet some people call counting-on a basic strategy!

In Block A, Unit 2 of the Planning section for Year 1 (DfES 2006b), it states that 'Later, they count on using a number line, then count on mentally'. The implication is that the former activity will facilitate the acquisition of the latter. To investigate this, you might like to try the following activity: imagine a number line and take note of the words you would say (perhaps sub-vocally) when using counting-on to calculate 5 + 4 on this line. Then use counting-on to find 5 + 4 in your head – again taking note of the actual words that you use. Finally, compare the two lists of number names and other aspects of the two processes.

It is likely that most readers moved along the line saying; 'One, two, three, four', noting that they landed on position 9. In the second situation they most probably said: 'Five . . . six, seven, eight, nine', noting that the last number name spoken was 'nine' – the answer to the addition. In these two situations they recited different number names while carrying out the activities, and they ascertained the answer from different contexts – the position on the line in the first case and the last word spoken in the second. This suggests that we are dealing with different strategies, even though, unfortunately to my mind, we use the same words to describe them. ('Counting-along' is more accurate in a number line context – although perhaps more clumsy.) Counting-on along a number line and counting-on mentally are conceptually different activities.

Counting-on-from-larger
Steven (finding 5 + 6):

> Well, I took the big number first . . . I said six in my head and counted five more.

Plenty of experience of using counting-on from the first number has led to Steven's realizing that he will get the same answer – and save effort – if he starts from the larger of the two numbers. This method of solution illustrates the extent to which the drive for 'cognitive economy' – the desire to reduce the load on working memory – can affect the strategies that children develop. By adopting this method Steven shows that he has some implicit awareness of the commutative property of addition (i.e. 5 + 6 = 6 + 5), although he would not be able to articulate this explicitly. This use of commutativity becomes a more helpful labour-saving device as the difference between the two numbers to be added increases in size. All three of these counting strategies, plus related activities, are included in the *Supplement of examples: Reception* in the *Framework for Teaching Mathematics from Reception to Year 6* (DfEE 1999: 2–18). They are more difficult to find in the *Primary Framework for Literacy and Mathematics* (DfES 2006a: 94), but make their first appearance in Year 1.

Derived strategies

Near doubles
Hannah (calculating 5 + 6):

> I looked back in my memory . . . six and six is twelve, so it's one less.

The first number facts that young children learn tend to be the doubles. This might be because they meet many situations in real life where things come in pairs or because there is less of a load on working memory. Soon, children begin to make use of these doubles facts to find 'near doubles'. More often than not to find 5 + 6 they would argue to themselves that 'five and five is ten, and so since six is one more than five, then five and six must be one more than ten'. This strategy could be called the 'one more than a double' strategy, whereas Hannah above has used 'one less than a double'. The achievement of the early learning goal in the *Primary Framework for Literacy and Mathematics* (DfES 2006a: 70) 'Find one more or one less than a number from 1 to 10' is a pre-requisite for using this strategy, as is – obviously – a knowledge of doubles. This was the most common 'derived-fact' strategy used by the children in the research sample.

Some children had favourite doubles which they used in a variety of situations, while others used a doubles fact and then used counting-on. Ben (finding 5 + 7) said:

> Ten . . . eleven, twelve . . . I counted in my head [i.e. double five, count on two]

It is probably the case that other children use this calculating strategy, but the fact that they perform the count silently in their heads means that no one else becomes aware of this. Other responses involved a 'doubles-plus-or-minus-two' or even a 'doubles-plus-or-minus-three' approach. Jane was seen to put up three fingers while correctly working out 7 + 4 and, when asked how she arrived at her correct answer, replied:

> Four and four is eight . . . and then if you put a seven instead of the four it's three more . . . so it's three more than eight.

This extension of the near doubles strategy was much more rare!

Bridging-up-through-10
Mark (calculating 7 + 8):

> 15 . . . Well I had 8 and I knew that 8 and 2 was 10 . . . and then because 7 is an odd number it's got 5 more . . . and 10 and 5 makes 15.

One mathematical idea underpinning this strategy is 'complements in ten'. For example, 7 is the complement in ten of 3, and 1 is the complement of 9. This idea is covered in most mathematical schemes by the 'story of ten' type of activity, but very few of these schemes offer more than one or two such activities. The concept is not usually treated as the important building block for mental arithmetic that it would appear to be. Vicki worked out 8 + 5 by, in her own words,

> . . . taking the two off it and putting it there.

Clearly, she had decided to make the eight into a ten by adding the two that she had removed from the five. The subsequent addition of the ten and the three was then easier for her to do. Paul's explanation of his answer to the same problem was:

> I made the eight into ten and went 11, 12, 13.

Paul's strategy is clearly a combination of bridging and counting-on.

Another important mathematical idea underpinning this strategy is 'partitioning' – sometimes called the 'additive composition of number'. In many British commercial mathematics schemes, either pre- or post-NNS, the section covering early addition in the context of single-digit numbers will most likely focus on finding the sum of two numbers. Children may be working in real-life situations solving real problems that lead to finding sums, or they may be less fortunate and have to work through a page of calculations like 4 + 4 = or 7 + 8 =. The focus of the activity is on finding the sum of the two numbers. However, in the Netherlands the emphasis is very different. Because of the importance attached to partitioning when using strategies such as bridging (notice that Mark had to be able to partition 7 into 5 and 2), the Dutch tend to put more emphasis on children knowing that 7 is 4 + 3, 2 + 5 or 6 + 1. Finding all the partitions of a number is considered at least as important as finding sums.

The 'complements in ten' strategy, with or without counting, was used much more frequently with subtraction than with addition, and is considered below in more detail. In the *Framework for Teaching Mathematics from Reception to Year 6* (DfEE 1999: 40) this strategy had the grandiose title of 'Add or subtract a pair of numbers mentally by bridging through 10 or 100, or a multiple of 10 or 100, and adjusting'. Interestingly, the word 'bridging' does not appear in the *Primary Framework for Literacy and Mathematics* (DfES 2006a), although it is, perhaps, implicit in the phrase 'Teachers help children to identify and use multiples of 10 as landmark numbers in calculations using number lines to record steps' (p. 114).

Step-counting

Counting in multiples of two, three or indeed any number is what is meant by 'step-counting' (see Anghileri, Chapter 9). Children often learn this skill, and some teachers teach it, as a preparatory activity for the learning of 'tables facts'. Ben's answer to the calculation 4 + 5 was:

4 . . . 6, 8, 9.

It was difficult to ascertain exactly why Ben had tackled the problem in this way, but it related to his visualizing the five in standard 'domino' formation, then adding the two pairs of dots by counting-on in twos from four, and finally adding on the remaining dot.

Research on mental calculation strategies for subtraction

Several researchers discuss subtraction strategies, but the evidence of 'progression' is not as clear cut as in the case of addition. Six particular strategies for dealing with subtraction situations were identified in the research project: counting-out (separating from), counting-back-from, counting-back-to, counting-up, inverse properties, and bridging-down-through-ten.

Counting strategies

Counting-out
Patrick, working out 7 – 3, said:

Four . . . I just knock down skittles in my head.

Further into the interview, having just given the correct answer to 13 – 6, he explained: 'I just had a game of skittles'. Counting-out involves the modelling (usually on the fingers rather than with skittles) of the number to be operated upon (the minuend). In Patrick's calculation, it would normally be the case that seven fingers are raised, and then three are lowered one at a time while the child counts 'One, two, three'. The remaining fingers are then counted. This strategy can involve children in three separate forward counts, although some soon learn to set up or remove a given number of fingers quite quickly – sometimes in one movement – and then read off from their fingers how many remain.

This strategy can be very successful when dealing with numbers up to ten, but because of a finger-shortage problem, it is less useful with larger numbers. Many children perceive the need for a more sophisticated technique when dealing with numbers greater than ten. Others, however, show surprising ingenuity in modifying a strategy that has brought them success. Anna had been correctly using 'counting-out' to answer some simple subtractions, and was asked to calculate 11 – 6 with a view to helping her to realize the inadequacies of this technique with these particular numbers. Fingers were set up and the correct answer was given. When asked how she had worked out the answer even though she only had ten fingers, she replied: 'I counted the newspaper'. Anna had used my newspaper, which was lying on the table, as the eleventh object in her collection. She proceeded to 'remove' that object first before returning to the familiar territory of her ten fingers to deftly take away the remaining five objects. She later calculated 15 – 9 by imagining five extra objects.

Counting-back-from
Richard found 7 – 3 by saying:

$$7 \ldots 6, 5, 4$$

He raised a finger as he said each of the words 'six', 'five' and 'four'. Similarly, Rebecca correctly worked 23 – 9 by counting backwards starting from 22 and tallying the count on nine of her fingers: not an easy task! 'Counting-back-from' is obviously more efficient for calculations where the difference between the two numbers is small.

This strategy was actually the most common subtraction procedure used by the children in this sample. However, an analysis shows that it is quite a sophisticated strategy. Children need to be able to execute successfully the following sub-skills: count backwards from a specified number; count backwards a specific number of steps; and employ some suitable 'keeping track' device. They must also have already perceived the need to keep track of the numbers being counted. Because this procedure involves a forward count during the keeping-track phase, 'counting-down-from' involves two simultaneous processes which in effect go in opposite directions. This fact could account for the occasional errors that were made by children using this technique. Graham gave the answer 'five' when finding 7 – 3. His counting-back strategy had let him down because he had counted '7 . . . 6 . . . 5' instead of '6 . . . 5 . . . 4'. The backward and forward count and the keeping-track method had all been correctly executed; Graham had simply started his count at the wrong place. This error was made by several other children in the sample.

Counting-back-to
Janine (7 – 3):

$$7 \ldots 6, 5, 4, 3. \text{ It's four}$$

Janine was the only child in the research project to use this strategy, which involves counting down to the subtrahend (here 3). While reciting the number names she raised a finger as each number after 'seven' was said. In this procedure the answer is the number of fingers raised rather than the last number spoken, as is the case with the seemingly easier 'counting-back-from' (see Wright, Chapter 14).

Counting-up

Carpenter and Moser (1984) suggest that children prefer to use the 'counting-up' rather than the 'counting-down' strategy – what used to be called 'shop-keeper arithmetic' in the days when tills did not tell you how much change to give. This does appear to be borne out by their data, since only 18 per cent of their sample did not use this strategy at all. Baroody (1984), on the other hand, argues that children use the 'counting-down-from' strategy more frequently because it provides a more accurate model of their informal concept of sub-traction as 'take away'. The results of my study confirm Baroody's (1984) position, since only *three* of the 103 children interviewed used this procedure.

A consideration of Gillian's answer to 7 – 3 should clarify the way in which this procedure operates:

3 . . . 4, 5, 6, 7 . . . It's four.

The final part of her answer came from her reading off the number of fingers she had raised while tallying her forward count. Here we have another 'count-and-tally-and-then-count-the-tally' procedure. What is being counted in this case is the number of counting words from three to seven. This strategy demands that, in this case, the finger that is normally mapped onto the count-ing word 'one' is, instead, mapped onto the word 'four'. This is quite a subtle adaptation of the basic counting procedure. These counting strategies for sub-traction, plus related activities, can be found in the *Supplement of examples: Reception* in the *Framework for Teaching Mathematics from Reception to Year 6* (DfEE 1999: 2–18). In the *Primary Framework for Literacy and Mathematics* (DfES 2006a: 72) counting-up has been moved from Reception to Year 1.

Derived strategies

Bridging-down-through-ten

This strategy was used on many occasions and by a number of children. It employs aspects of two sub-strategies discussed in the section on addition: 'complements in ten' and 'partitioning'. Tim, working out 15 – 9, said:

I took away five from fifteen and then I took away four . . . that's six.

Vicki's account of how she calculated 23 – 9 provides a lucid explanation of the thinking involved in the execution of this procedure:

Three and six make nine . . . and I took three away to make twenty . . . and I had the six to make four . . . so it's fourteen.

Vicki mentions 'four' because it is the 'complement in ten' of six.

None of the children in the sample had been taught this strategy by their teachers, and yet an analysis of the technique suggests that it is very subtle and quite complex. The ones digit of the larger number tells you how many to take away first in order to reduce this number to ten or to a multiple of ten. You then have to split (partition) the smaller number into two parts, one of which is equal to the ones digit of the larger number. The other part tells you how much you still have to take away from the ten (or multiple of ten). The answer is the complement in ten of this number or the complement of a multiple of ten.

Inverse properties

Beth (explaining her correct answer to 7 – 4):

> Well, four and three makes seven . . . so it's three.

It is important that children come to appreciate the connection between addition and subtraction. When one operation 'undoes' the other the two operations are called inverses: adding five and then subtracting five has no effect, so addition and subtraction are inverse operations. The implications of this are that every known addition bond provides information on two subtraction bonds (as well as another addition bond because of commutativity). For example, because $7 + 4 = 11$, then $11 - 7 = 4$ and $11 - 4 = 7$. This is very useful information to have, and children need a range of classroom experiences to help them appreciate this relationship between the two operations. Anna explained her correct answer to $14 - 8$ by arguing that:

> Two sevens are fourteen . . . so you take away another one.

What she meant was that '$7 + 7 = 14$, so $14 - 7 = 7$, but because it is $14 - 8$, I have to take away another 1. So the answer is 6'. The strategy used by this competent 6-year-old has used doubles, inverses and partitioning.

Implications for teaching and learning

The reason for describing in some detail the wide range of calculation strategies used by young children is not to try to convince teachers that they need to teach all of them, but to enable them to recognize these strategies when they are used by their pupils; recognition is just the first step. The following section looks at some research on the teaching of mental strategies,

In 1997, a School Curriculum and Assessment Authority discussion paper (SCAA 1997: 15) wondered whether 'strategies for mental calculation can actively be taught to pupils, or whether pupils develop them for themselves as a result of either maturation or experience'. The fact that the research reported in this chapter was carried out before the NNS was introduced suggests that some young children do develop them for themselves. Later in the same document we read that the development of mental calculation strategies 'should not be left to chance' (SCAA 1997: 29). In a similar vein, the *Primary Framework for Literacy and Mathematics* (DfES 2006a: 68) states that 'It is crucial that mental methods of calculation are taught to children and not confined to starter activities in lessons'.

Askew et al. (2001) devised a successful intervention programme to improve the mental calculation strategies of a group of children operating at or below Level 2 according to their SAT results. The intervention significantly improved the profile of techniques used by the pupils to arrive at correct solutions, and the researchers concluded that 'Through carefully targeted teaching, pupils who have not developed these strategies for themselves can indeed learn them' (p. 9). Murphy (2004: 16) interviewed three young children after the direct instruction of a mental calculation strategy. She argued that 'mental strategies can be introduced to children through whole class instruction but ... their use of the strategies may be reliant on their personal knowledge'.

As has been suggested above in the analysis of calculation methods, there is always some prerequisite knowledge that children need before they are able to 'invent' or learn a new strategy. Two specific procedures, counting-on and bridging-up, are listed below along with some of the sub-skills, understanding and knowledge necessary for their successful execution.

Counting-on

The minimal requisite sub-skills to enable a child to carry out this strategy effectively are the ability to:

- continue the count from a number different from one;
- appreciate that it is possible to count the number names;
- keep track of how many numbers have been said as the count is continued.

Bridging-up

To use this strategy effectively, children need to be able to do the following:

- understand that numbers can be partitioned;
- ascertain what is needed to build one of the numbers up to ten;
- partition the other number into two appropriate parts;
- know how to add a single digit number onto ten or a multiple of ten.

In conclusion, to be an effective teacher of mental calculation, practitioners need to:

- create a classroom environment where children feel comfortable talking about the strategies they use;
- listen carefully to children's explanations of their personal calculation methods;
- be able to recognize the particular strategy that a child is using;
- appreciate the prior number knowledge and sub-skills required for the efficient execution of the relevant strategy;
- ensure that children have the requisite experiences to enable them to progress to more sophisticated strategies.

Teachers must ensure that all children work in a classroom environment that will provide them with a wide variety of mathematical activities and teaching approaches that will afford them the opportunity to make their own connections; to commit some simple number facts to memory; and to develop the confidence necessary to use these facts to figure out other number facts that they have not yet learned.

References

Askew, M., Bibby, T. and Brown, M. (2001) *Raising Attainment in Primary Number Sense: From Counting to Strategy*. London: BEAM Education.

Baroody, A.J. (1984) Children's difficulties in subtraction: some causes and questions, *Journal for Research in Mathematics Education*, 15(3): 203–13.

Carpenter, T.P. and Moser, J.M. (1984) The acquisition of addition and subtraction concepts in grades one through three, *Journal for Research in Mathematics Education*, 15(3): 179–202.

DCSF (Department for Children, Schools and Families) (2008) *Independent Review of Mathematics Teaching in Early Years Settings and Primary Schools* www.publications.teachernet.gov.uk/eOrderingDownload/Williams%20Mathematics.pdf (accessed June 2008).

DfEE (Department for Education and Employment) (1999) *Framework for Teaching Mathematics from Reception to Year 6*. London: DfEE.

DfEE/QCA (Department for Education and Employment/Qualifications and Curriculum Authority) (2000) *Curriculum Guidance for the Foundation Stage*. London: DfEE/QCA.

DfES (Department for Education and Skills) (2006a) *Primary Framework for Literacy and Mathematics*. Norwich: DfES.

DfES (Department for Education and Skills) (2006b) The standards site.

www.standards.dfes.gov.uk/primaryframework/mathematics/planning/
Year1/counting/Unit2/ (accessed 31 March 2008).

DfES (Department for Education and Skills) (2007) *Practice Guidance for the Early Years Foundation Stage.* Nottingham: DfES www.publications.teachernet.gov.uk/ eOrderingDownload/eyfs_guide12_07.pdf (accessed 31 March 2008).

Gray, E.M. (1991) An analysis of diverging approaches to simple arithmetic preference and its consequences, *Educational Studies in Mathematics,* 22(6): 551–74.

Murphy, C. (2004) How do children come to use a taught mental calculation strategy?, *Educational Studies in Mathematics,* 56: 3–18.

SCAA (School Curriculum and Assessment Authority) (1997) *The Teaching and Assessment of Number at Key Stages 1–3. Discussion Paper No. 10,* London: SCAA.

Steinberg, R.M. (1985) Instruction on derived facts strategies in addition and subtraction, *Journal for Research in Mathematics Education,* 16(5): 337–55.

Thompson, I. (1989) Mind games, *Child Education,* 66(12): 28–9.

9   Uses of counting in multiplication and division

Julia Anghileri

Introduction

> Count repeated groups of the same size
> Share objects into equal groups and count how many in each group
>
> (DfES 2006a: 70)

Children's first experiences of multiplication arise where they make groups with equal numbers of objects and recognize the possibility of counting the groups rather than counting individual items. Where there is a 'natural' link between the objects, like *pairs* of shoes or *sets* of wheels for model cars, this counting in groups is easiest; a line of shoes may be counted as individual items or as pairs, and the numerical connection is multiplication. Division is also practised by very young children as they share any collection into equal portions or divide a set of objects into equal subsets. Ideas of 'equal sets' and 'fair' portions are fundamental to an understanding of multiplication and division and these early activities can form a secure base from which understanding of the more formal operations with their specific language and symbols will be developed.

Everyday activities like laying places at a table involve grouping items and these groups can be counted. When a knife, a fork and a spoon are used for each setting, it would be somewhat artificial to count the individual pieces of cutlery, but the counting of groups may be associated with the number of people expected. Where there is no obvious link in the collection in each set, children must recognize the common property that enables groupings to be identified and must become aware of the importance of a one-to-one correspondence between the items in the sets. Repeating patterns will provide a visual image for equal groupings and opportunities to count items and sets of items. For a practical classroom activity, beads could be grouped in threes to make a coloured necklace. This would work equally well with repeated groups of different shaped beads or a 'Noah's Ark' activity with equal groups of different animals.

The importance of language

Much of the language used in talking about such activities is shared between multiplication and division (Anghileri 1995a), as the two arithmetic operations represent a different way of expressing the relationships that exist between three numbers. Whenever equal sets are put together and counted, reversing the procedure and reconstructing the original sets may be used to illustrate the way multiplication and division are inverse operations.

Early grouping and matching activities will encourage the use of important mathematical language, and although many people automatically think that this means words like 'multiply' and 'divide', there are more basic words that need to be understood before any formal language is introduced. Everyday words like 'grouping' and 'sharing' along with 'each' and 'fair' have early associations with the processes that will become multiplication and division.

To illustrate some difficulties with language that may not be expected, consider the following observations and revealing responses from young children. Using pattern sticks made of linking cubes in different colours, children were shown a stick using four colours with two cubes of each colour and asked, 'How many colours?' (Anghileri 1989). For many children the question 'How many . . .' led to a count of all the cubes and the response 'Eight'. When asked what the colours were, some children then realized the full implication of the question, but others were unable to count the groups and remained fixed on their understanding of eight cubes. When asked to 'make a pattern stick using five colours with three of each colour', common errors were to produce a stick with five different colours and a further three cubes added to the end, or a stick with three cubes in each of three colours (see Figure 9.1). Not only was it

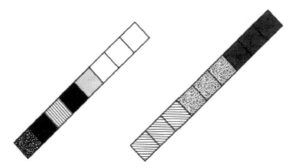

Figure 9.1 Incorrect responses to making a pattern stick with five colours using three of each colour.
  – A stick with five colours and a further three cubes
  – A stick with three cubes in each of three colours

difficult to identify the roles of the two numbers, five and three, but it was difficult for some children to recognize the importance of the word 'each' in the phrase 'three of each colour'. The word 'each' will be fundamentally important to understanding both multiplication and division.

One gets an idea of the scope and complexity of language when comparing such phrases as 'shared by three', 'shared with three', 'shared into three' and 'shared into threes'. Mathematical understanding will depend on detailed attention to the meanings of such phrases (and later phrases like 'divided by three', 'divided into three' and 'divided into threes') as it is clear that a collection like a bag of twelve apples can be divided differently 'by three', 'into three' and 'into threes' (see Figure 9.2).

As well as developing an understanding of the numerical relationships involved in multiplication and division, teachers will need to help children to focus on this language and the associated meanings. In practical situations, the ideas of multiplication and division as inverse operations may be explored:

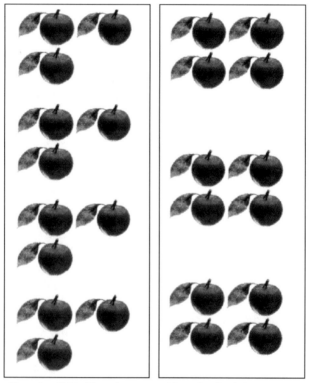

12 apples divided into threes   12 apples divided into three

Figure 9.2 Illustration of the complexity of the language of division.

a collection that is made up by putting together four groups of three may be partitioned again into four groups, or into three groups or just two groups. Such grouped collections can be counted in various ways and links in the numbers explored so that children begin to build up their understanding of the number relationships. For example, two lots of four can be reorganized as four lots of two. Where teachers recognize the wealth of relationships that can be found through such activities, they can guide children into appropriate use of language and begin to identify the arithmetic links that will be represented symbolically in later years.

Before 'multiplication' as a mathematical word is introduced, children may build up many ideas associated with 'equal sets' of objects, many 'lots of' items or actions, and experiences repeated 'many times'. For division, associated early language will involve 'sharing out' or 'repeatedly removing groups' of items to get 'equal portions', or 'dividing up' a collection with appropriate focus on words like 'each' and 'equal groups' and sometimes 'left-overs' and 'remainders'.

Patterns of numbers

Learning about patterns is an important aspect of Foundation Stage mathematics and the *Primary Framework for Literacy and Mathematics* (DfES 2006a: 70) states that at this stage most children learn to 'observe number relationships and patterns in the environment and use these to derive facts'. By talking about patterns, the language needed to understand multiplication and division will become familiar and young children can begin to learn the number patterns that are especially important. For most children, counting sequences like 2, 4, 6, 8 . . . will become familiar at an early age and a lot of satisfaction may be achieved by mastering this and other more difficult patterns of multiples. Number rhymes like 'One, two, buckle my shoe . . .' and 'One two, three, four, five . . . once I caught a fish alive' are enjoyed by children and encourage rhythmic pattern-making and counting. Both rhythmic counting in ones and *step*-counting in multiples will provide useful strategies for solving multiplication and division problems. Rhythmic counting with emphasis on some numbers will provide a link between the two, and by building on children's understanding and recognizing significant stages in the development of counting, teachers can encourage children to learn these patterns and the relationships that provide a framework for later formalization. A calculator is a practical resource to encourage exploration of patterns and a simple calculator will 'count', for example in the pattern of threes, by pressing the buttons '3', '+', '+' and then repeatedly pressing '='. It is not to say that multiplication has been mastered when the patterns of numbers become familiar, but that these may form the foundations of subsequent work enhancing children's overall number sense. It is not only for multiplication that these patterns are important; for example, the pattern of tens, '10, 20, 30, 40 . . .', is important for developing understanding of place value, and the pattern of fives, '5, 10, 15, 20 . . .', builds children's understanding of the role of five beyond the numbers they can easily count.

Counting procedures for multiplication

Step-counting and rhythmic counting are used when children have a large collection of items to count and the rhythm can act as an aid to memory. When children have been closely observed finding the total number of objects arranged in equal groups, it is evident that there is a gradual progression from counting individual items to more rhythmic counting and ultimately recognition of the significance of a number pattern. Earliest uses of a counting strategy involve a count of every individual item in a unitary counting procedure (counting in ones). Often this is accompanied by some tactile reinforcement, like touching the objects being counted or using fingers to keep a tally. It is helpful at this stage to encourage the systematic arrangements of objects so that the idea of a repeating pattern and a rhythmic count become familiar. At this stage, some children will answer simple multiplication problems by using their fingers to model their mental image.

At the next stage, this unitary counting becomes rhythmic with developing emphasis on the group subtotals:

$$1, 2, 3 \ldots 4, 5, 6 \ldots 7, 8, 9 \ldots$$

Again, some physical reinforcement like a nod of the head often accompanies this counting and children may start to use their fingers in growing independence from concrete objects.

It is interesting to observe the different ways that children use their fingers (Anghileri 1995b) and the balance between tactile and visual support that is provided as children develop mental imagery in their counting. In an investigation of children's solution strategies (Anghileri 1989), Key Stage 2 pupils' responses were recorded when they were presented with practical tasks involving multiplication of single-digit numbers. One of the tasks involved a card with one-pence coins stuck on it in a regular 6×3 array. After some discussion about the number of coins in each row and in each column, the card was turned over so that the coins could no longer be seen. After checking that the children remembered the number of rows and the number of coins in each row, individual children were asked to figure out how many coins were on the card altogether. Many different ways of counting and using fingers were observed and difficulties sometimes arose over the differing roles of the two numbers. A typical example was Jenny (aged 8 years and 11 months), who used three different finger methods in her attempts:

Attempt 1. Having counted the middle three fingers of her left hand, 'One, two, three', Jenny raised one finger on her right hand as a tally. She focused again on her left hand to count, 'four, five, six', and raised a second finger on her right hand. Using her left hand she counted, 'seven, eight, nine'. When she raised a third finger on her right hand, her gaze passed from the right-hand three fingers to the left-hand three fingers and back again. At this point, she abandoned her first attempt, apparently confused over the differing roles of the fingers on her right and left hands.

Attempt 2. Jenny counted rhythmically three fingers at a time, starting on her left hand and then proceeding onto her right hand and back to her left hand. She counted, 'One, two, **three**'. She then used the remaining two fingers of her left hand and one finger of her right hand to count, 'four, five, **six**'. She continued this rhythmic counting in threes until she reached 'twenty-seven', when she was interrupted and asked to recall the structure of the array she had seen.

Attempt 3. She now started again with three fingers of her left hand, 'One, two, three'. She clasped these together saying, 'one lot'. Now she extended the remaining two fingers of her left hand and one from her right hand saying, 'one, two, three . . . two lots'. She proceeded in this manner working across both hands, counting in ones all the fingers she extended, '. . . one, two, three . . . six lots'. Now she went back to the beginning and successfully counted in ones all the fingers she had extended for grouping, 'One, two, three, four, five, six, . . . sixteen, seventeen, eighteen'. (She must have memorized all the fingers she had raised.) In this final attempt, Jenny had kept a mental tally of the sets of fingers she had raised and counted in ones all eighteen.

Roles of the fingers

This example illustrates how finger methods for multiplication are more complex than for addition and subtraction because the two numbers have differing roles: one represents the number of items in a set, whereas the other represents the number of such sets (and sometimes a ratio between two sets). As in Jenny's first attempt, the fingers on different hands may be used to designate two very different counts that are taking place concurrently.

When counting of repeated sets is to be used as a solution strategy for multiplication, there are *three* concurrent counts that must be undertaken. Two such counts relate to the individual items: a primary count matches a counting word with each item, while a matching, internalized count monitors the fact that every set has the same number of elements.

Verbal count   1, 2, 3 ... 4, 5, 6 ... 7, 8, 9 ... 10, 11, 12
Internal count 1, 2, 3 ... 1, 2, 3 ... 1, 2, 3 ... 1, 2, 3

Here the fingers can give tactile and visual support to the matching count, allowing more attention to be focused on the ongoing count with the task of 'counting-on' from a subtotal. A third count is necessary to 'tally' the number of sets that have been accounted for.

Verbal count   1, 2, 3, ... 4, 5, 6, ... 7, 8, 9, ... 10, 11, 12
Internal count 1, 2, 3, ... 1, 2, 3, ... 1, 2, 3, ... 1, 2, 3
Tally   1   ...   2   ...   3   ...   4

This tallying must be done at the same time as monitoring the '1–2–3' count and it is this feature that causes problems for some children. In the case of Jenny, it is clear that in her second attempt she is maintaining two of the counts to produce groups of three numbers but is unable to implement the third 'tally' count. In her third attempt, Jenny found it more successful to keep repeating '1, 2, 3' as she kept a tally of the sets; she then went back to count the total number of fingers extended in her count. Other children's counting procedures often involve a greater degree of abstraction, as they are able to keep a silent tally of the sets or are able to count using a number pattern (e.g. 3, 6, 9, 12 . . .). The use of number patterns effectively reduces to two the number of concurrent counts to be maintained.

Children's methods may not be the same as those methods taught or those recommended in the schemes, but frequently involve 'invented' strategies that can be fascinating to watch. It is tempting to dismiss many of these strategies as inefficient and to attempt to replace them by the more conventional algorithms of arithmetic. It is true that more efficient strategies will need to be developed, but fingers often provide an important link between practical and mental methods, enabling abstraction to develop with understanding. The *Primary Framework for Literacy and Mathematics* (DfES 2006a: 3) notes that for effective teaching of mathematics 'children need to be introduced to the processes of calculation through practical, oral and mental activities'. Teachers may encourage discussion among pupils of the different solution strategies they use and take the opportunity to study their procedures in order to gain information of their understanding and develop teaching strategies to help them refine these methods (Beishuizen 2001).

When fingers are used to tally the number of groups counted, children have established a method for solving multiplication problems that is evident throughout the primary school years and beyond, as finger methods give access to widely used strategies for solving multiplication problems. Historically, finger methods for multiplication were used before pencil-and-paper algorithms became commonplace and 'advanced' methods of finger calculations were used by educated monks and priests. Watching children attempting arithmetic problems will give teachers an opportunity to *see* procedures that exemplify children's thinking and illustrate their stage of understanding.

Stages of development

Multiplication and division problems may be solved by building up repeated sets and the questions, 'How many objects in four sets of three?' and 'How many threes are there in twelve?', may both be tackled by counting up repeatedly groups of three using gradually more sophisticated strategies. The development of these strategies appears to run in parallel with children's developing strategies for addition and subtraction. Concrete objects will be used first to *model* each situation as the items are grouped and counted. While still counting in ones, many children start to count *rhythmically*, placing emphasis on the subtotal numbers (1, 2, 3 . . . 4, 5, 6 . . . 7, 8, 9 . . .); sometimes the spoken word is accompanied by a pause, a nod of the head or some other physical movement. The development from uniformly counting in ones to rhythmic counting in groups indicates that the child has some appreciation that it is the sets that are to be tallied as the count proceeds from one set to the next. This ability to count-on from the total for each set has been noted as a stage in the developing understanding of addition, where the child moves from counting-all of the objects to counting-on from the first subtotal. A more detailed account of this strategy can be found in Thompson (Chapter 8). Next, there is a stage of using number patterns which relates to the use of number facts in addition. Finally, number facts are used directly or related results are derived from facts that are known.

The links in a child's developing understanding of addition and of multiplication are illustrated in Figure 9.3. Although the counting procedures for addition and multiplication can be seen in many respects as developing in parallel, multiplication is more complex, as it involves many groups and each subsequent group to be counted must be constructed as a repeat of the first group with a tally of the number of times it is used also kept. In counting repeated sets, the child comes to recognize the need to terminate one count and start the next corresponding count, continuing until the set has been repeated a sufficient number of times. The transition from the first stage (unitary counting) to the next stage (rhythmic counting) is marked by the child's ability to recognize that the single word that ends the first count represents the totality of the group; that is, transfer is made from the *counting* meaning of the word to the *cardinal* meaning (Anghileri 2006) or recognition of the *composite* nature of numbers as well as the *component* nature (Steffe and Cobb 1988). This transfer has also been identified as the *cardinal principle* (see Maclellan, Chapter 6).

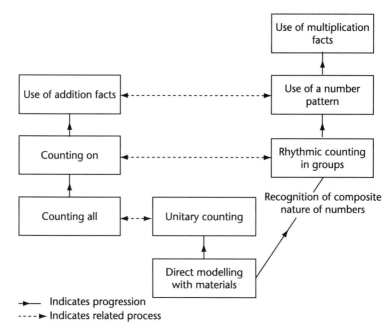

Figure 9.3   Relationships among addition and multiplication problem-solving strategies.

Some children count rhythmically but only say out loud the subtotal numbers (the interim numbers being internalized, their presence being detected sometimes as a whisper, a silent mouthed acknowledgement or a time lapse to indicate that counting is taking place). In this manner, further emphasis is placed on the subtotal numbers, with the result that the number pattern produced becomes familiar in its own right. The reciting of number patterns now becomes important for solving multiplication and division problems. Fingers may be used to tally the count but this method is much faster than counting in ones. Some children combine both a number pattern and counting in ones. When calculating how many counters there would be in six sets of three, Ruben (age 10 years 2 months) confidently began '3, 6, 9, 12 . . .', tallying by extending a finger each time to match the words. Now he continued '13, 14, 15', extending a fifth finger, and '16, 17, **18**'. He did not look at his fingers or extend the sixth finger but knew immediately he was at the required total. Clearly, his use of fingers gave a *tactile* support to his internal calculations.

Each of the methods described above show successful children's strategies are often related to their use of fingers. These methods show the child's confidence in understanding the structure of multiplication or division and illustrate different stages of progress towards recognition of the importance of number patterns and multiplication facts. Very few children in the primary years appear to use multiplication facts directly (Anghileri 1989), although many have access to them when they are asked. The security of counting in ones, or in groups, and using fingers, somehow reinforces their understanding of the structure of a problem, giving them a model rather than an abstract fact.

Counting on the number line

Experiences with a number line will help children to understand that the nature of multiplication and division as counting in groups is related to a visual image of *equal jumps*. With encouragement to verbalize the numbers associated with different size jumps, this can help reinforce the number patterns for multiplication and the way that counting groups may involve a tally of the number of jumps rather than the number of unit intervals involved. When the procedure is related to division, the number line may initially be used for counting 'backwards' as division is related to repeated subtraction but the patterns are not usually known so well in reverse. Even in doing division it is better to count in steps forward from zero so that familiar patterns of numbers are used. This can be helpful with division problems that do not give an exact answer, like 'How many threes are there in ten?', where remainders may be associated with the final interval that is shorter than the required jumps. In this example three jumps of three will get you to nine and there is one 'left over' to reach ten. Using a number line for doing multiplication and division will provide actions and a visual image that not only help children but also provide teachers with ideas for diagnostic assessment to establish understanding of the procedures for multiplication and division and the relationships between them.

Research in the Netherlands has shown that the 'empty number line' with no intervals and no numbers marked (except those written on by the child) enables children to be flexible in the size of jumps required (Beishuizen 1999) and can be used to illustrate jumps of fifty or a hundred as easily as smaller jumps. Since the children may decide the starting and stopping points and need not work to scale, they are able to develop mental imagery that goes beyond the unit intervals found on more traditional number lines.

Division by sharing or by repeated subtraction

Sharing and grouping are different procedures for dividing up a set and they correspond to different actions for solving a division problem. In the first instance, children will learn to share equally and systematically. In these early experiences it is not necessary for children to count for themselves and a common experience for young children is to undertake the practical sharing activity as an adult or more experienced child verbalizes an accompanying count. To properly understand division, however, children must also be helped to move on to removing equal groups in a procedure of repeated sub-traction. This latter process more easily identifies division as the inverse of multiplication as children address questions such as 'How many fours are in twelve?'. Counting groups in the process of repeated subtraction will relate to the patterns of numbers that have been built up in multiplication. The emer-gence of rhythmic counting and discussion of the different actions will enable children to begin to establish links between multiplication and division.

With large numbers of articles to be shared, a more efficient procedure that children will adopt is to share two or three at a time. The ability to guess or estimate the size of portions will help to identify a link between sharing and grouping, which will be necessary to solve such problems as one hundred shared between fifty. For such problems, sharing out one at a time between fifty portions will not be appropriate. Repeated subtraction of 'chunks' will be the basis for a method of written recording which is easier for children to understand than the traditional algorithm (Anghileri 2001) and which is found in government guidance on calculating (DfES 2006b).

Implications for teaching and learning

Counting involves skills that are successfully mastered by most children who can remember the consistent sequence of words and their association with numbers. Counting in multiples (e.g. 2, 4, 6, 8 . . . or 3, 6, 9, 12 . . .) also relies on memorizing consistent sequences of words that have a rhythm and pattern that can become very familiar. When these counts are associated with repeated groups of objects or equal intervals on the number line, they form a sound base upon which ideas of multiplication and division can be built.

Teachers can help children to focus on the diversity in language associated with equal groupings and sharing activities and how such language may be related to counting patterns. The particular words and procedures that enable children to solve practical problems will need to be refined to include more formal language, but the links that exist between multiplication and division must not be lost.

Children can show considerable initiative when attempting real problems that are presented to them within a familiar context. Opportunities for discus-sion will encourage comparisons between their different methods and may be used to focus on details of language that will be crucial for the precision needed in mathematics. It should be remembered that fingers are always available to support growing abstraction, which will facilitate progress with understanding. Confidence is crucial for successful problem-solving and the development from naive strategies to more formal and efficient procedures should not be at the expense of understanding or the gains may be very short term.

References

Anghileri, J. (1989) An investigation of young children's understanding of multiplication, *Journal for Research in Mathematics Education*, 20: 367–85.

Anghileri, J. (1995a) *Children's Mathematical Thinking in the Primary Years*. London: Continuum.

Anghileri, J. (1995b) Children's finger methods for multiplication, *Mathematics in School*, 24(1): 40–2.

Anghileri, J, (2001) *Principles and Practices in Arithmetic Teaching*. Milton Keynes: Open University Press.

Anghileri, J. (2006) *Teaching Number Sense*. London: Continuum.

Beishuizen, M. (1999) The empty number line as a new model, in I. Thompson (ed.) *Issues in Teaching Numeracy in Primary Schools*. Milton Keynes: Open University Press.

Beishuizen, M. (2001) Different approaches to mastering mental calculation strategies, in J. Anghileri (ed.) *Principles and Practices in Arithmetic Teaching*. Milton Keynes: Open University Press.

DfES (Department for Education and Skills) (2006a) *Primary Framework for Literacy and Mathematics*. Norwich: DfES.

DfES (Department for Education and Skills) (2006b) *Primary Framework for Literacy and Mathematics – Guidance Papers – Calculations* www.standards.dfes.gov.uk/primaryframeworks/library/Mathematics/guidance/resources/ (accessed 31 March 2008).

Steffe, L. and Cobb, P. (1988) *Construction of Arithmetic Meanings and Strategies*. New York: Springer-Verlag.

SECTION 5
Representation and calculation

In Chapter 12 Tony Harries and his colleagues argue that 'representations' in mathematics education can refer either to internal or external manifestations of mathematical concepts. They identify students' personal symbols, their natural language, visual imagery, problem-solving strategies and heuristics as examples of internal representations, and number squares, number lines and computer-based microworlds as examples of external representations. This section contains two chapters on internal representations – Chapters 10 and 11 – and two on external representations – Chapters 12 and 13.

In Chapter 10, Elizabeth Carruthers and Maulfry Worthington – whose taxonomy of children's mathematical graphics was adopted by the Williams review panel – argue that focusing on young children's use of graphicacy can help them to overcome potential difficulties that many children experience, and can lead to a deepened understanding of the language of written mathematics. Rooted in Vygotsky's research on semiotics, they begin by emphasizing the importance of young children's meaning-making within their imaginative play, allowing them to develop understanding of the relationship between marks, symbols and meanings. They then chart the development of children's own early written calculations as they move towards standard symbols and formats with understanding, mediated by dialogue and sensitive adult support. Examples discussed show how children's personal written methods for calculations reveal their intuitive personal strategies. This journey supports significant processes of learning such as mathematical thinking, creativity and problem-solving. Their findings challenge existing practices in many Foundation Stage and Key Stage 1 settings regarding this aspect of the curriculum and raise questions about the extent to which young children's experiences with written mathematics engage and challenge children's thinking at a deep level.

Ian Thompson (Chapter 11) continues the theme of children's mathematical graphicacy by starting from where the authors of the previous chapter left off. He addresses the fifth and final stage of their 'dimensions of mathematical graphics' model: 'calculating with larger numbers supported by jottings'. He describes a research project involving 117 nine-year-old Year 4 children who had not been taught traditional pencil-and-paper algorithms. He provides specific examples of children's responses to the problems they were asked to solve in order to introduce a discussion of specific aspects of young children's written calculation methods. These include: layout direction, that is whether they set out their work horizontally or vertically; calculation direction, that is whether they work from left to right or from right to left; place value issues, that is whether they understand the place value concept; and idiosyncratic jottings, that is whether they use any notation that is different from the norm.

In Chapter 12, Tony Harries, Patrick Barmby and Jennifer Suggate argue that there is a lack of clarity in the thinking about the nature of understanding in primary mathematics. They first explore the way mathematical ideas are represented, and come to the conclusion that they are represented in a variety of ways, and that understanding is related to the way in which the learner works both within and between the various representations of a concept. Second, they see reasoning as closely linked both to representations and understanding, and suggest that to understand mathematics is to make connections between internal mental representations of a mathematics concept, and that to reason is to make connections between different representations (internal or external) of a mathematical concept, through formal or informal processes. They then use the example of addition and subtraction in order to explore these ideas for a particular topic area in early mathematics. This leads to a suggestion for a pedagogy for understanding addition and subtraction through working with – or what they term 'interrogating' – representations of these concepts.

The final contributor to this section, Steve Higgins (Chapter 13) argues that information communications technology (ICT) is an integral aspect of life today, and yet there is still vigorous debate about its role in early childhood education. He presents an overview of research about the mathematical learning of young children with ICT, and suggests that if activities are planned with children's interests and mathematical development in mind, they can contribute significantly to mathematical learning. The chapter begins by setting the issues in the context of official guidance in England about the use of ICT for mathematics in the early years, including the use of calculators. It continues by reviewing recent research where the use of technology supports young children's mathematical learning, and argues that it is the match between the opportunities provided by the technology with developmentally appropriate mathematical challenges together with adult mediation that makes them effective. Steve then exemplifies these ideas with a case study where ICT was used to support the development of young children's counting skills with drawing and painting software. In this project, the teacher and research team planned a series of computer-based activities to engage the children in counting activities. These were structured with a progression in skills development based on the research on counting. The chapter concludes with recommendations for practice based on this analysis.

10 Children's mathematical graphics: young children calculating for meaning

Elizabeth Carruthers and
Maulfry Worthington

Introduction

To understand and use the standard written language of mathematics effectively, children need to build on their earliest awareness of relationships between objects, signs and meanings. The first discussion of this relationship originates in research on semiotics (the symbol-meaning-communication relationship) and was explored by the Russian psychologist Vygotsky (1978) in his research on children's early writing.

However, it is clear that children's early written mathematics often causes difficulties, resulting in only superficial understanding. Research has highlighted the fact that children as old as 9 who used standard mathematical symbols every day in school were reluctant to represent addition and subtraction with the same symbols, when given a situation other than a page of 'sums' (Hughes 1986).

Some of these difficulties may relate to a lack of clarity about the pedagogy: as one nursery teacher explained to us, 'Between the ages of three and seven there is a no man's land in the teaching of written mathematics'. This dilemma is confirmed by our findings from two studies we made with over 500 teachers (see Carruthers and Worthington 2006).

The theoretical basis underpinning this chapter is socio-cultural: children's homes, cultures, communities and early childhood settings provide authentic contexts in which meanings are made and negotiated.

Underpinning context

Using clinical studies in which young children played an invented game with tins, Hughes's (1986) significant research broke new ground. His work revealed how young children could use their own marks and symbols to represent and communicate quantities in personally meaningful ways. Hughes's findings suggested that this might reduce some of the difficulties that young children experience with early written mathematics, although the children's development from their earliest marks through to standard written mathematics was not a feature of his research.

Publication of Hughes's book coincided with interest in 'emergent' writing approaches in England and by 1990 there were the beginnings of interest in 'emergent mathematics'. In emergent approaches children build on their earliest understandings of written symbols in meaningful contexts with sensitive adult support. However, rather than exploring letter symbol and sound correlation to communicate meanings, children's mathematical marks and representations carry meanings about quantities and the number system.

In a study with young children, Munn (1997) repeated Hughes's 'tins game' and explored the relationship between emergent writing and emergent mathematics. Identifying *communicative purposes* as an important feature of emergent writing, she questioned the extent to which the children understood that they could use their symbols to communicate meanings about quantities. She found the exception were children who used standard written numerals they had been taught, arguing that such learning:

> is set in the context of interaction that closely conveys the quantitative reasoning of these symbols. When children invent ways of depicting quantity based on drawing, this is not necessarily so . . . (Pre-schoolers) . . . were unlikely to have had any conversations about the meaning of their activity simply because such activity has no widespread cultural meaning.
>
> (Munn 1997: 94)

The children's difficulty appeared to stem from the fact that they were unlikely to have engaged in *dialogue* with adults about their symbols to negotiate 'cultural meanings'. And unlike literacy in the nursery and school, mathematics is not always embedded in meaningful social contexts that can help children make sense of the value of symbols as communicative tools.

Against this background of emergent writing and Hughes's research, 'emergent mathematics' appeared to offer a positive way of supporting young mathematicians.

Children's mathematical graphics

As teachers working in the Foundation Stage, we had developed our pedagogy to support the children's emergent writing and valued its benefits for their learning. However, we eventually rejected the term *emergent mathematics* – and not only because these two symbolic languages are inherently different. During the 1990s the term *emergent writing* had developed negative connotations when Reception or Year 1 teachers sometimes lacked professional pedagogical knowledge to support children's progression towards standard forms. We also wanted to use a term that went beyond suggesting that children's understanding *emerges* on its own with little pedagogical support. It was clear that the numerous examples of children's mathematical marks and representations we had collected (scribble marks, drawings, personal and standard symbols, letters, words and numerals) could be described as 'graphics'. This led us to originate the term *children's mathematical graphics* (Worthington and Carruthers 2003).

Developing meanings

Central to our thinking about children's mathematical graphics is the premise that from birth children are constantly trying to make meaning of their world. Rooted in a social cultural perspective, children use whatever they can within the culture of their own lives to make personal meaning. This view of cognition moves beyond the idea that development consists of acquiring skills. Rather, 'a person develops through participation in an activity, changing to be involved in the situation at hand in ways that contribute both to the ongoing event and to the person's preparation for involvement in other similar events' (Rogoff 2003: 254). The belief is that all higher order functions such as learning grow out of social interactions.

Symbolic tools

One of the most significant aspects of children's development that Vygotsky explored was his research on 'symbolic tools': symbol systems that include language, writing, diagrams, maps, algebra, counting, road signs, and so on. Just as hammers, screwdrivers and spades aid physical tasks, *symbolic tools* mediate learning and help us to resolve cognitive problems. Indeed, mathematics as a subject has been described as 'really a matter of problem solving with symbolic tools' (van Oers 2001: 63).

In school the standard symbolic tools of mathematics include numerals and operations, leading to standard calculations. However, in addition to Hughes (1986), a number of other researchers have identified written work as the main aspect of mathematics that young children find difficult. Ginsburg (1977: 129) observed that 'while they make many errors in [standard] written arithmetic, children may in fact possess relatively powerful informal knowledge. This can be used as the basis for effective instruction'. Yet children's learning and the pedagogy of early written mathematics remain poorly understood.

Our research has focused on effective ways of building on children's 'powerful informal knowledge'. Its success allows bridging of the 'gap' in understanding between informal and standard written mathematical symbols, identified by Hughes (1986). Where children's representations are valued and where there is collaborative dialogue about meanings and symbols, children will develop understanding of written mathematics at a deep level.

Children's mathematical thinking

Vygotsky (1978: 116) observed that there is 'a unified historical line that leads to the highest forms of written language'. He traced young children's understanding from their symbolic (pretend) play, identifying their appropriation of objects to which they gave alternative meanings. We follow this line of development as it meanders from young children's meaning-making in play to calculations.

Children's own mathematical graphics are 'thinking on paper', and uncovering their meaning is crucial in supporting their journeys towards conventional mathematical symbols. The marks and representations that children use reveal their thinking. Their graphics are personal thinking tools and are key to their development. This is not *recording* following a practical activity; for example, drawing the cubes following their use in a practical context. Children's own mathematical marks and representations also assist them in moving from mathematics with concrete materials into more abstract mathematical thought and symbols.

We found that when children are given the opportunity to use paper and pens to support their thinking, they develop effective personal strategies. Not only do these strategies work for them in solving mathematical problems but much more importantly they understand what they do (Carruthers and Worthington 2006). We want children to understand written mathematics rather than hurdle blindly through a set of 'tricks' that they have memorized.

Uncovering children's development

Perhaps the most illuminating aspect of our research on *children's mathematical graphics* is that the data revealed a pattern of development. As we sorted through the 700 examples of children's own written mathematics, significant categories were revealed, leading to our taxonomy tracing development from birth to eight years (Figure 10.1). Explanations of each aspect of the taxonomy are outlined below.

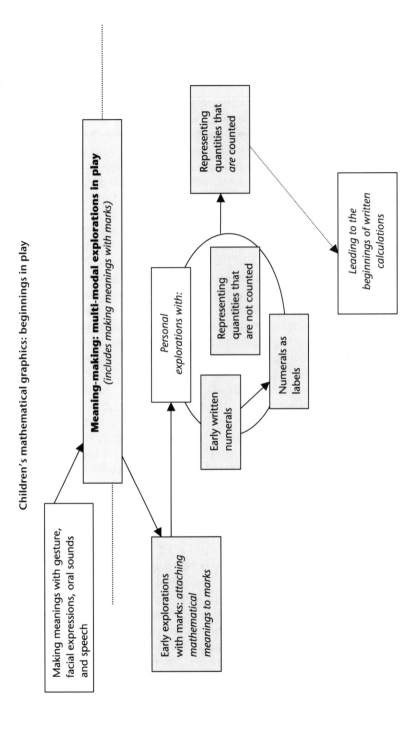

Children's mathematical graphics: beginnings in play

Making meanings with gesture, facial expressions, oral sounds and speech

Meaning-making: multi-modal explorations in play
(includes making meanings with marks)

Early explorations with marks: *attaching mathematical meanings to marks*

Personal explorations with:

Representing quantities that are not counted

Early written numerals

Numerals as labels

Representing quantities that *are* counted

Leading to the beginnings of written calculations

Figure 10.1 The development of written number and quantities. (see page 136 for second half of taxonomy)

Source: Carruthers and Worthington 2006

Taxonomy of children's mathematical graphicacy development from birth to eight years

Beginnings in play: making meanings

As young children explore their world, they play in many ways with different objects, materials and people. The work of Kress (1997) in describing and explaining his observations of children's *multi-modal* play provides the foundations of children's journey into all symbol systems including mathematics. In play children have available many modes of representation for make-believe: these include role play and small-world play; block play and junk modelling. Kress's focus on making meanings 'with lots of different stuff' relates to Vygotsky's research on symbolic tools.

Three-year-old Sol gave his teacher what appeared to be a piece of screwed-up paper, declaring that it was a telescope. His teacher said, 'Oh! Tell me about this' and pointing to a narrow crack in the paper Sol said, 'Look! There's the hole'. Through this simple act Sol signified the act of 'looking through' a telescope. When children are engaged in free, child-initiated play with an abundance of open materials such as cloth, cardboard boxes, cubes, cylinders, buttons and straws, they create personal meanings, and the materials and objects they choose then become all sorts of things with which they can play. Meanings often take on a fluid quality and children transform them from day to day (Worthington 2007).

Children also make meanings with marks in their play. In the nursery 4-year-old Naadim was playing 'shops'. Seeing some paper and pens nearby, he made some marks across a page that resembled the letter 't' and then read what he clearly intended to be a shopping list: 'spaghetti, carrots and potatoes'. With his list in his hand Naadim picked up a shopping basket and went 'shopping'. His mother told his teacher that her son shopped with his parents regularly and that they wrote a shopping list to take with them. In his play Naadim had drawn on this important cultural aspect of experience.

Early exploration with marks

Young children's first marks, sometimes referred to as scribbles, are a major development in a child's step towards multi-dimensional representations of her world. Very early marks can be ignored by adults and scribbles may be seen as random accidents. However, in his study of young children's drawings and paintings, Matthews (1999) argues that rather than haphazard actions scribbles are products of a systematic investigation. Malchiodi (1998) suggests that if children give meaning to their scribbles, then they may be moving forward in their development of representational images. This is supported by our research.

Between the ages of 3 and 4 years children begin to differentiate between their marks for drawing and writing, and those to which they attach mathematical meanings. For example, 3-year-old Matt (Figure 10.2) was at home and his aunt was sitting at a table near him and writing postcards. Matt wanted to be a part of this literate activity and covered numerous pieces of paper with his marks: some he referred to as drawings and for some he 'read' their written content. On two pages Matt referred to mathematical meanings for his marks 'reading' the marks on one page as 'I spell 80354'. His parents thought that his

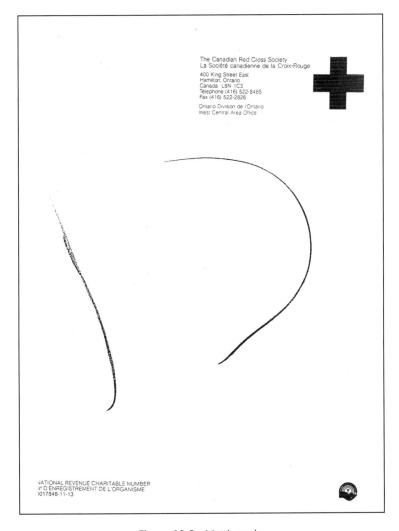

Figure 10.2 Matt's marks.

reference to spelling may have related to family talk about how to spell his brother's name and that it was possible that he had heard someone refer to a string of numbers for a telephone number.

Early written numerals

Children refer to their marks as numbers and begin to explore ways of writing numerals. Their perception of numerals and letters is of symbols that mean something, first differentiated in a general sense: 'this is my writing, this is a number'. Young children's marks gradually develop into something more specific when they name certain marks as numerals. At this stage their marks may not be recognizable as numerals but may have number-like qualities. This development is similar to the beginning of children's early writing.

Numerals as labels

Young children are immersed in print and see symbols and texts in their environment, in the home, on television and their community. They often attend to these labels and are interested in how they are used; they can write in contexts which make sense to them (Ewers-Rogers and Cowan 1996). Children look at the function of written numerals in a social sense and by the time they enter school, understand the different meanings of numbers. In our research we found that children moved from knowing about these symbols in the environment to writing them down for their own purposes. This is a significant shift, since when they choose to write these numbers they have converted what they read into a standard symbolic language and used them in meaningful contexts.

Representing quantities that are not counted

Young children's marks are often lively and at first give the sense of something without needing to be too exact. When children *represent quantities that are not counted*, their graphics almost have an impressionist air about them as they focus on a particular aspect at the time. For example, Joe, aged 3 years, represented a spider with many legs and said the spider had eight legs. Joe did not represent the eight legs exactly; neither did he count the legs he had drawn. He had the sense of a spider and the many legs featured prominently in his drawing. This was an exciting and imaginative drawing of a spider because Joe was unrestricted by influences of school. When children *represent quantities that they do not count*, it is their personal sense of quantity that they represent.

Representing quantities that are counted

Our analysis of young children's marks also showed that they *represent quantities that they count*. For example, 3-year-old Jenna drew vertical lines with coloured pens naming them 'raindrops', and counting them when she had finished. Our evidence shows that *quantities that are not counted* precede those that are, although there is often an overlap of these two aspects. This aspect of development leads children directly to the beginnings of written calculations. Hughes's (1986) analysis of the children's representations in the 'tins game' revealed aspects of their development that we categorized as *representing quantities that are counted*.

The development of early operations: children's own written methods and strategies

Written calculations

The dimensions of children's development described above provide the crucial foundations of written calculations. Children need to continue to have plenty of opportunities to explore their mathematical ideas on paper as they explore calculations. As children move on to explore calculations in diverse ways, their own representations support their mental methods and help them to work out calculations. Counting features a large part in the beginnings of written calculation and children's preference for counting persists even though schools may choose to present calculations with other strategies. The variety of graphical responses that children choose also reflects their personal mental methods and intuitive methods developed from 'counting-all'.

Counting continuously

We use this term 'counting continuously' to describe this aspect of children's early representations of calculation for addition and subtraction. Several studies have shown that young children can carry out simple additions and subtractions (with objects and verbally) and that they can do this through counting strategies. The most common strategy is to 'count-all' or to count the final number of items (Carpenter and Moser 1984; Thompson, Chapter 8).

Since the 'counting-all' strategy is not one that children are taught, Hughes suggests that we can infer that it is a self-taught strategy (Hughes 1986: 35). When children are given a worksheet with two sets of items to add, they count the first set and then continue to count the second set. This is misleading for teachers because although such a page will be termed 'addition', children will only be using it to count and do not recognize the separation and combining of the sets. However, when children choose to represent

Children's mathematical graphics: the development of calculations

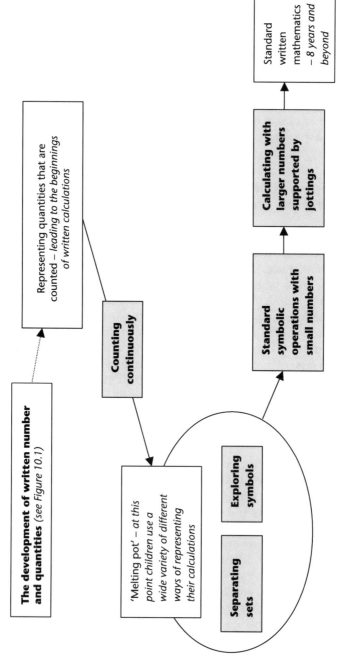

The development of written number and quantities *(see Figure 10.1)*

Representing quantities that are counted – *leading to the beginnings of written calculations*

Counting continuously

'Melting pot' – *at this point children use a wide variety of different ways of representing their calculations*

Separating sets

Exploring symbols

Standard symbolic operations with small numbers

Calculating with larger numbers supported by jottings

Standard written mathematics – *8 years and beyond*

Figure 10.3   Early operations: the development of children's own written methods.

Source: Carruthers and Worthington 2006

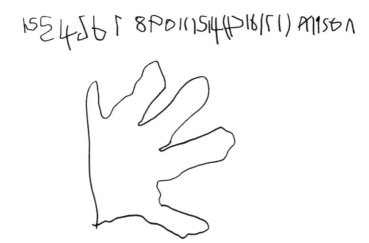

Figure 10.4 Alison.

addition by a *continuous count* they have begun to understand the need to separate the two sets and are developing a sense of addition by combining them. This is an important distinction and also a good reason to give children opportunities to use their own methods and representations. In the reception class Alison (Figure 10.4) wanted her friends to each bring a teddy to the café that her class had organized, and her teacher asked her to work out what the total would be (i.e. seven children plus seven toys). Counting the children and then their toys she represented the total using numerals. Alison decided to check what she had written: finding that she had written numerals to 17, she put brackets round the numbers she did not need. The hand she drew may denote the action of adding although we cannot be sure.

The 'melting pot'

As children explored different ways to calculate, we found a variety of different representations of operations which we refer to as a 'melting pot'. Carpenter and Moser (1984) studied the range of strategies children use to add and subtract and found that a variety of informal counting strategies persist through the primary years. Children's choices of ways to represent operations do not remain static since discussion and modelling alter individuals' perspectives, introducing them to further possibilities. Since children seem to find the standard algorithms and calculation difficult to understand (Hughes 1986; Ginsburg 1977), it is not surprising that at this stage we can see children explore many strategies. It is important that children are free to work out their own sense of calculations in ways they understand. It is this continual striving for personal understanding that we must encourage in mathematics from the beginning.

Separating sets

We found that children use a range of strategies to show that the two amounts that they are adding (or subtracting) are separate, for example, by:

- grouping the two sets of items to be added, perhaps by leaving a space between them or by representing them on opposite sides of the paper;
- separating the sets with words;
- putting a vertical line between them;
- putting an arrow or personal symbol between the sets;
- drawing rings (boxes) around each set.

These strategies indicate that children are moving into new ways of working.

Exploring symbols

As children explore the role and use of symbols, they use a range of personal or invented symbols, or an approximation of standard symbols, and their development is strengthened by three additional and significant strategies: implicit symbols, code-switching and narrative action.

Implicit symbols

Children who have been used to representing calculations in their own ways may have an understanding of '=' or '+' but have not represented these standard symbols. The marks they make or the arrangement of their calculation show that the symbol is *implied*: their understanding is revealed when often they 'read' their calculation as though to include absent features. This is where mental and written calculations combine to make meanings fluid: children are not encumbered by set rules to write the calculation in one 'correct way' but combine everything they know. The examples in this section are from children in Reception who were adding grapes.

Some children omit the operator sign altogether: by leaving a space Jack (Figure 10.5) implied the operation for addition (the 'doing' of the calculation) and used a single line for the equals sign. In Figure 10.6 William implied an equals sign by leaving a space between his numerals 1 and 6. Jax's space between the six and the four dots she drew also implied the addition sign. Finally she added a letter 'T' to signify 'ten' (Figure 10.7).

These examples are different, but all show that the children were able to work out the calculation and know the function of the missing symbol although they chose not to include one. At this point in their development,

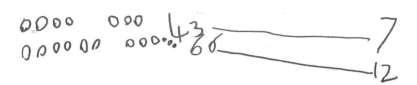

Figure 10.5 Jack.

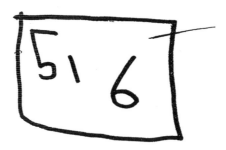

Figure 10.6 William.

Figure 10.7 Jax.

their calculation skills are in advance of their written knowledge of standard operations. This has parallels with very early counting and when children are sometimes pressurized into writing the correct numeral; they may be unable to write numerals in standard forms, resulting in adults failing to recognize their current number knowledge. The move in England to mental methods has helped to resolve this to some extent, since assessment of children's early mathematical knowledge is judged more on their ability to calculate mentally. This is particularly pertinent for very young children when they first enter an educational setting, when their mathematical knowledge may not always be acknowledged and teachers may over-emphasize skills and correctly written numerals rather than uncover children's existing mathematical knowledge.

Code-switching

'Code-switching' is a term used in second-language learning: as learners develop fluency in their second language they substitute features of their first language (such as familiar words) for those they do not yet know. In their early written mathematics we found many examples when children *code-switch* within calculations, switching between their personal symbols and representations and standard symbols. This intuitive strategy allows children to use ways of representing their understanding as they move towards using increasingly standard forms of calculations. John (Figure 10.8) was adding the grapes in two dishes that he had chosen (and that he would eat after he had worked out their total). He chose to use a written response to help his thinking, switching between writing and numerals: '2 grapes, there is two; 4 grapes there is four' before adding the total (6) on the left of the page. Learning about effective layout develops through collaborative dialogue as children's understanding grows.

Narrative action

This is a particularly significant feature: our term describes individuals' decisions to include either hands or arrows in their calculation to signify the operation. This feature has been identified by other researchers, which they term *dynamic schematization*: such representations indicate 'higher levels of understanding' since they have the potential to show 'the relationship between drawing and object, sign and meaning transformation' (Poland and Van Oers 2007: 271–2).

Narrative action appears to support internalized *mental* images of earlier concrete operations of addition or subtraction calculations: the hand or arrows they include allow them to reflect on the operation and its function. In the following activity the children were in their first term in Year 1. Barney (Figure 10.9) drew an arc of arrows signifying his former action of 'taking away' to support his thinking about a subtraction game with beans.

Figure 10.8 John's grapes.

Other children chose to explore the hand and arrow symbols that their peers had introduced: playing the beans subtraction game Kristian explored Barney's arrow symbol in his own way (Figure 10.10). In the same game Alex (Figure 10.11) introduced the idea of using a hand to signify the same 'taking away' action and subsequently Barney explored Alex's hand symbol as an alternative to his arrows (Figure 10.12).

In an interesting adaptation, Emma appropriated Alex's hand symbol and made it her own by combining it with arrows (Figure 10.13). Checking her first calculation she noticed that she had not shown the quantity she was subtracting and rectified this in her second example.

Using *narrative action* to signify the operation, children are effectively moving into their *zone of proximal development* or 'ZPD', which Vygotsky (1978: 86) describes as '*the distance between the actual development level as determined by*

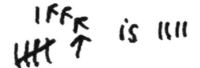

3 is 2

1 is 1

Figure 10.9 Barney – subtracting beans.

is IIII

Figure 10.10 Kristian.

Figure 10.11 Alex.

Figure 10.12   Barney.

independent problem solving, and the level of potential development as determined through problem solving under adult guidance or in collaboration with more capable peers' (italics in the original).

Narrative actions appear to serve a dual purpose:

- They have an important *bridging function* between concrete and mental operations, and between physical *actions* with concrete materials and the operations within written calculations.
- They enable children to move from exploring a range of personal symbols for operations to understanding what operations signify and what their function is within a calculation.

Standard symbolic operations with small numbers

By this point children have already been introduced to standard symbols and ways of working through a range of models (see Carruthers and Worthington 2006, Chapter 10). They understand the complex roles and functions of various mathematical symbols and have developed a wide range of strategies that they can use flexibly to solve problems.

In a mixed Reception/Year 1 class the teacher had planned a dice game for children to play in pairs. Individuals playing the game rolled the two dice in turn, providing an opportunity for children to either count or add the dots and to use paper to help them think about the symbols if they wished. Amelie had just started school and explored her ideas in a very

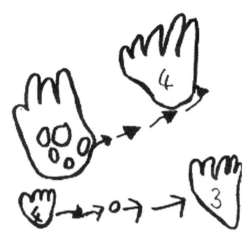

Figure 10.13   Emma.

spontaneous way. Her teacher observed and listened as she carefully counted the dots each time and then counted out loud as she marked them on the right of her paper (Figure 10.14). In her first term in Year 1, Anna chose to use the opportunity to use standard symbols in horizontal written calculations (Figure 10.15).

Calculating with larger numbers supported by jottings

Calculating with larger numbers is more challenging, since now children will need to have a feel for the larger numbers involved and may need to manipulate several steps. This is where mental methods and some taught 'jottings' can be of value. For example, 7-year-old Miles's class was going on a residential trip and was to have a picnic on their journey. His teacher used this opportunity for some problem-solving, inviting the children to help work out how many trays (with three nectarines in each) they would need for 26 children. Miles had chosen to orientate his paper in 'portrait' format and quickly understood that he would run out of space on his empty number line: his highly adaptive solution was to double several of the jumps that he made as he worked from right to left (Figure 10.16).

From this point in their development, children move naturally to standard written mathematics and have deepened their levels of understanding written calculations and problem-solving.

Figure 10.14   Amelie.

Implications for teaching and learning

The *Independent Review of Mathematics Teaching in Early Years Settings and Primary Schools* recommends that:

> To secure effective pedagogy in early years mathematics, local authorities, leaders, managers and head teachers should provide the following key elements . . .
>
> - A culture with a significant focus on mathematical mark-making . . .
> - A learning environment that encourages children to choose to use their own mathematical graphics to support their mathematical thinking and processes.
>
> (DCSF 2008: 37)

The report concludes (DCSF 2008: 34) that 'The role of (mathematical) mark-making in children's cognitive development' is exemplified by the taxonomy (from Carruthers and Worthington 2006) – a version of which is illustrated in

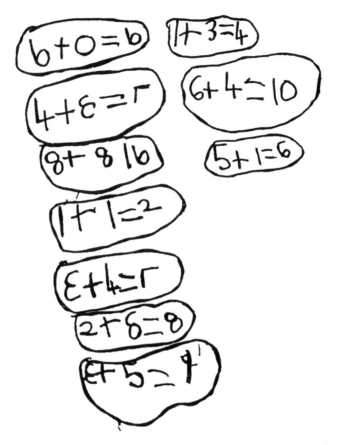

Figure 10.15 Anna.

Figure 10.16 Miles.

Figures 10.1 and 10.3. The report's authors also raise concerns about the use of the Foundation Stage Profile (FSP) arguing that 'Relatively few children attain point 8: *"uses developing mathematical ideas and methods to solve practical problems"* in any of the three mathematical assessment scales' (DCSF 2008: 41, original italics).

These aspects of the report raise significant questions about the teaching of early written mathematics. It is encouraging that children's mathematical graphics have been given precedence in the early years' section of this important mathematics report. However, its impact will depend on the dissemination not being 'lost in translation'. We can only wait and see!

While we have highlighted a number of implications for teaching and learning in this chapter, we would like to give prominence to three that we see as the most essential:

1   The foundations of early written mathematics begin in children's make-believe play, for it is here that children begin to understand the relationship between meanings and symbols.
2   Teachers need to consider that *all* young children's mathematical marks and representations are significant: their scribble-marks and early drawings, for example, have as important a role in children's development as later personal strategies they use in their calculations.
3   Finally, if children can calculate or solve a problem mentally, they do not need to *record* the mathematics they have done. Recording places the emphasis on marks and drawings as a *product* and is a lower level of cognitive demand. The difference between recording a mathematical activity and *representing mathematical thinking* is one of quality and depth of thinking.

References

Carpenter, T. and Moser, J. (1984) The acquisition of addition and subtraction concepts in grades one through three, *Journal for Research in Mathematics Education*, 15(3): 179–202.

Carruthers, E. and Worthington, M. (2005) Making sense of mathematical graphics: the development of understanding abstract symbolism, *European Early Childhood Education Research Journal*, 13(1): 57–79.

Carruthers, E. and Worthington, M. (2006) *Children's Mathematics: Making Marks, Making Meaning*, 2nd edn. London: Sage Publications.

DCSF (Department for Children, Schools and Families) (2008) *Independent Review of Mathematics Teaching in Early Years Settings and Primary Schools* www.publications.teachernet.gov.uk/eOrderingDownload/ Williams%20Mathematics.pdf (accessed June 2008).

Ewers-Rogers, J. and Cowan, R. (1996) Children as apprentices to number, *Early Childhood Development and Care*, 125(15): 15–17.

Ginsburg, H. (1977) *Children's Arithmetic*. New York: Van Nostrand.

Hughes, M. (1986) *Children and Number: Difficulties in Learning Mathematics*. Oxford: Blackwell.

Kress, G. (1997) *Before Writing: Re-thinking the Paths to Literacy*. London: Routledge.

Malchiodi, C. (1998) *Understanding Children's Drawings*. London: Jessica Kingsley.

Matthews, J. (1999) *The Art of Childhood and Adolescence: The Construction of Meaning*. London: Falmer Press.

Munn, P. (1997) Writing and number, in I. Thompson (ed.) *Teaching and Learning Early Number*, 1st edn. Milton Keynes: Open University Press.

Poland, M. and Van Oers, B. (2007) Effects of schematizing on mathematical development, *European Early Childhood Education Research Journal*, 15(2): 269–93.

Rogoff, B. (2003) *The Cultural Nature of Human Development*. Oxford: Oxford University Press.

Van Oers, B. (2001) Educational forms of initiation in mathematical culture, *Educational Studies in Mathematics*, 46: 59–85.

Vygotsky, L.S. (1978). *Mind and Society: The Development of Higher Mental Processes*. Cambridge, MA: Harvard University Press.

Worthington, M. (2007) Multi-modality, play and children's mark-making in maths, in J. Moyles (ed.) *Early Years Foundations: Meeting the Challenge*. Maidenhead: Open University Press.

Worthington, M. and Carruthers, E. (2003) *Children's Mathematics: Making Marks, Making Meaning*, 1st edn. London: Paul Chapman Publishing.

11 What do young children's mathematical graphics tell us about the teaching of written calculation?

Ian Thompson

Introduction

In Chapter 10, Carruthers and Worthington provide the second part of their taxonomy of children's mathematical graphics and chart the development of children's own early written calculations. In the course of their analysis a pattern of development appeared which the authors grouped into non-hierarchical categories of children's own early written calculations:

- counting continuously;
- separating sets;
- exploring symbols;
- calculating with small numbers using standard symbols;
- calculating with larger numbers supported by jottings.

The authors have used examples of personal mathematical strategies from children in the 4 to 8 age range to illustrate this development. This chapter looks in more detail at the final dimension – 'calculating with larger numbers supported by jottings' – and focuses initially on my own research investigating the idiosyncratic written calculation strategies used for two-digit addition by 9-year-old children.

One problem with working with older children in this area is that many have already received a substantial amount of exposure to formal, compact written methods by the time they reach Year 3 or 4. In an attempt to avoid this potential problem, I worked with a sample of 117 nine-year-old children in Year 4 from four schools involved in the Calculator Aware Number (CAN) Curriculum Project. The basic principle underlying the philosophy of schools involved in this project was that children should have unrestricted access to calculators from Year 2 onwards, and that traditional pencil-and-paper algorithms should not be formally taught. It was obvious from talking to the children and from some of their mathematical marks that many of them *had* encountered standard methods either in school textbooks or at home while working with keen (or perhaps, worried) parents or carers.

In the study (Thompson 1994), the children were presented with word problems commensurate with their age and ability. They were informed that the key to the calculator cupboard had been lost and were asked to write down their solutions to a collection of problems, setting out their working in such a way that a friend could understand the method they had used. They were also told that it did not matter whether their answers were right or wrong, as I was more interested in learning about the methods that they had used. This latter point could well have influenced their keenness to provide a written explanation along with their numerical solution. The children were deliberately asked to work on their own, as it was felt that this request was more likely to generate a wider range of solution strategies.

This chapter will comprise specific examples of children's responses to the problems they were asked to solve. The examples chosen are representative of others in the sample, and have been selected in order to introduce a discussion of the following aspects of young children's written calculation methods: direction – both of layout and calculation process; place value issues; and idiosyncratic jottings.

Direction

Layout direction

Of the sample of 117 children involved in the research project, 71 per cent set out their work horizontally. They were generally loth to write down the original numbers involved in the problem they were attempting, preferring instead to launch straight into their solution. Rashid's work (Figure 11.1) illustrates both of these points. It is quite clear that he has added the multiples of ten separately from the ones (the 'units'), and, although he probably worked it out in his head, has actually forgotten to write down the final answer of 216, that he probably found by adding the two subtotals together. His strategy – often called 'partitioning', or, mainly in the research literature, '1010' – resembles the example (Figure 11.2) shown in the *Guidance Paper – Calculation* (DfES 2006a). However, there are subtle but important differences between the

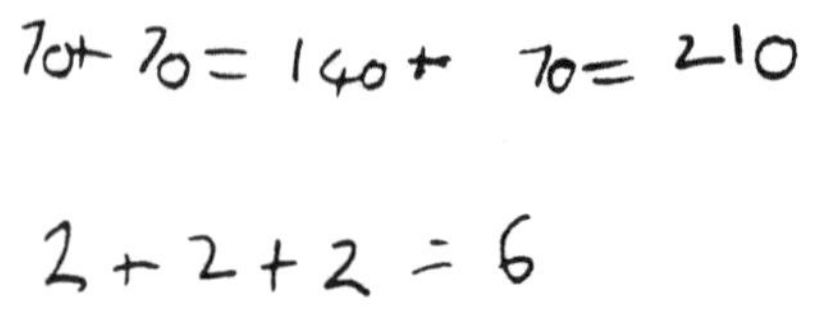

$$70 + 70 = 140 + 70 = 210$$

$$2 + 2 + 2 = 6$$

Figure 11.1   Rashid finding three lots of 72.

$$47 + 76 = 40 + 70 + 7 + 6 = 110 + 13 = 123$$

Figure 11.2 Guidance paper example 1 – using partitioning.

two layouts. One motive the authors of the report had for recommending the format illustrated in Figure 11.2 was to try to ensure that children do not make 'incorrect' statements in their working out, despite the fact that they may have actually calculated correctly and produced the right answer. In Rashid's case both his working and his answer are correct, but the statement $70 + 70 = 140 + 70$ is actually mathematically unsound. (However, the pedant in me wants to point out to the authors that it is also mathematically unsound to have more than one equals sign per line as we have in Figure 11.2!)

Also, the layout of the example in Figure 11.2 is in effect suggesting that children should set out their plan of attack before they execute it. The mathematical notation is really shorthand for the following: 'The problem I have to solve is $47 + 76$ . . . I have partitioned both the numbers into multiples of ten and ones, and reorganized them so that I can more easily add the tens together before adding the ones . . . $40 + 70$ is 110 and $7 + 6$ is 13 . . . 110 and 13 is 123.' On the other hand, Rashid's written marks are almost a running commentary on his thinking and calculation procedure as they happen in real time. Discussion with Rashid suggested that his approach was more on the lines of: 'Take the 70 out of the 72 . . . Double 70 is 140 (write down $70 + 70 = 140$) . . . add another 70 . . . that makes 210 (write down $+ 70 = 210$) . . . now $2 + 2 + 2 = 6$ (write this down)'. The partitioning step, where we would rewrite 72 as $70 + 2$, is treated differently by many young children, who just 'take out' the tens, operate on them and then retrieve the ones later. This strategy accounts for the major difference between the children's layout and the recommended one.

Marc (Figure 11.3) uses a different strategy from Rashid, but he does actually write down the calculation before proceeding to work it out. He leaves the first addend unaltered, adding to it appropriate chunks of the partitioned second addend; that is, first the 200 and then the 9. Researchers call this procedure the 'sequencing' strategy or N10 (shorthand for 'add the multiple of 10 of the second number to the whole of the first number' [see Rousham 2003]). The *Guidance Paper – Calculation* (DfES 2006a) models Marc's strategy in Figure 11.4. However, the paper describes this procedure as a 'partitioning'

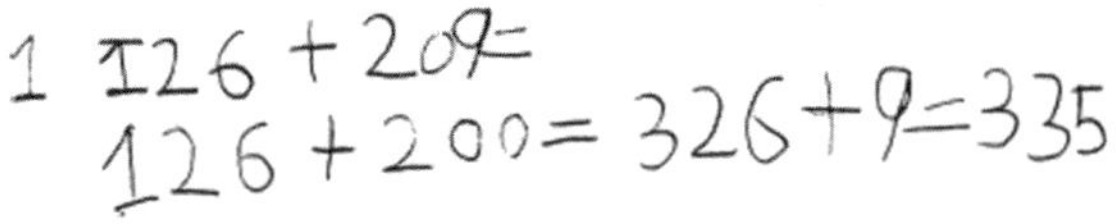

Figure 11.3 Marc adding 126 and 209.

$$47 + 76 = 47 + 70 + 6 = 117 + 6 = 123$$

Figure 11.4 Guidance paper example 2 – using partitioning.

strategy, exactly as it did in the example in Figure 11.2, perpetuating a misconception perpetrated in the original National Numeracy Strategy (NNS) *Framework for Teaching Mathematics from Reception to Year 6* (DfEE 1999: Section 6, page 40).

The guidance paper has failed to make the very important distinction that exists between the two calculation strategies: procedures that involve the partitioning of both numbers, as in Figures 11.1 and 11.2, cannot be carried out on an empty number line (just try it!). Interestingly, Marc was the only child in the research under discussion to use the 'single partitioning' strategy (i.e. the sequencing strategy). Similarly, Jones (1975), researching the written methods of 10- and 11-year-olds, found that less than 4 per cent of his sample used this procedure.

Calculation direction

As might be expected, almost all the children who wrote down their calculations in a horizontal format worked from left to right, beginning the calculation with the most significant digit. Of the 117 scripts in the sample there were just 21 that included one or more calculations set out in the more traditional vertical format using conventional mathematical symbols. However, of these 21 children, only eight worked consistently from right to left, with ten always working from left to right, using non-standard methods. The remaining three varied the direction of their working.

Emma (Figure 11.5) is finding the sum of 39 and 37, and chooses to set her working out vertically. She partitions the two numbers, taking the two 30s and adding them together, before writing the remaining ones underneath the 60. Her sentence 'I added the rest of the numbers' does not tell us how she added them. However, further questioning revealed that to add the seven she '. . . took one off to make 70 . . .'. This means that she has added the nine and the seven separately to the 60. First of all she adds the nine to get 69, then

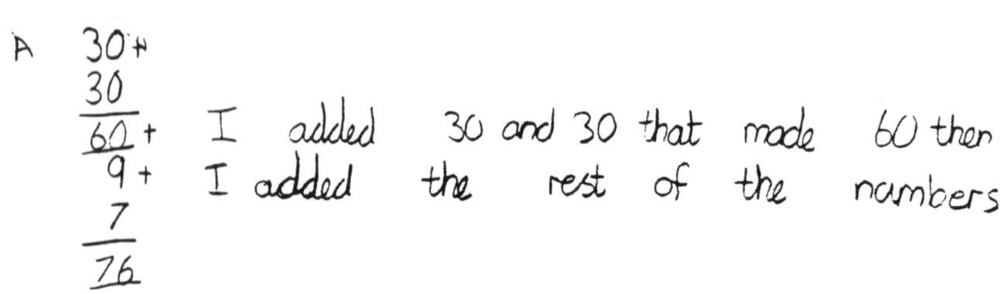

Figure 11.5 Emma working vertically from left to right.

splits the seven into six and one so that she can make the 69 into a multiple of ten before adding the remaining six to give the answer 76.

Emma has used the mental strategy of 'bridging-up' (see Thompson, Chapter 8) to complete her calculation. This is an excellent example of a written algorithm clearly based on the mental calculation strategies of partitioning, sequencing, bridging and working from left to right. In research that followed the progress of children from their second to their fifth school year, Hedrén (1999) also reported this propensity to base written calculation procedures on mental methods.

Place value issues

When people hear the phrase 'place value' they usually think of 'hundreds, tens and units', where a number such as 144 is interpreted as '1 in the hundreds column, 4 in the tens column and 4 in the units column'. Kate (Figure 11.6) clearly interprets 144 differently. She appears to have used a very complex-looking algorithm for her calculation of the number of bricks in four rows given that there are 144 bricks in each row. However, closer inspection suggests that it is a very logical algorithm, showing quite clearly the various stages in her thinking. The idiosyncratic arrows pointing to the 400 show that: the 1 has been interpreted as 100; the adjacent 4 has been treated as forty (four of them equalling 160); and the final 4 has been dealt with as four ones. The crossings-out to the right of the calculation show that one hundred has been transferred from the 160 to the 400, and that a ten has been transferred from the almost illegible 16 to the 60. This re-partitioning has made the resulting addition (500 + 70 + 6) much simpler to complete.

Thompson (2003) has argued that it is important to distinguish between the two different interpretations of place value outlined above. He describes the interpretation illustrated by Kate's work (and, incidentally, that of every other example in this chapter) as the *quantity value* aspect of place value, and

Figure 11.6 Kate's highly idiosyncratic partitioning algorithm.

$$47$$
$$\underline{+76}$$
$$110$$
$$\underline{13}$$
$$123$$

Figure 11.7 Recommended expanded algorithm.

the 'standard' interpretation (also observed in Figure 11.8) as the *column value* aspect. In the former case, a number like 47 is interpreted as '40 plus 7', whereas in the latter it is seen as '4 in the tens column and 7 in the ones column'. The *Guidance Paper – Calculation* (DfES 2006a) includes an 'expanded' written method for addition at Stage 3 (Figure 11.7) which is a 'tidied-up' version of Kate's 'quantity value' algorithm. At Stage 4 the document describes a 'column value' algorithm (Figure 11.8). This is variously called the 'column', the 'compact' or the 'standard' method (see Thompson 2007 for a discussion of the shifting terminology for this algorithm).

Traditionally, the 'patter' to accompany the calculation in Figure 11.8 runs something like this: 'Seven and six make thirteen . . . Put down the three and carry the one . . . Four and seven is eleven . . . Eleven and one makes twelve'. While this rigmarole is being performed, various digits are written down, and finally the number 123 appears in the designated place. The patter for the expanded method in Figure 11.7 would be: 'Forty and seventy makes one hundred and ten . . . Seven and six makes thirteen . . . One hundred and ten and thirteen makes one hundred and twenty-three'. The compact algorithm treats each number to be added as a collection of discrete digits, where those set out underneath each other in the same column have to be combined as if they were actually ones digits. This leads us to say, 'Four and seven makes eleven and one more makes twelve' part way through calculating 47 + 76, when we actually mean 'Forty and seventy makes a hundred and ten, and ten more makes a hundred and twenty'. Use of the compact written algorithm obliges users to disregard the meaning that the individual digits possess by dint of their position in the number, and forces them to indulge in pure symbol manipulation.

Column (i.e. standard) written methods were created so that everyday arithmetic could be carried out with the minimum of fuss and bother, and there is little doubt about the efficiency and elegance of these procedures. Several decades ago, Plunkett (1979: 2) suggested that standard algorithms are

$$47$$
$$\underline{+76}$$
$$\underline{123}$$
$$1$$

Figure 11.8 Recommended compact algorithm.

widely taught because they are, among other things, written, standardized, contracted, efficient, automatic, symbolic, analytic and general. However, being extremely compact they inevitably conceal much of what is actually going on in a calculation.

These compact methods summarize several steps involving commutativity, associativity and distributivity, whereas, because they contain more detail, non-standard informal methods record the successive stages of the calculation, thereby allowing children to keep track of where they are, as well as enabling them to ascertain more easily where they have gone wrong if the answer is incorrect. I would therefore question the wisdom of attempting to teach the column method to all primary children given that the expanded, left-to-right method of addition is more easily understood because it builds on the 'double partitioning' method used by most young children for mental calculation. Like the more complex standard algorithm, it is also generalizable to the addition of larger numbers.

Idiosyncratic jottings

Some children produced interesting and original ways of using notation to help them execute and communicate their work. Figure 11.9 lucidly illustrates Kelly's partitioning strategy. The lines linking corresponding tens digits and ones digits clearly show that she has added these separately, although without her written explanation we would not have known which she added first. Denise's algorithm (Figure 11.10) shows clearly which parts were added horizontally and which were added vertically, and constitutes an excellent written record of her calculation procedure. Her idiosyncratic use of the addition symbol adds to the originality (and charm) of this algorithm.

The *Framework for Teaching Mathematics from Reception to Year 6* (DfEE 1999: Section 1, page 7) argues that when children find it difficult to hold the intermediate steps of a calculation in their head they should make informal pencil and paper notes. Most discussions of jottings appear to refer only to the empty number line (for addition and subtraction) and the grid structure (for multiplication). However, in 2004 a Primary National Strategy numeracy

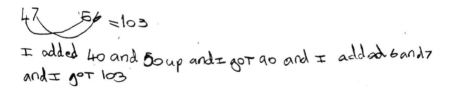

Figure 11.9   Kelly finding the sum of 47 and 56.

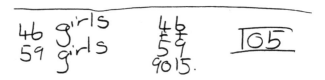

Figure 11.10 Denise finding the sum of 46 and 59.

consultants' discussion paper (no longer accessible on the Internet) posed the question *Are jottings what we need?* Consultants were asked to consider whether or not it was time to move on from just encouraging children to decide the nature of their own jottings to *teaching* them how to jot. Loaded adjectives such as 'messy', 'unstructured' and 'scribbled' used in the paper left little doubt as to what the expected answer should be: an answer that would effectively dismiss in one fell swoop the children's work illustrated in this and the previous chapter.

To argue for the teaching of specific, taught jotting techniques rather than letting children choose their own methods appears to contradict the original NNS approach to the early stages of the acquisition of calculation skills and strategies, where the emphasis is clearly on the development of a range of mental methods from which children are expected to choose those that best model their own ways of thinking. What in the NNS are appropriately described as *informal jottings* would now become *formal jottings*; to my mind, this latter phrase is an oxymoron!

The whole raison d'être of a 'jotting' is to provide support for the individual performing the calculation. Consequently, given the range of strategies that people use to execute such calculations, we would expect an individual's jottings to be a function of the mathematical operations involved; to be influenced by the size of the numbers; to relate to the (perceived) relationship between these numbers; and, inevitably, to be extremely personal, variable and idiosyncratic. Jottings need to be seen as a personal record of any intermediate steps in a calculation that the person doing the calculating feels the need to record in order to facilitate the execution of the calculation. In order to solve the 'four rows of bricks with 144 bricks in each row' problem discussed above, I, personally, would interpret the problem as 144 × 4, and would probably want to jot down 400; calculate 44 × 4 as 88 × 2, giving 176; and then mentally add this to the 400, writing down the answer 576. The only numbers written down in my case would be 400 and 576. Kate, on the other hand (Figure 11.6) would probably want to jot down a little more!

One approach to teasing out what is involved in an 'informal versus formal jottings' debate is to utilize an idea taken from the teaching of literacy, namely, the concept of *audience*. The English section of the *National Curriculum* (DfEE/QCA 1999: 49) requires that children in Key Stage 1 write for '(their) teachers, other adults, children and the writers themselves', and for Key Stage 2 children this audience widens to include '(their) teachers, the class, other children, adults, the wider community and imagined readers' (p. 58). So, in the teaching of English it is expected that children will be taught techniques for adapting their written and oral communication to suit their audience.

If we extend this concept to the teaching of mathematics, it seems reasonable to accept that when the children themselves are the sole audience for their work, they should record in their own way, writing down just those things that support them in their thinking. These are what we currently call *jottings*. With a different audience, for example, other children, teachers or markers of National Curriculum test questions, children need to be taught how to ensure that this audience can make sense of their recording; this is what we call *working*. For 'supporting' thinking we use jottings; for 'explaining' thinking we show our working. So, we still need the term 'jottings', even though it is not to be found in the *Primary Framework for Literacy and Mathematics* (DfES 2006b) nor the *Practice Guidance for the Early Years Foundation Stage* (DfES 2007)! But we also need to develop children's explanatory skills, helping them to make their thinking explicit to a wider audience (see Thompson 2004 for further discussion of jottings).

Fortunately, the *Independent Review of Mathematics Teaching in Early Years Settings and Primary Schools* (DCSF 2008: 37) may well have rescued the concept of 'jottings' by recommending 'A learning environment that encourages children to choose to use their own mathematical graphics to support their mathematical thinking and processes'.

Implications for teaching and learning

So, what *do* young children's mathematical graphics tell us about the teaching of written addition? It is important to remember that the children involved in this research had not, in theory, been taught written methods, and, in the vast majority of cases had invented their own written methods. There are several implications that follow from the above discussion.

- It is important to let children set out their calculations horizontally so long as this layout is not becoming unwieldy or leading to unnecessary errors.
- Even when a vertical layout is used, children should not be obliged to work from right to left, but encouraged to start from the left, summing the most significant digits first. Working from left to right also means that the initial stages of the calculation provide a useful first approximation to the answer.

- Children should be encouraged to base their written methods on their own preferred mental calculation methods.
- They should be working in an environment that attaches value to idiosyncratic written methods, and should be praised for inventing their own notation or jottings.
- As mentioned earlier, only one child in the research sample used the sequencing strategy: the basic strategy that underpins the use of the empty number line. This would suggest that teachers need to carry out a substantial amount of preparatory work to enable children to use what this research suggests is a strategy that not very many children invent for themselves.
- Teachers should not be in a rush to teach what is described above as the 'column value' aspect of place value (56 interpreted as 5 in the tens column and 6 in the ones column). All the examples illustrated in this chapter show children using the 'quantity value' aspect (56 interpreted as 50 plus 6). Thompson (2003) has shown that all mental calculation methods and all informal written methods for the four basic operations seem to make use of the 'quantity value' aspect of place value. It is only when making the final step (some might say 'leap in the dark') to standard (or compact) algorithms that the column value aspect is involved.

These suggestions also obtain to a certain extent for subtraction, multiplication and division. But that is another story!

References

DCSF (Department for Children, Schools and Families) (2008) *Independent Review of Mathematics Teaching in Early Years Settings and Primary Schools* www.publications.teachernet.gov.uk/eOrderingDownload/ Williams%20Mathematics.pdf (accessed June 2008).

DfEE (Department for Education and Employment) (1999) *Framework for Teaching Mathematics from Reception to Year 6*. London: DfEE.

DfEE/QCA (Department for Education and Employment/Qualifications and Curriculum Authority) (1999) *National Curriculum: Handbook for Primary Teachers in England*. London: DfEE/QCA.

DfES (Department for Education and Skills) (2006a) *Guidance Paper – Calculation* www.standards.dfes.gov.uk/primaryframework/mathematics/Papers/ Calculation (accessed 31 March 2008).

DfES (Department for Education and Skills) (2006b) *Primary Framework for Literacy and Mathematics*. Norwich: DfES.

DfES (Department for Education and Skills) (2007) *Practice Guidance for the*

Early Years Foundation Stage. Nottingham: DfES www.publications.teachernet. gov.uk/eOrderingDownload/eyfs_guide12_07.pdf (accessed 31 March 2008).

Hedrén, R. (1999) The teaching of traditional standard algorithms for the four arithmetic operations versus the use of pupils' own methods, in I. Schwank (ed.) *European Research in Mathematics Education 1*, Osnabrück: Forschungsinstitut für Mathematikdidaktik.

Jones, D.A. (1975) Don't just mark the answer – have a look at the method, *Mathematics in School*, 4(3): 29–31.

Plunkett, S. (1979) Decomposition and all that rot, *Mathematics in Schools*, 8(3): 2–5.

Rousham, L. (2003) The empty number line: a model in search of a learning trajectory, in I. Thompson (ed.) *Enhancing Primary Mathematics Teaching*. Maidenhead: Open University Press.

Thompson, I. (1994) Young children's idiosyncratic written algorithms for addition, *Educational Studies in Mathematics*, 26: 323–45.

Thompson, I. (2003) Place value: the English disease? in I. Thompson (ed.) *Enhancing Primary Mathematics Teaching*. Maidenhead: Open University Press.

Thompson, I. (2004) To jot or not to jot, *Mathematics in School*, 33(3): 6–7.

Thompson, I. (2007) The Revised Framework: an exercise in consultation?, *Primary Mathematics*, 11(1): 3–5.

12 What's in a picture? Understanding and representation in early mathematics

Tony Harries, Patrick Barmby and Jennifer Suggate

Introduction

During primary education, pupils are introduced to a number of big ideas. In early primary, these ideas are mainly focused on counting, addition and subtraction. In teaching addition and subtraction, there has been a clear use of representations such as number squares and number lines, with number lines being the most appropriate representation for demonstrating the essential characteristics of these operations. Furthermore, in the Year 2 objectives, there is a specific mention of the array as a way of representing multiplication. In the renewed *Primary Framework for Literacy and Mathematics* (DfES 2006: 67), the guidance notes talk about the need for pupils to '. . . understand the underlying ideas . . . develop ways of recording to support their thinking and calculation methods' and also to gain a 'good knowledge of numbers or a "feel" for numbers'.

There is a suggestion in the guidance that these two ideas are 'the product of structured practice and repetition'. While we do not deny the importance of practice and repetition, in this chapter we are taking a different approach. We first look at issues related to how we represent ideas in mathematics, then we link this to a view of what it means to understand an aspect of mathematics, and finally we look at the specific topic of addition and subtraction in order to illustrate the idea of using representations to gain understanding.

Role of representations in mathematical learning

Researchers world-wide have discussed the importance of representations in developing mathematical competence. Representations in mathematics education refer to both internal and external manifestations of mathematical concepts. Hiebert and Carpenter (1992) state that communicating mathematical ideas requires external representations (e.g. spoken language, written symbols, pictures or physical objects), whereas to think about mathematical ideas requires internal representations. Goldin and Shteingold (2001) also identified computer-based microworlds as external representations, and students' personal symbols, their natural language, visual imagery, spatial representation, problem-solving strategies and heuristics as internal representations.

Goldin and Shteingold's (2001) work on representations suggests that representational systems are important to the learning of mathematics because of the inherent structure contained within each representation. This structure can shape or constrain learning. Furthermore, different representations emphasize different aspects of a concept and so the development of an understanding of a particular concept comes from having a range of representations and being able to move both within and between them. For example, if we take the two representations of 27 in Figures 12.1 and 12.2, the first emphasizes the idea of place value and the way numbers can be built up, whereas the second emphasizes numbers as part of an infinite counting system.

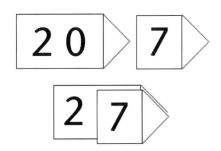

Figure 12.1 Arrow cards representation for 27.

Figure 12.2 Number line representation for 27.

Goldin (2002) suggests that representations contain a number of characteristics:

- First, they contain what might be called *primitive components* such as signs, symbols and objects. For young children this may include blocks, number cards or the digit themselves.
- Second, they contain *configurations* which are ways of combining the primitive components. These, for example, might be the way that blocks are arranged in order to represent numbers in such a way that place value is embedded in the configuration.
- Sometimes they contain *higher level structures* such as mathematical operations and rules which need to be adhered to in working with a particular representation.
- They also have *conventional and objective characteristics* so that once the conventions of a system have been agreed, there are then specific characteristics that exist because of this. For example, once the conventions of a base 10 system are accepted, then the properties of numbers within the system can be found from those conventions.

We would also add two more important characteristics that are required by a representation, particularly for the young learner:

- *Consistency*, both as we move from one operation to another and as the number domain extends through natural numbers, integers and rational numbers.
- *Transparency*, so that the characteristics of the operation are clearly available for the learner to visualize and use.

However, Harries and Suggate (2006) suggested that representations are not always self-evident, but actually they need to be 'worked on' so that the essence of the representation is understood. As Mason has written:

> ... to get much educational benefit, students need to be active in processing images; they need to work on images, not just look at them. They need to probe beneath surface reactions. Working on and with mental imagery supports this development.
>
> (Mason 2005: 78)

Kaput (1994: 530) maintained that the ability to see links between different representations (both iconic and symbolic) is a powerful problem-solving tool, and he suggested that linking notational systems helps pupils to extend their reasoning processes from concrete to more abstract systems: '... all aspects of a complex idea cannot be adequately represented within a single notation system, and hence require multiple systems for their full expression ...'.

These ideas from Mason and Kaput suggest that we need to investigate ways in which young learners can explore representations and how this exploration may be a way in which understanding is developed.

Understanding, reasoning and representations

The previous discussion touched on the fact that using representations can develop children's understanding of mathematics. Let us consider in more depth the link between representations of mathematical concepts and how we come to understand these concepts. We begin by examining some definitions or explanations of 'understanding' in mathematics. Skemp (1976) identified two types of understanding: relational and instrumental. He described relational understanding as 'knowing both what to do and why' (p. 2), and the process of learning relational mathematics as 'building up a conceptual structure' (p. 14). Instrumental understanding, on the other hand, was simply described as 'rules without reasons' (p. 2).

Nickerson (1985), in examining what understanding is, identified some 'results' of understanding: for example, agreement with experts; being able to see deeper characteristics of a concept; looking for specific information in a situation more quickly; being able to represent situations; and visualizing a situation using mental models. However, he also proposed that 'understanding in everyday life is enhanced by the ability to build bridges between one conceptual domain and another' (p. 229). Like Skemp, Nickerson highlighted the importance of knowledge and of relating knowledge: 'The more one knows about a subject, the better one understands it. The richer the conceptual context in which one can embed a new fact, the more one can be said to understand the fact' (pp. 235–36). Hiebert and Carpenter (1992) specifically defined mathematical understanding as involving the building-up of the conceptual 'context' or 'structure' mentioned above:

> The mathematics is understood if its mental representation is part of a network of representations. The degree of understanding is determined by the number and strength of its connections. A mathematical idea, procedure, or fact is understood thoroughly if it is linked to existing networks with stronger or more numerous connections.
>
> (Hiebert and Carpenter 1992: 67)

Therefore, this idea of understanding being a structure or network of internal mathematical ideas or representations comes out clearly from the literature. We also see reasoning as the process of linking between different representations of a mathematical concept, both internally or externally. Thus, we can use the following definitions for understanding and reasoning:

- To understand mathematics is to make connections between mental (internal) representations of a mathematical concept.
- To reason is to make connections between different representations (internal or external) of a mathematical concept, through formal processes (e.g. logic, proof) or informal processes (e.g. examples).

We can therefore see the close links between understanding and reasoning, and why in establishing links through reasoning, we might develop understanding of a mathematical concept. We have also established some connection between the internal representations that make up our understanding and the external representations that we use to communicate mathematics. Going back to the ideas of Mason and Kaput discussed earlier, by encouraging children to explore and reason between representations, what we are doing is providing the opportunity for understanding to develop.

Types of situation leading to addition/subtraction and key ideas

The literature suggests that there are essentially two situation types that lead to addition and four which lead to subtraction. For addition, Haylock (2001) names the situations as aggregation and augmentation. The first one concerns the joining together of two quantities or sets, whereas the second concerns situations where a quantity or set is increased by a certain amount. For subtraction, Haylock identifies four broad situations that give rise to subtraction. First, there is partitioning which in a sense is the inverse of aggregation, whereby we start with the whole and remove a quantity/set and want to know how much is left. Second, we have the inverse of augmentation where we reduce the quantity set by a given amount. Third, there is comparison, where the objective is to compare the relative size of two quantities, and fourth, there is the general idea of subtraction being the inverse of addition. These different situations may be more appropriately illustrated by different representations. Also, a key idea within addition is that of commutativity, which again is more easily shown using particular representations.

The situations above are what might be termed 'key developmental understandings' – KDUs (Simon 2006). He suggests two important characteristics of KDUs. First, they involve a 'conceptual advance on the part of the student' by which he means that it allows the student to think about the concept in a different way. Second, they are not acquired as a result of 'explanation or demonstration' but require a multiple range of experiences through which understanding can be built. This resonates with Nuñes and Bryant's (1996: 140) idea that students' understanding of addition and subtraction develops as they 'use different systems of signs (or tools for thought) when reasoning about addition and subtraction'.

Characteristics of the main representations for addition/subtraction

In addition to being helpful tools, researchers have suggested that representations play a more profound role in the learning of mathematics. Lesh et al. (1983: 268) suggested that 'to do mathematics is to create and manipulate structures'. During problem-solving, subjects 'frequently change the problem representation from one form to another . . . at any given stage, two or more representational systems may be used simultaneously, each illuminating some aspects of the situation' (p. 264).

There are many representations of numbers, but for the purposes of working with addition and subtraction, we have identified the representations in Figures 12.3 and 12.4 as being the main ones with which pupils need to work. Each representation shows the calculation 26 + 38.

For addition, the first representation is the one which would seem to most naturally represent the idea of aggregation, where the two sets to be joined are clearly indicated by the different shading. The second representation most naturally represents the idea of augmentation where there is a clear starting point and a movement which takes the learner to the augmented position. We can argue in a similar way for subtraction. Thus, in terms of Nuñes and Bryant's (1996) and Simon's (2006) ideas on KDUs, developing an understanding of addition and subtraction requires the students to work on reasoning activities related to the representations shown.

Using representations of addition and subtraction

If the idea of representation is crucial to developing understanding, then this would suggest that there needs to be a change in emphasis to the way in which we engage pupils in mathematical thinking. We suggest that pupils need to be able to use representations in a variety of ways in order to develop their understanding of a mathematical topic. We suggest that they need:

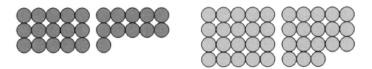

Figure 12.3　Counters representation of 26 + 38.

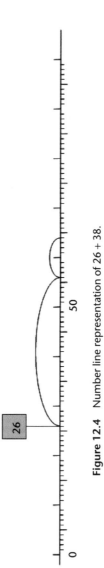

Figure 12.4 Number line representation of 26 + 38.

- to have a range of images or representations with which they make sense of numbers;
- to be able to explain what they 'notice' about particular representations;
- to be able to explain characteristics of the representation;
- to be able to discuss connections between different representations;
- to be able to discuss what they can use the representations to do;
- to be able to explain how they use the representations to perform the different calculations.

Looking at addition and subtraction specifically, as young children explore the nature of these operations, there seem to be three number domains that they work through initially – number bonds up to 10, number bonds up to 20 and two-digit numbers. As indicated above, pupils need to experience a range of representations which illustrate the operations in these domains. Examples of these are shown in Figure 12.5.

Some of these – counters, tens and ones blocks, abacus, number squares, beads and the number line – are particularly helpful for illustrating addition and subtraction. In the sections below, we examine some of the

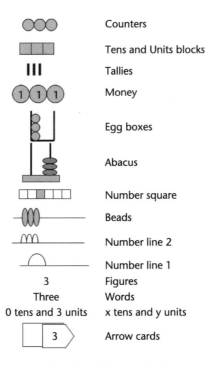

Figure 12.5 Possible representations for addition and subtraction.

representations associated with number bonds up to 10, number bonds up to 20 and two-digit numbers, in order to see how pupils can use them to develop their understanding,

Number bonds up to 10

Fuson (1992) suggested that there are essentially three ways in which children develop their competence within this domain. First, there is direct modelling involving count-all methods for addition, then abbreviated counting procedures such as counting-on, and finally procedures using known facts (see Thompson, Chapter 8). These ideas can be modelled in a variety of ways; for example, using fingers where all fingers can be counted, or a number can be held 'in the head' and fingers used to count on. A key representation for addition and subtraction is the number line, and a useful way of introducing young children to this representation is shown in Figure 12.6 – frogs on a lily pad.

Now, what would we expect the pupils to 'notice' from these representations? Some possible suggestions are shown below:

- lots of lily pads;
- solid and dotted arcs;
- frog on number 9 in both pictures;
- only solid arcs in the second diagram;
- a flag on 4 in the second diagram.

In trying to make sense of the two representations (e.g. explaining characteristics or connections between the representations), these ideas provide a starting point for focusing on addition as counting, and then different starting points for counting (i.e. explaining how the representations can be used).

In the first example, we see the count-all strategy being illustrated, with

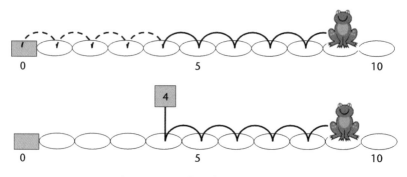

Figure 12.6 Lily pad representations.

each count being shown as a jump. In the second example, we see the number 4 being identified as a starting point and then the extra 5 jumps being shown separately. Similarly with subtraction, the frogs on the lily pad can be used to illustrate different ways of working – subtraction as taking away, finding the difference where two positions are identified and we need to find the distance between them either by counting-up or counting-down.

Number bonds up to 20

Research by Canobi (2005) examined the mathematical understanding that was important within the topic of addition and subtraction. This is applicable for the domain of number bonds up to 20. The concepts explored by Canobi were:

- commutativity $(a + b = b + a)$;
- subtraction complement $(a – b = c$ implies that $a – c = b)$;
- inversion principle $(a + b = c$ implies that $c – a = b$ and $c – b = a)$;
- three-term inverse problem $(a + b – b = a)$.

All the concepts essentially explored the idea of a number triple which gives rise to a number of possible calculations. The main points noted in the research were that, first, these were all related to the types of addition/subtraction word problems that pupils are required to engage with, and which can be expressed symbolically by the equations above. Second, the notion of part–whole relationships was a key developmental issue, and third, there was a tendency for pupils to be located in extreme groups – conceptually strong or conceptually weak.

We can demonstrate how representations can be used to explore these ideas. All the ideas can be illustrated/represented on the 'number blocks on a line' idea, as shown on page 170, for the number triple $9 + 7 = 16$. Ideally, this can be shown dynamically within a computer environment. Figure 12.7 shows that $9 + 7$ gives the same result as $7 + 9$. Figure 12.8 shows $16 – 7 = 9$. Figure 12.9 shows $16 – 9 = 7$.

Again, we can ask what we might expect children to notice about the three pictures on page 170:

- in each case there are two numbers shown by shaded and white blocks;
- there are 7 white blocks and 9 shaded blocks;
- two rows of blocks in each picture;
- in the first picture the colours are swapped round, but still end on 16;
- in the second and third diagrams, one set of blocks is lifted from the top line of blocks.

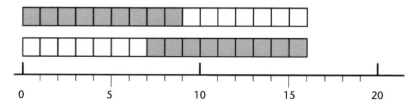

Figure 12.7   Number blocks on a line (1).

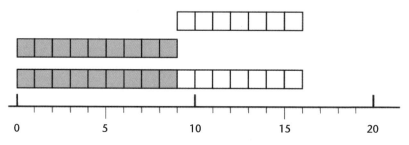

Figure 12.8   Number blocks on a line (2).

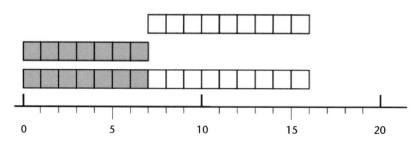

Figure 12.9   Number blocks on a line (3).

We can again use these comments as a starting point for focusing on the idea that the three numbers give rise to four addition/subtraction calculations. The representations can encourage discussion to explore these ideas. The moving parts of the representation allow us to illustrate all the equations in the previous section. In the representation there are three parts – the total and the two parts which make up the total. All the equations are asking that given two of the parts, what is the third part of the equation?

Addition of two-digit numbers

When we move on to consider the domain of two-digit numbers, the key development here is the use of flexible partitioning of numbers. Again, different representations will facilitate this in different ways. Consider the representations in Figures 12.10 and 12.11, which are illustrations of adding 28 and 47 using the number line.

Once again, what might pupils notice about the representation given in Figures 12.10?

- The arcs join the flag at 28 to the number 75.
- We jump 2 from 28, to get 30, then a jump of 40 to 70, then a final jump of 5 to 75.

Now we can move to explore different illustrations using the same representational system (Figure 12.11). They also represent the same calculation. In examining the connections between the representations, pupils might conclude that:

- they all represent addition or subtraction;
- they all have same start and end points;
- they show different ways of partitioning the number to be added or subtracted.

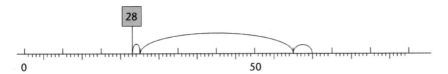

Figure 12.10   Number line 1.

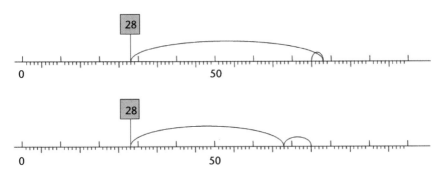

Figure 12.11   Number lines 2 and 3.

Therefore, comparing the different representations and explaining the similarities and differences might be used to illustrate the idea of partitioning numbers in addition and subtraction.

We could extend the exercise to consider an illustration within a different representational system – in this case using counters as shown. Clearly, this is quite a different image of addition, using counters (Figure 12.12). What might pupils notice now and what connections might they make with the previous representations? In this case, the way of completing the calculation is first to join the groups of ten and then the units into a group of ten with some units left over as shown. We see that both numbers being added have been 'split up', unlike in the number line representation. We could discuss the relative merits of the different methods.

We now have four different representations of addition for 28 + 47. Discussing the representations allows us to explore the concept of addition, through reasoning about the calculations in terms of some of its multiple representations.

Conclusion

In all the examples above, we have been trying to let the pictures/representations speak. In a sense, we have replaced the starting question of 'what do I have to do?' with 'what does it look like?' For numbers, we have several representations, an analysis of which allows us to talk about the characteristics of a number, so that the picture becomes both a tool to think with and a focus for discussion. Similarly, with operations such as addition, we have a number of representations which become our tools for thinking and discussion. In particular, we have a key representation – the number line – which allows us to operate in a variety of ways. Again, we can explore similarities and differences between representations and consider how we move from one representation to another.

So, we may have a pedagogy for understanding through representations, and the key questions seem to be:

- What does the object/operation look like?
- Is there more than one way of representing the object/operation?
- What are the characteristics of the various representations?
- What is the same and what is different about the various representations of the same object/operation?
- How do we move from one representation to another?
- What are the most useful characteristics of a particular representation?

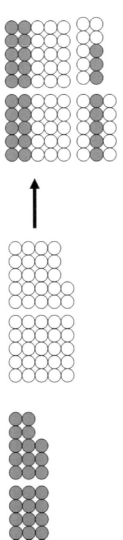

Figure 12.12 Addition with counters.

These questions, which are essentially an interrogation of the representations, provide the basis for developing an understanding of the concept being explored.

References

Canobi, K.H. (2005) Children's profiles of addition and subtraction understanding, *Journal of Experimental Child Psychology*, 92: 220–46.

DfES (Department for Education and Skills) (2006) *Primary Framework for Literacy and Mathematics*. Norwich: DfES.

Fuson, K. (1992) Research on whole number addition and subtraction, in D. Grouws (ed.) *Handbook of Research on Mathematics Teaching and Learning*. New York: Macmillan.

Goldin, G.A. (2002) Representation in mathematical learning, in L.N. English (ed.) *2002 Handbook of International Research in Mathematics Education*. Hillsdale: NJ: Lawrence Erlbaum Associates.

Goldin, G.A. and Shteingold, N. (2001) Systems of representation and the development of mathematical concepts, in A.A. Cuoco and F.R. Curcio (eds) *The Roles of Representation in School Mathematics*. Reston, VA: National Council of Teachers of Mathematics.

Harries, T. and Suggate, J. (2006) Exploring links across representations of numbers with young children, *International Journal for Technology in Mathematics Education*, 13(2) online journal available at www.icme-organisers.dk/tsg08/harries.doc (accessed 31 March 2008).

Haylock, D. (2001) *Mathematics Explained for Primary School Teachers*. London: Paul Chapman Publishers.

Hiebert, J. and Carpenter, T.P. (1992) Learning and teaching with understanding, in D.A. Grouws (ed.) *Handbook of Research on Mathematics Teaching and Learning*. New York: Macmillan.

Kaput, J. (1994) Technology and mathematics education, in D.A. Grouws (ed.) *Handbook of Research on Mathematics Teaching and Learning*. New York: Macmillan.

Lesh, R., Landau, M. and Hamilton, E. (1983) Conceptual models and applied mathematical problem-solving research, in R. Lesh and M. Landau (eds) *Acquisition of Mathematical Concepts and Processes*. London: Academic Press.

Mason, J. (2005) Micro-structure of attention in the teaching and learning of mathematics, in *Mathematics Teaching 2005 Conference Report*, Edinburgh Centre for Mathematical Education.

Nickerson, R.S. (1985) Understanding understanding, *American Journal of Education*, 93(2): 201–39.

Nuñes, T. and Bryant, P. (1996) *Children Doing Mathematics*. Oxford: Blackwell Publishers.

Simon, M.A. (2006) Key developmental understandings in mathematics: a direction for investigating and establishing goals, *Mathematical Thinking and Learning*, 8(4): 359–71.

Skemp, R. (1976) Relational understanding and instrumental understanding, *Mathematics Teaching*, 77: 20–6.

13 Mathematical learning and the use of information and communications technology in the early years

Steve Higgins

Introduction

In the debates about early childhood and the influence of technology, there have been broadly two schools of thought about information and communications technology (ICT) and the learning of young children. The first is that these technologies are potentially detrimental to children's social and intellectual development, contrasting with the opposite view that technology offers a range of experiences that may be beneficial depending on how meaningful the activities are to the children involved and how they contribute to wider development (for a review of this debate, see Hall and Higgins 2002: 301).

The National Numeracy Strategy (NNS) seemed to endorse the former view with the only mentions of computer use in the Reception framework (DfEE 1999) to help children recognize numerals on the keyboard (p. 8), and to talk about and make patterns and shapes with appropriate software (pp. 18 and 26). Similarly the *Practice Guidance for the Early Years Foundation Stage* (DfES 2007) recommends the use of programmable toys and computers to support children's learning (pp. 76 and 81–2) but without particular mathematical goals. This chapter therefore explores the research about the role of technology in children's mathematical learning in the early years. It argues that there is evidence that a range of approaches involving ICT can be of benefit, but that there are a number of challenges in ensuring that the learning which results from young children's engagement with ICT is mathematically meaningful (Clements 2002: 171).

The impact of technology on learning

Although the impact of ICT on learning is about the same as the average for all educational interventions (Higgins 2003: 5), there is some evidence that in the area of mathematics and for younger children it is more beneficial. Fletcher-Flinn and Gravatt (1995) reviewed early work in this field and reported that computer-assisted instruction was more effective than traditional teaching for a wide range of skills in reading, writing, mathematics and science, but with a rather low overall average effect. The study did, however, identify a number of areas where the use of technology was more effective and the greatest benefits were found for young and pre-school children for mathematics.

More recent studies have been designed to have a greater impact by grounding the activities in the existing research evidence about how young children learn mathematics. This is consistent with the idea of developmentally appropriate experiences (Clements 2002: 161) and developmentally appropriate practice (discussed in Hall and Higgins 2002: 309). One example of this is the use of computer-based activities included in the 'building blocks' programme (Sarama and Clements 2004). In this approach children are provided with a range of experiences to build a solid foundation for mathematics. The research used a design and development model drawing on theory and previous research in the field. The team assumed that curriculum and software design can (and should) have an explicit theoretical and empirical foundation, but that it also should inform further development of both theory and research.

Their approach included design of mathematical objects, or computer 'manipulatives', and specific mathematical processes and skills embedded in software 'tools' and interactions. It included extensive field-testing from initial ideas through to large summative evaluation studies. Children undertook a range of numerical activities on screen including counting, adding to, taking away, combining quantities, and the like. The actions on geometric shapes included rigid transformations (slide, turn and flip tools) as well as duplication, combination and decomposition (with 'glue' and 'axe' tools). One game involved similar activities undertaken on screen and practically with a teacher or adult. Mrs Double, an on-screen character (or the teacher working with small groups) puts out three chips and asks the child to 'make it six', encouraging counting-on or adding for children who could use more sophisticated strategies. At the level of addition of small numbers, the teacher introduces a socio-dramatic play area, the dinosaur shop, and encourages children to count and add during their play. Children help to run a dinosaur shop on the computer as well. At one of the more challenging levels a customer orders two types of item, and children label these two collections in two separate boxes (such as two red triceratops and three yellow brontosauruses for example). The customer asks for one box and children move all the dinosaurs into a new one and label it with the calculation.

The test results suggest that such an approach can result in significant learning gains in mathematics for young children. The development work was based on building an explicit model of children's thinking, including 'learning trajectories' with the specific aim of 'finding the mathematics in, and developing mathematics from, children's activity' (Sarama and Clements 2004: 183). The research team believes that their qualitative research suggests that the goal for the early years should be 'mathematical literacy', not 'numeracy'. They argue that the 'latter usually is (mis)understood as dealing mainly with numbers' (p. 187) and argue that other areas of mathematics such as geometry and patterning are foundational for mathematics learning as they build on the interests and competencies of young children as well as supporting the learning of other mathematical topics.

A number of studies indicate the importance of adult involvement and mediation through discussion in children's learning with technology. The support of adults in talking to children about what they were doing on computers has been shown to help children's learning in mathematics, both using structured programs and in a more open-ended problem-solving environment, such as Logo (Klein et al. 2000). Logo is a computer programming language simple enough for young children to use, particularly when defining and drawing shapes, but advanced enough for adults to be challenged. Some versions of the software let children control robots in the classroom through a computer or keypad (for an overview, see Clements 2002). In Klein et al.'s (2000) research, when adults supported the children through discussion, three specific approaches were found to be of benefit to the children's learning:

1   asking them to *expand* on what they were doing ('How else can you draw this . . .?' 'Which is the easiest way to do it?' 'Why?');
2   *encouraging* them ('Good, how did you do it?', 'What did you do to get this . . .?', 'How can you correct this?');
3   giving them prompts to *regulate* what they were doing at the computer ('What does the computer tell you?', 'Is it correct?', 'How can you tell?', 'How do you know that you did well?', 'What did you learn from this mistake?').

The findings support the conclusion that integrating adult mediation and interaction in early years learning environments using computers supports more effective use of such technologies and has positive benefits in terms of children's performance and learning of mathematics.

Other recent work suggests that ICT can help young children who have been identified as 'at risk' in term of their learning (Fuchs et al. 2006). The purpose of this study was to assess the potential for computer-assisted instruction to enhance number combination skill for children 'at risk for math disability and reading disability'. At-risk students were assigned randomly to computer-assisted instruction in mathematics or in spelling, which they received in 50 sessions over 18 weeks. The research specifically looked for both the acquisition of skills and any transfer effects to other areas of mathematics (or literacy). It therefore aimed to identify the value of computer-assisted instruction on early addition and subtraction in terms of number combination skills with an assessment of story-problem questions among 5- and 6-year-olds. This was set within the context of wider classroom instruction focused on the development of number sense.

The activities the children undertook involved the repetition of a calculation that appeared on screen with its answer to help the children remember the calculation. The computer-mediated treatment, which was referred to as FLASH by the research team, briefly presented the calculation (or word for the reading group), then the computer asked the child to retype the calculation (or word) from memory. The length of time the calculation remained on the screen was determined by the children's previous success. The better they performed, the shorter the time it remained on screen. If the response was correct, positive reinforcement was provided; if not, corrective feedback was provided. The results indicated that this instruction was effective in supporting recall but that the transfer of these skills to story problems with similar calculations did not occur. This is consistent with the research discussed above and suggests that the mathematical experiences were not sufficiently meaningful to the children for them to be able to use the mathematical recall skills that they had developed. There was no adult mediation or development of the applicability of what they knew in a new context. The research clearly suggests the limits of what this kind of computer-assisted instruction can do. It may support the development of more automatic recall, or the improvement of specific skills, but these need to be embedded in a child's experience and interest to develop mathematical understanding and the facility to use the skills they have acquired.

Calculators

One further example of mathematical technology which has been researched but which has not been included in this overview is calculators. Desktop calculators are perhaps the cheapest of all forms of ICT and there has been considerable debate about their value in the teaching and learning of mathematics in schools. Unfortunately, this debate has rarely been informed by research into the impact of such use, which suggests that, when used to support and challenge mathematical thinking in young children, it can have a lasting benefit on children's competence in number (Ruthven et al. 1997).

Williams and Thompson (2003) describe the situation concerning the use of calculators in Key Stage 1 at the time of the introduction of the NNS in 1999 as being one of 'extreme confusion for teachers' (Williams and Thompson 2003: 153). Most research findings and some official publications – including Ofsted reports – were quite positive about their use. However, the *Framework for Teaching Mathematics from Reception to Year 6* stated clearly that 'schools should not normally use the calculator as part of Key Stage 1 mathematics . . .' (DfEE 1999: 8). Even the British Educational Communications and Technology Agency (BECTA 2001) discouraged the use of calculators at Key Stage 1 arguing that children at this stage were still developing skills such as mental calculation, rounding and checking results, all of which were necessary skills for using calculators effectively. Research suggests that the assumption that all of these skills have to be well developed before children can use calculators effectively ignores the fact that using calculators can actually help the development of these very skills at all ages and Key Stages.

The *Guidance Paper – The Use of Calculators in the Teaching and Learning of Mathematics* (DCSF 2007) sets out the current approach to calculators taken by the Primary National Strategy (PNS). Objectives that promote the use of calculators as a tool for calculations are included for Years 4, 5 and 6; no objectives are provided for other year groups. However, we are informed that 'in the context of exploring numbers and the number system, the calculator can be used with other age groups as a teaching and learning tool' (DCSF 2007). It does, however, argue that Foundation Stage children should become familiar with calculators in their play activities, exploring what the keys do and entering familiar numbers. Year 1 children are expected to be able to key in two-digit numbers and investigate what happens when ten is added or subtracted. Year 2 children are to be introduced to the constant facility in order to benefit from the range of activities that can be built around its use.

There is even an acknowledgement that 'The calculator can be used to sharpen and secure mental calculation' (DCSF 2007), although this is slightly watered down by the statement that their use is for '*consolidating* children's learning of number facts and calculation strategies' (my italics). Unfortunately, the document is not quite enlightened enough to argue that they can actually be used to stimulate and develop, rather than just 'consolidate', mental calculation strategies. However, this document is a big step in the right direction in encouraging teachers to use technology to support children's skills, confidence, competence and understanding of number.

The benefits of technology have therefore been found with both more structured approaches using mathematical games and practice software as well as more open ended or creative activities and with both simple and complex technologies. Research indicates that there are some clear limits on what can be achieved with skills teaching without developing children's interest and engagement in making sense of their experiences mathematically. There is no clear implication from the research that one approach is more effective than another; rather, it is necessary to engage children's interest and involve them in mathematical discussion in order to develop effective use of ICT in the early years.

Recent developments in technology

A range of new technologies is being developed and used in schools and early years settings. In the UK there has been a significant take-up of interactive whiteboards. These are large display screens for a computer mounted on a classroom wall which can be controlled by touch. While these are popular with both teachers and children, there is no clear evidence that they are beneficial for learning (Higgins et al. 2007), at least as measured by tested attainment. They clearly have potential for teachers to introduce mathematical ideas and representations and for children to discuss their experiences mathematically with groups and the whole class. Evidence is not yet available to show how this might benefit the mathematical learning of young children. It seems likely, however, that such technologies can be of value if the activities are planned to help children think and talk about the mathematical aspects of their learning as appropriate to their current level of mathematical skills and understanding. The PNS in England has invested heavily in supporting such technology and has developed a series of interactive teaching programs (ITPs) for mathematics. Some of these are appropriate for teaching young children aspects of number (*Counting On and Back, Difference, Twenty Cards*) as well as aspects of shape and space (*Symmetry, Polygon*) or measures (*Tell the Time, Measuring Cylinder*). They are available to download at www.standards.dfes.gov.uk/primary/publications/mathematics/itps/ (accessed 31 March 2008).

Most early years teachers prefer young children to be using technology rather than using it themselves in such settings (Higgins and Moseley 2001). In this research a level of scepticism about ICT by teachers of young children was associated with better learning outcomes for their pupils. There have been a number of innovative projects where young children have used digital video cameras, for example, to record aspects of their learning (Somekh et al. 2007); however, there is little evidence concerning the impact on their learning, particularly in areas such as mathematics. Without planned and structured activities designed to support and enrich the development of children's mathematical skills and understanding, it seems unlikely that the technology itself will be of any benefit.

Developing counting skills with young children

In the section which follows, there is a description of a research project which used evidence about the development of early number capabilities to devise with the class teacher a series of activities using ICT to improve the children's counting and early number skills. The school where the research took place was in an inner-city area in the north-east of England. A characteristic of the area was high parental unemployment and it has been subject to several government-funded regeneration initiatives over the past few decades. Over 70 per cent of pupils receive free school meals. Pupils were achieving below national expectations on entry to the school; however, the school was recognized as being effective at raising standards of achievement. The teacher had been at the school for six years when the project took place and had usually taught the Reception Year (4- and 5-year-olds). When planning activities, she liked to make links between different activities and to draw out connections for the children. During an interview she remarked:

> ... they might need work on number recognition, or using number lines, and it isn't always linked. But usually we do something that is to do with counting, a counting rhyme or acting out a song which is linked to other activities.

At the beginning of the summer term, when a baseline test was conducted, some pupils were making errors in reciting the number names accurately (particularly in terms of stable but inaccurate counting sequences in the numbers from 13 to 19 and at the decade transitions such as 29 to 30). Some children also had unstable number word sequences from 8 to 20. Most had inaccurate touch counting skills and strategies which led them to give an incorrect total at the end of a count, particularly for collections of 6 to 15 objects, and were also unable to identify the correct written numeral to go with a number name in various counts up to 20. This is consistent with a developmental sequence for early counting, though is more typically found with slightly younger children (3- and 4-year-olds). For further information about the development of counting skills see Threlfall (Chapter 5).

The research team and the teacher therefore agreed to tackle these particular areas of counting skills using some computer-based activities. After negotiation and discussion, the focus for the project was the development of pupils' counting skills using a painting and drawing program (Kid Pix – Broderbund Software). Like many painting programs aimed at young children, the software has the facility to let children stamp a variety of pictures onto the screen. Children choose a stamp and then click with the mouse to place it. An additional feature of Kid Pix is that it has numeral stamps with sounds, so when the stamp for the number three is selected, for example, the computer voice says 'three'. The teacher therefore planned to use the software over the course of the term to create a range of counting pictures (see Figure 13.1).

Using the painting software in this way enabled her to use the computer in the classroom and in the school's computer room more flexibly than previously. The programs she had used for counting before had focused only on numeral recognition and set-to-symbol or symbol-to-set skills and matching

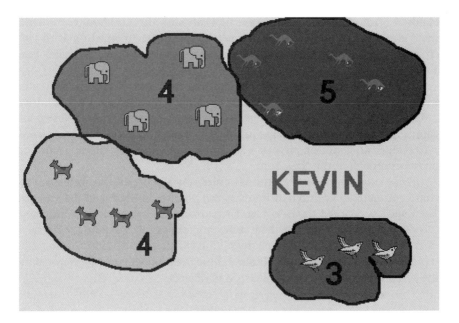

Figure 13.1 A child's counting picture.

tasks. As many of the children had incorrect stable portions or unstable portions in their counting sequences up to 10, this was inappropriate for the majority of the children. The teacher commented: 'The Kid Pix program was quite different from anything I've used before, because the programs we've used before to support numeracy have been very closed.'

The children were introduced to the software systematically. Small groups of five or six children were taught how to use the program in the school's computer room by the teacher or the teaching assistant. They then had an opportunity to practise these skills on the computer in the classroom in pairs or individually. Towards the end of the project larger groups were able to use the computer room and even on some occasions even the whole class of 28 children were using 15 computers with the support of two adults.

The teacher also used diagnostic information from the baseline test. It gave her detailed information about the particular counting errors that specific children were making. These were discussed as part of the research and development work. In particular the typical error patterns were analysed and a range of skills tasks were identified as potentially helpful for groups or for individual children. In addition to the work using ICT, she planned other number activities to support particular skills for groups of children in the class. The teacher wanted children to be able to practise specific aspects of counting and therefore emphasized different aspects of counting skills with different children. Although the tasks were similar and the children considered them the same – 'making counting pictures' – in her interaction with the children the focus of discussion and specific practice of skills varied (see Table 13.1).

The teacher thought that having children create these mathematical pictures, and count out loud as they did so, enabled them to use the ICT more independently. The children were able to use the software to make a variety of counting pictures over a period of just over two months. Each child completed on average two counting pictures each week, either in the computer room or on the computer in the classroom.

Once the children started the activities, the teacher encouraged them to count the number of different items in the pictures as they used the stamps. Then she encouraged them to count again once the picture was completed through reviewing what they had done; sometimes this was undertaken as a class activity using printed versions of the pictures. In addition, using the numeral stamps enabled the children to hear the number names and associate the correct symbol with their collection of objects.

Table 13.1 Targeting specific counting skills

Skill	Activities	Focus
Reciting number names up to 10	Counting, stamping and repeating numbers Clicking along the numeral stamps and saying the numbers with the computer Counting with other children's pictures	Number name sequence: • Correct portion • Stable/incorrect portion • Unstable portion
Touch and count practice to 10	Counting co-ordinated with stamping (clicking), recounting by touch or point on screen, counting by touch or point on print-out	Enumeration Check for 'skim' (too few counting words) and 'flurry' (too many counting words) errors
Number words to 20	'More than 10' pictures Making animal/field pictures 'Counting house' pictures	Number name sequence: • Correct portion • Stable/incorrect portion • Unstable portion • Extend current limit
Touch and count practice to 20	Counting co-ordinated with stamping (clicking), recounting by touch or point on screen, counting by touch or point on print-out or with a peer	Check for 'skim' and 'flurry' errors

These activities were chosen to complement other class and group counting activities which the teacher had also planned. She was able to integrate the creative and exploratory activity that the children did in the computer room with counting and number activities in the classroom. She felt that in the past she had focused on activities for sorting, comparing and matching, and had not developed the children's use of language in number and counting sufficiently. The teacher reflected on what she saw as the value of the approach: 'We didn't have much in the way of numeracy materials, whereas using the painting program has really helped, and the children have used a lot more mathematical language.'

The teacher valued the opportunity to use key mathematical vocabulary as she worked with children. She also felt it was important to review the finished pictures with them so that their work had a purpose and so that she could assess their counting skills. This could be done with an individual, a small group or with individuals in whole class review time.

The pictures were also saved and incorporated into a further resource for the classroom. They were printed out and laminated for the children to complete number tasks with dry-wipe pens (see Figure 13.2).

One further benefit from this approach was that the children could create counting pictures to use away from the computer, or to take home to share with parents. This aspect was valued by the children and encouraged them to create a range of pictures. Part of the development of the pupils' skills may therefore have come from this home–school contact as well as the practice and sense of achievement that resulted from this.

This is an example of the kind of technology-supported learning which is consistent with developmentally appropriate practice and research on children's mathematical development. The children's level of understanding and skills were sensitively observed and extended by the teacher through the range of activities offered by the technology. The children had ownership and agency in the management of the activity and in their learning, as well as enjoying the experience and talking about it spontaneously with their peers. The results from standardized test data suggest that the teacher was able to use the computer-based activities effectively as part of her teaching to support the development of her pupils' counting skills, as the mean standardized score of the class increased from 82.6 to 97.3 in three months.

Look at Rachel's picture. Count how many.

clouds

ducks

cows

hens

bugs

flowers

Figure 13.2 A teaching resource created from a child's counting picture.

Implications for teaching and learning

- Technology itself will not benefit children's mathematical learning on its own, but it can play a part in supporting and extending their learning experiences and the mathematical meaning that they derive from this.
- Technology supported activities in mathematics should be based on research about how children learn mathematics in order to support, stimulate and challenge their thinking, and develop specific mathematical skills and understanding.
- Such activities should engage children's interest in pursuing the mathematical ideas involved and should involve adults in regulating their interaction with technology, encouraging their interest and expanding on what they can do and understand.
- Both structured and more open-ended activities can support learning; however, children are unlikely to make connections with other mathematical experiences without further support and interaction.
- The activities should promote mathematical talk and discussion, and the role of adults or more experienced children is likely to be crucial in developing this.

References

BECTA (British Educational Communications and Technology Agency) (2001) Calculator activities for primary schools, *Micromath*, 17(3): 20–34.

Clements, D.H. (2002) Computers in early childhood mathematics, *Contemporary Issues in Early Childhood*, 3(2): 160–81.

DCSF (Department for Children, Schools and Families) (2007) *Guidance Paper – The Use of Calculators in the Teaching and Learning of Mathematics* www.standards.dcsf.gov.uk/primaryframework/mathematics/Papers/ Calculators (accessed 31 March 2008).

DfEE (Department for Education and Employment (1999) *Framework for Teaching Mathematics from Reception to Year 6*. London: DfEE.

DfES (Department for Education and Skills) (2007) *Practice Guidance for the Early Years Foundation Stage*. Nottingham: DfES.

Fletcher-Flinn, C.M. and Gravatt, B. (1995) The efficacy of computer assisted instruction (CAI): a meta-analysis, *Journal of Educational Computing Research*, 12: 219–42.

Fuchs, L.S., Fuchs, D., Hamlet, C.L., Powell, S.R., Capizzi, A.M. and Seethaler, P.M. (2006) The effects of computer-assisted instruction on number combination skill in at-risk first graders, *Journal of Learning Disabilities*, 39(5): 467–75.

Hall, E. and Higgins, S. (2002) Embedding computer technology in developmentally appropriate practice: engaging with early years professionals' beliefs and values, *Information Technology in Childhood Education Annual 2002*, 301–20, ISSN 1522–8185 (Annual).

Higgins, S. (2003) *Does ICT Improve Learning and Teaching in Schools?* Nottingham: British Educational Research Association.

Higgins, S., Beauchamp, G. and Miller, D. (2007) Reviewing the literature on interactive whiteboards, *Learning, Media and Technology*, 32(3): 213–25.

Higgins, S. and Moseley, D. (2001) Teachers' thinking about ICT and learning: beliefs and outcomes, *Teacher Development*, 5(2): 191–210.

Klein, P.S., Nir-Gal, O. and Darom, E. (2000) The use of computers in kindergarten, with or without adult mediation: effects on children's cognitive performance and behaviour, *Computers in Human Behavior*, 16: 591–608.

Ruthven, K., Rousham, L. and Chaplin, D. (1997) The long-term influence of a 'calculator-aware' number curriculum on pupils' mathematical attainments and attitudes in the primary phase, *Research Papers in Education*, 12(3): 249–82.

Sarama, J. and Clements, D.H. (2004) Building blocks for early childhood mathematics, *Early Childhood Research Quarterly*, 19: 181–9.

Somekh, B., Underwood, J., Convery, A., Dillon, G., Jarvis, J., Lewin, C., Mavers, D., Saxon, D., Sing, S., Steadman, S., Twining, P. and Woodrow, D. (2007) *Evaluation of the ICT Test Bed Project Final Report June 2007*. Coventry: British Educational Communications and Technology Agency (BECTA).

Williams, H. J. and Thompson, I. (2003) Calculators for all?, in I. Thompson (ed.) *Enhancing Primary Mathematics Teaching*. Milton Keynes: Open University Press.

SECTION 6
Assessing young children's progress in number

This section, which comprises just two chapters – one by Bob Wright and one by Ian Thompson – is concerned with assessment. Until the mid-1990s assessment was either 'summative' or 'formative'. Summative assessment is carried out periodically, at the end of a unit of work, a term, a year or – particularly with reference to the English education system – at the end of a key stage. Results of this type of assessment are reported in terms of marks, grades or levels to a range of different audiences. Formative assessment, on the other hand, takes place in the classroom at all times, and is concerned with the generation of information that can be used as feedback to influence the nature of the teaching and learning activities taking place. The key message is that formative assessment is about using the information gathered to improve learning in the classroom. More recent terminology for these two aspects of assessment is 'assessment *of* learning' (summative) and 'assessment *for* learning' (formative).

The percentage of children in England leaving primary school at Key Stage 2 with Level 4 and above rose from 59 per cent in 1998 to 77 per cent in 2007. Despite this, the percentage of pupils who attained no higher than Level 2 was stable at around 6 per cent during that period. This statistic led to a renewed interest in the concept of 'intervention'. The approach of the Primary National Strategy (PNS) to children who experienced difficulties in mathematics took the form of 'waves' of intervention: wave 1 involved the effective inclusion of all children in high-quality learning and teaching in the daily mathematics lesson; wave 2 dealt with short-term provision in the form of small-group intervention; and wave 3 was concerned with individualized intervention involving teaching activities focused on fundamental errors and misconceptions.

In 2007 the government, working in partnership with a new charity, *Every Child a Chance*, announced a new initiative, *Every Child Counts*. The aims of this new initiative were to provide wave 3 intensive intervention for around 5 per cent of children and less intensive intervention for the next 5 to 10 per cent of lower-attaining learners, with the intensive intervention being delivered by a numeracy intensive support teacher. The programme included a development phase from 2008 to 2010, leading to the implementation of a national programme from 2010 onwards.

One of two major intervention programmes singled out for special consideration in the final report of the Williams review panel in the context of the *Every Child Counts* initiative was the Mathematics Recovery (MR) Programme. MR had its origins in a research and development programme in Southern Cross University in New South Wales, Australia, between 1992 and 1995, and Bob Wright, the author of Chapter 14, was heavily involved in the development of this programme. A key feature of the programme is the intensive, individualized teaching of low-attaining young children for a cycle of 10–15 weeks. Children are presented with numerical tasks in an interview situation with the aim of determining the extent of their knowledge and the level of sophistication of the strategies they are using. Assessment and teaching are fully integrated, in that the one informs the other.

In his chapter, Bob provides detailed descriptions of assessment tasks that can be used to document children's early number knowledge via one-to-one interview-based assessments. Tasks are described for three important domains of learning: (a) facility with number words and numerals; (b) counting as a problem-based activity; and (c) spatial patterns and configurations and finger patterns. Also included are tasks that can be used to assess more advanced knowledge such as knowledge of formal arithmetic in the range 1 to 20, facility with tens and ones, and knowledge of two-digit addition and subtraction. Discussion of each of these areas includes an overview of its relevance and importance. The chapter has the purpose of providing a means by which teachers and schools can develop systematic programmes of instruction in early number, based on a detailed understanding of their students' current levels of number knowledge. This approach can result in number learning that is significantly more advanced for given ages and grade levels.

Bob Wright's chapter addresses the issue of intervention for children experiencing difficulties in mathematics. As mentioned above, the third wave of the PNS's approach to intervention is concerned with individualized work that focuses on fundamental errors and misconceptions. In Chapter 15, Ian Thompson looks at young children's errors and misconceptions from the perspective of 'assessment for learning'. He begins by considering some of the recommended approaches to dealing with children's mistakes, before finding them not particularly relevant for working with young children. He argues that it might make more sense to view the errors that children make in the early stages of the Foundation Stage and Key Stage 1 as being a function of their developing understanding of some of the difficult aspects of the structure of the number system. He then considers what some of these 'difficult aspects' might be, focusing in particular on a comparison of the English and the Asian number word systems and on one particular source of potential difficulty, namely, the numbers from ten to twenty: the 'awkward teens'. The chapter concludes with a consideration of one way of instigating discussion with children in the early stages of learning about number, with a view to generating information that can be used for formative assessment purposes.

14 Interview-based assessment of early number knowledge

Robert J. Wright

Introduction

For many years, basic arithmetic has been an important instructional goal for primary schools and today this is as important as ever. Accompanying this is the belief that early number knowledge provides an essential foundation for learning basic arithmetic. Thus number learning continues to hold a central and key position in the early years of school. In the 1960s and 1970s, curricula in early number were strongly influenced by educators' and psychologists' interpretations of Piagetian theory and its implications for education. From the late 1970s onwards, researchers began to look critically at the sense that had been made of these interpretations. Resulting from these research efforts was a better understanding of and a greater focus on the role of counting in children's early number learning (Carpenter and Moser 1982; Fuson 1988; Steffe and Cobb 1988). Around 1990, researchers also focused on documenting in detail, the number knowledge of school entrants (4- to 6-year-olds) and how number learning progressed in the early years (Young-Loveridge 1991; Aubrey 1993; Wright 1994).

Collectively, these research efforts provide strong theoretical bases for current early number curricula and programmes. A consequence of this is that, compared with the teaching of early number 20 to 30 years ago, the teaching of this topic today can be more closely attuned to children's early number development; can be much more sensitive to differences among children in their number knowledge; and can result in number learning that is significantly more advanced for given ages and grade levels. Nevertheless, achieving these features does not occur automatically. A critical ingredient for the development of strong instructional programmes in early number is a strong programme of assessment to inform teaching. This is because teaching of early number is most likely to be successful when it is closely attuned to children's current levels of knowledge and is strongly informed by a very clear understanding of where children's learning will next progress to.

In the case of early number learning, in the last 10 to 15 years, there has been an increasingly strong recognition on the part of school systems and educational leaders of the importance of assessment and its key role in informing teaching. This recognition has occurred simultaneously with, or has closely followed recognition of, the critical role of assessment in early literacy. In several countries and jurisdictions, this has resulted in major systemic initiatives focused on new approaches to assessing early number knowledge. A feature of many of these initiatives is the use of one-on-one, interview-based assessments. Often, these have the dual purposes of enabling teachers to document and profile children's knowledge via a learning framework (Wright et al. 2006a) and providing a basis for teachers' professional learning that is collegial and school-based (Bobis and Gould 1998). The next section provides a detailed overview of some of the key elements of these approaches to assessing early number that have become increasingly widely used in recent years.

Domains of early number learning

Children's early number knowledge is complex and multifaceted. At the same time, this knowledge is characterized by significant interrelatedness of its many facets. Further, there are several ways early number knowledge might be analysed or organized into interrelated topics. The approach taken here involves describing three important domains: (a) facility with number words and numerals; (b) counting as a problem-based activity; and (c) spatial patterns and configurations and finger patterns. Also included is a section on assessing more advanced knowledge. Detailed descriptions of relevant assessment tasks are provided. This has the purpose of enabling teachers to come to know an approach to assessing that results in a rich picture of children's early number knowledge and can strongly inform instruction.

Facility with number words and numerals

One of the most important domains of early number learning concerns number words, that is the names of numbers; sequences of number words; and numerals, that is the written symbols for numbers (6, 14, 37, etc.). This domain is described first here because, as well as being important, it includes significant very early learning. Thus, some of the important learning of this domain typically begins in a significant way from age 2 or 3.

Number word sequences

Assessing facility with forward number word sequences (FNWSs) concerns three main factors. First is the fluency with which a child can say a forward sequence. Is the sequence said smoothly with little effort and with neither hesitancy nor errors? Second is the range of numbers in which the child has fluency. Can the child say the words to 10, to 30 or to beyond 100? Third is the extent to which the child can name the next number in a sequence. Can this be done for all words in the range one to ten? If so, how far does this range extend? In a similar vein, assessing facility with backward number word sequences (BNWSs) concerns fluency, range and saying the number word before a given number. Children's facility with number word sequences is critically important as a basis for counting as a problem-based activity (see below).

Numerals

Children of ages 4 and younger, as well as encountering individual number words and number word sequences, will encounter numerals, and often these will co-occur with spoken number words. They will begin to make tentative associations between these. This has similarities with, and differences from, how they begin to associate the spoken and written forms of letters and words. Numerals (e.g. '4') stand for whole words (four) whereas letters (e.g. 'f') typically do not stand for whole words. The extent to which a young child has learned to name numerals is important as a basis of early number learning. This importance extends well beyond naming numerals in the range 1 to 10. Learning to name multi-digit numerals earlier rather than later is very important and is quite separate from notions of place value.

Assessment tasks

FNWSs

Assessment tasks used to assess facility with FNWSs involve (a) counting forwards from a given number: 'start counting from one', 'start counting from 47 and I will tell you when to stop', and so on; and (b) within a range of numbers, such as 1 to 10, 11 to 30; 30 to 100, stating the number after a given number (numbers are not presented in numerical order): 'I am going to tell you a number and I want you to tell me the next number after the one I say – fourteen! eleven! eighteen! sixteen!', and so on.

BNWSs

Tasks to assess BNWSs involve (a) counting backwards from a given number: 'count from ten down to one'; 'start from 23 (42, 94) and count backwards and I'll tell you when to stop' and (b) again within a range of numbers (1 to 10; 11 to 30; 30 to 100) stating the number before a given number: 'I am going to say a number and I want you to tell me the number that comes before the one I say – seven! four! nine! six!', and so on.

Numerals

Assessing facility with numerals can involve several different tasks (Wright et al. 2006b). Tasks based on naming a displayed numeral are easily adminis- tered and seem to be a good indicator of children's facility with numerals. These tasks are also referred to as reading or identifying numerals, and involve presenting singly, some or all, the numerals in a given range (1 to 10, 11 to 20, 20 to 100, etc.) and asking, 'What number is this?'. The numerals are not presented in numerical order. An alternative task is to put the numerals from a selected range (1 to 10, 46 to 55) in a random arrangement on the desk (the numerals should be upright) and to ask the child to put them in order starting from the smallest. Another task, again with the numerals in random arrange- ment, involves asking the child to select a named numeral: 'Which is the number eight?'.

Counting as a problem-based activity

The previous section outlined approaches to assessing children's facility with number word sequences (and numerals). The term 'counting' was not used in that section because, as used in this chapter, counting refers to situations where the child uses a FNWS or a BNWS to solve a problem – typically a problem about quantities or items of some description. From here on the term 'counting' will be used in this sense. The psychological model of children's development of counting from research by Steffe and Cobb (1988) underlies the approach to assessment that is outlined here. Steffe and Cobb observed qualitative differences in children's use of counting (see also Wright et al. 2006a). Drawing on this model, three major milestones in children's devel- opment of counting are: (a) perceptual counting; (b) counting on and count- ing back; and (c) facile. A critical goal of assessment is to establish where the child is along this progression. In doing so, it is important to keep in mind that a child who is at a level significantly more advanced than perceptual counting, for example, might nevertheless use a perceptual counting strategy out of con- venience. Thus, an important facet of assessment is to determine the child's upper limit on this progression. A consequence of this is that, at some point in the assessment interview, the child will be presented with tasks that, for them, are very challenging. This is the key to determining the upper limits of the child's early number knowledge, that is, the cutting edge of knowledge and learning. When this is determined, it can be a specific focus of instruction.

Assessment tasks

Three main types of assessment tasks are used to assess children's counting: (a) tasks based on a single, visible collection of counters; (b) additive and sub- tractive tasks involving screened collections; and (c) bare number tasks. For a relatively young child or a child with only the beginnings of early number knowledge, tasks of type (a) will be most significant. For an older child or a child with significant early number knowledge, tasks of type (c) will be most significant. Thus, from (a) to (c), there is a progression in the arithmetical sophistication of the tasks. At the same time, for the vast majority of young children, it is useful to use assessment tasks of a reasonable range in sophistication, in order to gain a strong sense of the relative ease for the child of a range of tasks.

Tasks based on a single, visible collection

This type of task is widely used in early number assessment, and has the purpose of establishing if the child has reached the first milestone – perceptual counting. The child who succeeds well at these tasks is at least at the level of perceptual counting. There are two main forms of this type of task and the two forms are in a sense complementary to each other. One form involves placing out a collection of counters (10, 15, 18 counters) and asking the child how many counters in all. Using counters all of one colour is advocated. For one thing, this will avoid possible distractions such as comparing the numbers of the various colours. The other form of task involves presenting a collection of say 40 blue counters, and asking the child to get, say, 16 counters from the collection. The child who does not succeed on these tasks is labelled an emergent counter (Wright et al. 2006a). The emergent counters either do not know the required number word sequence or cannot properly co-ordinate the words with the items (counters). They might say two number words for one item or move (or point at) two items for one number word (see Thompson, Chapter 15).

Additive and subtractive tasks involving screened collections

This type of task is presented to a child who is at least a perceptual counter, and has the purpose of establishing the extent to which the child can use counting-on and counting-back. This type of task includes an additive task and at least three forms of subtractive tasks – missing addend, removed items and missing subtrahend. According to the choice of numbers involved, these tasks can be construed so that, if the child does count on or count back, the number of counts will be in the range two to five. This is because, be it assessment or teaching, it is not considered productive to engage children in long counts by one, to solve additive or subtractive tasks (Wright et al. 2006b). The four forms of task just mentioned can be illustrated in the following way. From a pedagogical perspective, the teacher's goal is to present a task (problem) based on the following sum, $9 + 4 = 13$, using screened collections. Each of these four forms (a, b, c and d) is now described.

(a) Additive tasks. The teacher proceeds as follows. She briefly displays and then screens a collection of nine red counters. Then she briefly displays and

then screens a collection of four blue counters, telling the child in turn, the number in each collection. She then asks the child how many there are in all. There are five main levels of children's response to this task: emergent, perceptual, figurative, count-on and facile. The perceptual child has no means of proceeding. Observing this, the teacher removes the screens (or perhaps the second screen only), and at this point the child counts the red counters and then the blue counters and says, 'Thirteen!'.

The emergent child proceeds similarly but (as described above) does not count the counters correctly. When the signal behaviour of the emergent or perceptual counter is clearly established, there is little point in presenting more of these tasks (additive or subtractive). The figurative counter's solution is labelled as 'counting-from-one' – they count from 1 to 9, and then from 10 to 13. According to Steffe's model, for the figurative counter, counting-from-one is necessary to give meaning to 9. To find 9 + 4, the count-on child says, 'Nine . . . ten, eleven, twelve, thirteen!'. Steffe and Cobb (1988) call this the 'counting-up-from strategy', whereas in the UK, it is called 'counting-on'. The facile child has a solution that does not involve counting by ones; for example, an add-through-ten strategy: 9 + 1 + 3 (see Thompson, Chapter 8).

(b) Missing addend task.   The teacher briefly displays and then screens a collection of nine red counters, 'I have nine counters under here'. Then she moves four green counters to beneath the same screen but neither announces the number nor displays the counters. 'I had nine red counters under here, then I put some more counters under here and now there are 13 in all. How many more counters did I put under the screen?'. This task and the two tasks below are probably too difficult for the figurative counter. The count-on child uses a strategy called 'counting-up-to': 'Nine –, ten, eleven, twelve, thirteen – four!'. As before the facile child might use an add-through-ten strategy.

(c) Removed items task.   The teacher briefly displays and then screens a collection of 13 red counters, 'I have 13 counters under here'. She then removes four counters, briefly displays and then screens them saying, 'I had 13 counters and I took away four. How many are left?'. The count-on child typically will also be able to count back to solve these tasks: 'Thirteen . . . twelve, eleven, ten, nine!'. This is called 'counting-down-from'. The child has counted down four from 13, to get the answer nine. As before the facile child typically will not count by ones.

(d) Missing subtrahend task.   The teacher briefly displays and then screens a collection of 13 red counters, 'I have 13 counters under here'. She then removes and screens four counters but neither announces the number nor displays the counters. 'I had 13 counters, I took some away, and now I have nine (briefly displaying the nine counters). How many did I take away?'. The

count-on child says: 'Thirteen . . . twelve, eleven, ten, nine – four!'. This is called 'counting-down-to'. The child has counted down to nine, and kept track of her counts. She stops because she has reached nine. Again, the facile child will not count by ones.

Advanced counting-by-ones strategies
The four strategies of counting-up-from, counting-up-to, counting-down-from and counting-down-to are collectively labelled advanced counting-by-ones strategies (Wright et al. 2006b). According to Steffe's model, counting-down-to is conceptually more sophisticated than the other three strategies, and for that reason, in some cases, the child will be observed to use those strategies but not use counting-down-to.

Settings, contexts and bare numbers
The preceding sections involve the use of collections of counters, and this is an example of the general approach of using what are referred to as 'settings' (materials, etc.) or contexts (materials and/or scenarios) when posing arithmetical tasks. In this approach, instruction progresses from the setting or context to formal mathematics. Thus, formal mathematics, characterized by little or no use of settings or contexts, is regarded as an ultimate goal of instruction, that is, the child's knowledge of the topic in question now extends to abstract mathematics. In the case of the arithmetical topic at hand, that is, children's counting, assessment tasks can also be presented at the level of formal mathematics, and this is particularly relevant for older children (e.g. 1st or 2nd grade (Year 2 and Year 3)) and children more advanced in their development of early number knowledge. A typical example is to present addition or subtraction tasks in horizontal format ($9 + 4$, $9 + \Delta = 13$, $13 - 4$, $13 - \Delta = 9$). Assessment tasks in these forms also have a role in the assessment of counting.

Spatial patterns and configurations, and finger patterns

Spatial patterns
The term 'subitizing' was first used by psychologists in the 1940s to describe the phenomenon of the immediate correct assignation of number words to small collections of perceptual items (see von Glasersfeld 1982; Aubrey, Chapter 1). The term as used in early number instruction today has taken on a broader meaning than originally intended, to the extent that any setting involving a spatial pattern or configuration is labelled as involving and being mainly about subitizing, and therefore intrinsically useful for learning. The approach taken here is that subitizing is somewhat tangential to the significant topic of the role of spatial patterns and configurations in early number learning. Certainly, the young child typically learns to ascribe number names to standard spatial configurations for numbers in the range one to six that

appear on dice, playing cards, dominos, and so on. Thus a 4-year-old can learn to name the standard dot pattern for five as 'five' but doing so, at least initially, does not necessarily involve much in the way of concepts of quantity. Nevertheless, learning names for spatial patterns in that way is a critical first step.

The assumption here is that spatial configurations have a key role to play in early number learning (Bobis 1996) (see also Harries et al., Chapter 12). Further, important instructional settings include: (a) initially dice, domino patterns, etc., and (b) subsequently, ten frames (5 × 2 grids with dots), and arithmetic racks or double ten frames. Initially, the standard patterns, particularly for numbers up to six, can provide a basis for young children's numerical reasoning involving combining and partitioning small numbers without counting; for example, five is made up of three and two, four and two make six. Subsequently, ten frames provide a basis for reasoning numerically in the range one to ten using doubles and five as a base. Finally, with the use of settings such as arithmetic racks and double ten frames, this reasoning can extend to the range one to twenty. This domain of learning provides a basis for learning to add and subtract without counting by ones, that is, developing facile number knowledge (see above).

Finger patterns

For almost all young children, finger patterns are significant in their early number learning. Typically, children use finger patterns in conjunction with arithmetical strategies involving counting. In particular, the advanced counting-by-ones strategies (see earlier) frequently involve the use of finger patterns to keep track of counting. For numbers in the range one to ten, there is also a homomorphism (correspondence in form) between finger patterns and standard configurations on a ten frame. Just as six can be displayed as three fingers on each hand or five on one hand and one on the other, so can six be displayed as three dots on each row of a ten frame or five on one row and one on the other. For this reason, many of the assessment tasks described for spatial patterns have corresponding forms involving finger patterns.

Arithmetic rack or double ten frame

In a similar vein to the way a ten frame is used to develop number knowledge in the range one to ten, an arithmetic rack (or double ten frame) can be used to develop number knowledge in the range one to twenty. The arithmetic rack has five beads of one colour and five beads of another colour on each of two rows. Prominent on the rack are the five-, ten- and pair-wise structures of numbers up to twenty.

Assessment tasks

Dice patterns
Knowledge of standard patterns for numbers in the range one to six can be assessed by flashing the pattern and asking the child how many dots they see.

Five-wise patterns on a ten frame
These are patterns made by successively filling first along one row, and then the other. Thus, four consists of four dots on one row; similarly, seven is five dots and two dots, and so on. As for dice patterns, children's knowledge of these structures can be assessed by a flashing activity. Of interest is whether the child answers immediately, that is, whether the structures constitute automatized number knowledge. Alternatively, the child might apparently visualize the flashed pattern and count, for example, for eight counting from one or counting on from five, that is, the child visualizes the pattern for eight on a ten frame, and then counts the eight dots from one, or alternatively says 'five' for the first row, and then continues to count the three dots on the second row: 'six, seven, eight'.

Pairs on a ten frame
In a similar vein, the child's knowledge of the standard patterns for the even numbers from two to ten can be assessed by a flashing activity.

Adding two numbers on a ten frame
As above, this can be assessed by flashing. Each row on the frame shows a number in the range one to five. There are 25 such sums ($1 + 1, 2 + 1 \ldots 5 + 1, 1 + 2, 2 + 2 \ldots 5 + 5$).

Finger patterns
These include making patterns on one hand for numbers in the range one to five; using five fingers on one hand and fingers on the other hand to make patterns for numbers in the range six to ten; and using two hands to show the doubles from one plus one to five plus five. When a child builds finger patterns, issues of interest are: (a) Does the child need to look at their fingers? (b) Can the child raise fingers simultaneously (e.g. for seven, simultaneously raising five fingers on one hand and two on the other)? There are differences among children in the extent to which they use finger patterns when adding and subtracting. Nevertheless, comprehensively documenting the child's facility in making finger patterns is an important part of assessing early number knowledge.

Arithmetic rack or double ten frame
These tasks are obvious extensions of the tasks above that involve combining and partitioning numbers in the range one to ten using a single ten frame.

Structures for numbers can be displayed and the child's task is to state the number of beads. This could include ten-wise structures for the teen numbers and pair-wise structures for the even numbers from 12 to 20. More difficult tasks can be presented by flashing rather than displaying the structure. Addition tasks involving two numbers in the range one to ten (one on each row) can also be used.

Assessing more advanced knowledge

Described below are three areas of assessment tasks that are particularly suited to children who are successful on all or most of the above tasks.

Formal arithmetic in the range 1 to 20

These tasks are referred to as bare number tasks (see above) and are presented as written expressions in horizontal format (9 + 6) or equations with an unknown ($9 + \Delta = 15$). A range of tasks involving addition and subtraction can be presented. It is assumed that the children to whom these tasks are being administered routinely use non-counting strategies to add and subtract in the range 1 to 20. Of particular interest is the range of strategies the child uses and the child's facility with different strategies.

Doubles and ten-plus
This includes the following facts: 6 + 6, 7 + 7 . . . 10 + 10 and 10 + 1, 10 + 2 . . . 10 + 9. Children with facile strategies are likely to use doubles and ten-plus facts to work out other combinations. Thus, it is useful to establish to what extent the child has automatized knowledge of these facts.

Using doubles, five and tens
The purpose of these tasks is to establish to what extent the child uses doubles and the five and ten structure of numbers to work out other facts. On one hand, it is appropriate to present facts with particular strategies in mind. Thus the task 6 + 7 is presented with a view to eliciting the strategy of doubles-plus-one (or doubles-minus-one): 6 + 6 + 1, 7 + 7 − 1. On the other hand, one needs to be very open to strategies different from what might seem to be the obvious strategy. Alternatives include: (a) adding through 10: 6 + 4 + 3; and (b) using fives: 5 + 5 + 1 + 2. Tasks such as 9 + 6 and 6 + 9 can have the purpose of eliciting add through ten: 9 + 1 + 5, and compensation: 6 + 10 − 1, respectively. The range of tasks can be extended to include: (a) subtraction and (b) addition and subtraction where two of the three numbers (addends and sum, etc.) are greater than ten; for example, 12 + 5, 4 + 14, 19 − 3, 17 − 15.

Facility with tens and ones using a setting

The initial assessment tasks involve the use of a setting involving tens and ones; for example, base-ten blocks, bundling sticks or ten strips (strips of ten dots and strips of dots for numbers less than ten). Of interest is the child's facility to increment and decrement flexibly by tens and ones in the range one to one hundred. As with the tasks to assess the relative sophistication of the child's counting strategies (see above), the technique of screening is again used. Typically, this approach involves the following: (a) an initial task of incrementing a number in the range one to ten, by single tens (6, 16, 26, 36). The child's task is to state the number of dots in all after each increment; and (b) tasks with a progression of increments of increasing complexity; for example, ten and six more, two more tens, one ten and three ones, and so on (Cobb and Wheatley 1988). This can be extended to include increments in conjunction with decrements.

Bare number tasks involving two-digit addition and subtraction

The following are examples of bare number tasks to investigate whether the child has already developed facile mental strategies for two-digit addition and subtraction and the nature and extent of such strategies. (a) 42 + 24. Does the child use a split (40 + 20 = 60, 2 + 4 = 6) or a jump (42 + 20 = 62, 62 + 4 = 66) strategy or some other strategy? (b) 57 + 19. Does the child use compensation (57 + 20 = 77, 77 − 1 = 76)? (c) 52 − 25. Does the child use double 25 (25 + 25 + 2, so it's just 25 + 2)? (d) 64 − 57. Does the child use adding up (i.e. complementary addition) to subtract (57 + 3 = 60, 60 + 4 = 64, so it's 7)?

Implications for teaching and learning

In the case of early number learning, detailed assessment of children's current knowledge and strategies is an essential first step in the development of successful instructional programmes. The assessment tasks set out in this chapter can provide a basis for approaches to assessment that determine children's current levels of knowledge and provide clear indications of the appropriate progressions in their number learning. A way forward for teachers and schools is to take a collegial approach to developing and learning to use these assessment tasks in one-to-one interviews with their students. Developing expertise in this approach to assessment of early number learning is strongly advocated and in this endeavour, video-taping and reviewing assessment interviews can be a very useful learning tool for teachers (Wright et al. 2006a). In this way, schools where this approach has not been used can work towards the goals of being sensitive to differences among children in their early number knowledge and closely attuning early number instruction to children's early number development.

References

Aubrey, C. (1993) An investigation of the mathematical knowledge and competencies which young children bring into school, *British Educational Research Journal*, 19(1): 27–41.

Bobis, J. (1996) Visualisation and the development of number sense with kindergarten children, in J. Mulligan and M. Mitchelmore (eds) *Children's Number Learning: A Research Monograph of MERGA/AAMT*, pp. 17–33. Adelaide: Australian Association of Mathematics Teachers.

Bobis, J. and Gould, P. (1998) The impact of an early number project on the professional development of teachers, in C. Kanes, M. Goos and E. Warren (eds) *Proceedings of the 21st Annual Conference of the Mathematics Education Research Group of Australasia*, Vol. 2, pp. 106–13. Brisbane: Griffith University.

Carpenter, T.P. and Moser, J.M. (1982) The development of addition and subtraction problem solving skills, in T.P. Carpenter, J.M. Moser and T.A. Romberg (eds) *Addition and Subtraction: A Cognitive Perspective*. Hillsdale, NJ: Lawrence Erlbaum Associates.

Cobb, P. and Wheatley, G. (1988) Children's initial understandings of ten, *Focus on Learning Problems in Mathematics*, 10(3): 1–24.

Fuson, K.C. (1988) *Children's Counting and Concepts of Number*. New York: Springer-Verlag.

Steffe, L.P. and Cobb, P. (1988) *Construction of Arithmetic Meanings and Strategies*. New York: Springer-Verlag.

von Glasersfeld, E. (1982) Subitizing: the role of figural patterns in the development of numerical concepts, *Archives de Psychologie*, 50: 191–218.

Wright, R.J. (1994) A study of the numerical development of 5-year-olds and 6-year-olds, *Educational Studies in Mathematics*, 26: 25–44.

Wright, R.J., Martland, J. and Stafford, A. (2006a) *Early Numeracy: Assessment for Teaching and Intervention*, 2nd edn. London: Sage Publications.

Wright, R.J., Stanger, G., Stafford, A. and Martland, J. (2006b) *Teaching Number in the Classroom with 4- to 8-year-olds*. London: Sage Publications.

Young-Loveridge, J.M. (1991) *The Development of Children's Number Concepts from Ages Five to Nine, Vols 1 and 2*. Hamilton, NZ: University of Waikato.

15 Addressing errors and misconceptions with young children

Ian Thompson

Introduction

It is now over 30 years since Brown and Burton (1978) produced their seminal paper on 'bugs' in American secondary school children's basic mathematical calculation procedures, and even longer since Ashlock converted his long-standing research into the fascinating book *Error Patterns in Computation* (1976). Substantial British contributions to the knowledge base in this area in the 1980s came from the Assessment of Performance Unit (APU); the Concepts in Secondary Mathematics and Science (CSMS) research project; and the Shell Centre for Mathematical Education. This work was focused mainly on children in Key Stages 3 and 4, but after a gap of several decades, a renewed interest developed in the mathematical mistakes made by younger children. This interest extended to trying to ascertain the reasons why children might make these mistakes and to a search for ways of dealing with them.

To this end, the Primary National Strategy (PNS) produced a very comprehensive in-service pack as part of its Wave 3 intervention materials (DfES 2005) with the aim of supporting children who were underachieving in mathematics. The materials focused on the most commonly occurring mathematical difficulties, and one of the stated aims of this detailed material was 'to increase children's rates of progress by using targeted approaches to tackle fundamental errors and misconceptions' (DfES 2005: 5). Each of the 45 booklets, which vary in size from 8 to 16 pages, identifies a potential area of difficulty, such as 'Misunderstands the meaning of "one more" and "one less" '. It then lists resources, key vocabulary and a range of detailed teaching activities that will 'correct' the identified misunderstanding. This chapter considers errors and misconceptions from a different perspective.

Approaches to focusing on children's errors

Children can make mathematical errors for a wide variety of reasons. The following are just some of them:

- a loss of concentration;
- misremembering number facts;
- memory overload;
- a lack of knowledge of the necessary mathematics;
- an 'incorrect' interpretation of the problem to be solved;
- changing the order of the steps in a calculation procedure;
- a misconception – an alternative or immature interpretation of a mathematical idea developed as a result of over-generalization from previous experiences.

There appear to be several different schools of thought on how to deal with such errors. According to the 1998 DfEE requirements for courses of initial teacher education, this role is straightforward. Trainees must be taught 'to recognize common pupil errors and misconceptions in mathematics, and understand how these arise, how they can be prevented, and how to remedy them' (DfEE 1998: 57). However, later advice for teacher trainers is less prescriptive, with only the occasional reference to this topic. For example, a section of the document discussing what assessors may wish to consider when judging trainees' teaching includes the question: 'Can the trainee identify common misconceptions and intervene to address pupils' errors?' (TTA 2003: 33).

One approach to addressing errors and misconceptions, which has an underlying philosophy very different from that of the TTA (later to become the TDA: The Teacher Development Agency), is that taken by mathematics educators at Nottingham University's Shell Centre for Mathematics Education who advocate a teaching approach they call 'diagnostic teaching'. In this approach, misconceptions are considered to be 'alternative frameworks'. As Swan (2003: 113) says: 'These (errors) are often called *misconceptions*, but more accurately they should be referred to as *alternative* conceptions as they are rarely "completely wrong", more often they are valid generalizations that are true in more limited circumstances'. This approach involves getting children to work individually on tasks designed specifically to focus on some well-known conceptual obstacle, and then having them share their methods and compare their findings. The materials are designed to create 'cognitive conflict', causing the children to become aware of, and confront, the inconsistencies in their own and others' methods and interpretations. Classroom studies that compared 'diagnostic teaching' with more traditional teaching methods showed that, although both methods achieved short-term gains, only the diagnostic approach, with its emphasis on discussion methods, achieved significant longer-term learning (Bell 1994). However, the mathematical content of the Shell Centre work is aimed at secondary school students.

Spooner (2002) devised a different method for generating the discussion of 'alternative interpretations' with Key Stage 2 children. He developed the idea of giving children the completed work of an 'unknown child', and asking them to mark the work and establish which examples were incorrect; discuss why the 'unknown child' might have made the errors; and suggest ways in which they would help the child overcome the problems they had exhibited. The work of the 'unknown child' was created to demonstrate error patterns that could be linked to specific misconceptions and/or common errors. Because it was the work of someone they did not know, the children engaged with the material more than they probably would have done had it been that of a classmate.

Neither of these approaches to errors and misconceptions seems suitable for using with very young children. Consequently, the remainder of this chapter is based on the view that in the Foundation Stage and early Key Stage 1, it makes more sense to view the mistakes that children make as being a function of their developing understanding of some of the difficult aspects of the structure of the number system. Rather than call these mistakes 'misconceptions', or even Swan's 'alternative conceptions', it might be more appropriate to describe them as 'limited conceptions'. The chapter discusses some of the potential difficulties with the structure of the counting word system, focusing on a comparison between the English and the Asian systems and on one particular source of potential difficulty: the 'awkward' teens. The chapter concludes with an account of one particularly successful way of generating discussion with children in the early stages of learning about number.

The structure of the counting word system

The complexity of the counting process has been discussed in earlier chapters (see Threlfall, Chapter 5; Maclellan, Chapter 6) as has the sophisticated and complex manipulation of numbers revealed in children's idiosyncratic mental calculation strategies (see Thompson, Chapter 8). However, as children progress from working with single-digit to two-digit numbers there are other potential pitfalls awaiting them. The *Trends in International Mathematics and Science Study 2003 International Mathematics Report (TIMSS)* (Mullis et al. 2004) showed that the increase in the average score of English 10-year-olds since the last TIMSS in 1995 was the largest of any of the participating countries. However, the mathematical attainment of English primary school pupils was still worse than that of their fellow pupils in Singapore, Hong Kong or Japan.

Smaller-scale studies in the USA have also shown that even at the age of 6, the mathematical performance of American children is significantly lower than that of Japanese children, and that Chinese 4-year-olds are able to count to a much higher limit than their American peers. However, one seemingly trivial but, quite possibly, important contributing factor that appears to have been ignored in many of these discussions concerns the structure of the counting word system of Asian languages.

Oral counting in Japanese and Chinese begins as in English by proceeding from *one* to *ten*. However, this is then followed, not by *eleven*, but by the equivalent of *ten one, ten two, ten three . . . ten nine, two ten, two ten one, two ten two*, etc. After *two ten nine* comes *three ten*, and the decade numbers (30, 40, etc.) continue this pattern up to *nine ten*. Within this system, the number which is one less than a *hundred*, for example, is *nine ten nine*. The structure can therefore be seen to be highly regular, logical and systematic, and such consistency and regularity are likely to facilitate the appreciation and absorption of the recurring pattern that underlies this counting system. Chinese number words are brief, and, on average take about a quarter of a second to say; English words take about a third of a second. Also, the average Chinese speaker has a numerical memory span of nine digits compared with seven for English speakers.

Another issue is that the English counting word system contains several number words that conceal the basic *tens and ones* pattern of the system. For example, the teens contain words which reverse the underlying *tens and ones* pattern: we say *fourteen* and *sixteen*, but *twenty-four* and *thirty-six*. The problem is further exacerbated when we express numbers in symbolic form, because the spoken reversal of the teens is not extended to the written representations of these numbers. So, even though we say the 'four' before the 'ten' in *fourteen*, we then proceed to write the number as 14, with the 'teen' before the 'four'. Is it any wonder that many young children, when learning to write numbers, tend to reverse the digits in the teens, writing 41 for 14 or 61 for 16, or sometimes confuse 14 and 40? English also has the two idiosyncratic number words *eleven* and *twelve*, which give no indication whatsoever of the fact that they mean *ten and one* and *ten and two*, respectively. The problem is exacerbated by the fact that there are further irregularities: *thirteen* and *fifteen*, with their idiosyncratic pronunciation of *three* and *five*, do not even follow the straightforward 'digit-teen' pattern associated with the numbers from *sixteen* to *nineteen*.

A further important difference between Asian languages and English concerns the frequency of use of the word for 'ten'. In Japanese, the teens and the decade words all involve the conspicuous presence of the word *ju* (ten) to describe numbers such as *ten-two* (12), *three-ten* (30) or *nine-ten* (90), whereas English uses two differently spelled and differently pronounced variations of the basic word *ten*, namely *-teen* within the second decade and *-ty* in successive decades. Neither of these factors is likely to make it obvious to a young mind searching for a pattern that the concept of *ten* is involved. In fact, a close scrutiny of Asian languages shows that because of the completely logical structure of the number word system, the word *ju* is used in *ninety* of the numbers below one hundred (all except the first nine numbers), thereby helping to reinforce the basic underlying regularity of the number word system. In contrast, the English word *ten* appears only once in those same ninety-nine numbers.

A further potential source of error is the irregular pronunciation of the decade words *twenty, thirty* and *fifty*. Because they do not have the regular form *two-ty, three-ty* and *five-ty*, as do *sixty* and *seventy*, these particular number words do not make it easy for children to see the way in which the words *two, three*, and so on are reused in the naming of the decades. The words conceal the relationship between the decade names and the first nine counting numbers – a connection that is more clearly observed in larger numbers such as *sixty, seventy, eighty* and *ninety*. This relationship is greatly emphasized in the highly logical structure of the counting word sequence found in Asian languages.

It is also unfortunate that all these irregularities occur in the early teens and decade names – *twelve, fifteen, twenty, thirty* – the very numbers that young children are experiencing and coming to terms with in their early number work at home and at school. This also means that English-speaking children have to memorize a long sequence of seemingly unrelated number names before the patterns become visible. Indeed, research does exist to show that there is a long period of months, extending to years in some cases, during which young children continue to learn the teen and decade names. English-speaking children have also been found to make more errors in reciting the counting words than do their peers operating with the Chinese regularly named sequence.

Even if it were to be found that this linguistic difference did contribute towards the inferior performance of English-speaking children, it is highly unlikely that any changes would ever be made to the counting words that we use. However, it is important for teachers to be aware of the likely difficulties to be encountered by young children learning to count, and also to be in a position to offer them activities and support for their learning. The remainder of this chapter contains suggestions of some suitable activities for this purpose.

Generating discussion of errors with young children

The approaches to errors and misconceptions described above, that is, the suggestions of the PNS (DfES 2005), Swan (2003) and Spooner (2002), are not particularly suitable for young children. However, researchers have found that a useful way of generating a meaningful discussion between an adult and young children when interviewing them is to introduce a 'naughty teddy' or some such device. Children are more likely to argue with or correct the mistakes made by a puppet than they are to confront or question an adult authority figure. Using this research idea for teaching purposes can generate stimulating learning experiences, and can provide a suitable context for involving children in some interactive discussion. The *Independent Review of Mathematics Teaching in Early Years Settings and Primary Schools* (DCSF 2008: 67) argues that 'The critical importance of engaging children in discussing mathematics is widely recognised'.

Maclellan (Chapter 6) describes Gelman and Gallistel's model for the development of counting competence in young children. Schaeffer et al. (1974) offer a different analysis, and develop a four-stage theory which includes the concepts of recitation and enumeration (see Threlfall, Chapter 5). *Recitation* involves the ability to say the number words in the correct order on each occasion, whereas *enumeration* describes the use of this sequence to find the number of objects in a collection.

Recitation

When children first learn the counting word sequence, they often treat it as a continuous sound string (*wontoothreefore* . . .), and only later do they come to realize that the sequence actually comprises separate words. For children at this stage of their understanding, the sequence can only be recited by starting at the beginning: it cannot yet be broken into and generated from an arbitrary starting point. For these children, starting a count from 'four' is beyond their capability. With experience, they come to treat the counting word sequence as a breakable chain, and learn to continue reciting from a given point within it. This is a necessary skill for children to acquire before they can progress at a later stage to using the calculation strategy known as 'counting-on'.

Introducing Miss Count
Miss Count is a puppet whose favourite pastime is counting. Unfortunately, however, she is not particularly good at it, and the children are invited to help correct any mistakes that she might make. The following suggestions for possible errors to be made by Miss Count are based on those mistakes which young children have been found to make when learning to recite the counting numbers (although see Threlfall, Chapter 5):

- *one, two, four, five* . . . (word omitted);
- *one, two, three, five, four, six* . . . (words in the wrong order);
- *one, two, three, three, four* . . . (repeating a word);
- *three, four, five* . . . (not starting from the beginning);
- . . . *thirteen, fourteen, fiveteen* . . . (error by analogy);

- *. . . eighteen, nineteen, tenteen . . .* (error by analogy);
- *. . . twenty-nine, twenty-ten . . .* (error by analogy).

When children spot Miss Count's 'miscounts', they can explain to the rest of the class why the puppet is incorrect, and the ensuing discussion can provide useful feedback for the class teacher on individual children's level of understanding. The activity also helps to improve the recitation skills of those children who are having difficulty mastering the sequence.

To make sense of the system, children need to appreciate that words such as *x-ty-nine* signal a change in the structure of the sequence, and that the sequence as a whole is a repetitive system. Even when they have come to understand that *x-ty-eight, x-ty-nine* is followed by a different *x-ty, x-ty-one, x-ty-two . . .* children often do not know the order of the *x-ty* words. Some practice in reciting the multiples of ten is a useful way of developing this necessary knowledge. Miss Count can also be used to focus on these particular aspects of the counting process. For example, she might incorrectly count . . . *twenty-eight, twenty-nine, forty . . .*, offering the wrong multiple of ten, or she could count in tens reciting the decade numbers in the incorrect order. It is also important that teachers ensure that Miss Count occasionally gets things right!

Enumeration

Enumeration involves assigning the correctly ordered number words in one–one correspondence with the objects being counted. Miss Count can provoke discussion among the children concerning enumeration mistakes. Some of the errors that the puppet can make while enumerating a collection of objects include:

- pointing at one of the objects without saying a number word at the same time;
- co-ordinating the recitation with the pointing but missing out one of the objects;
- pointing correctly at each object, but saying an extra number word;
- saying a number word without pointing at a specific object and then continuing;
- co-ordinating the recitation with the pointing but counting one object twice;
- correctly enumerating five objects and then saying, 'There are six'.

Another error that children sometimes make involves the matching of the syllables in the counting number words to the objects rather than the actual words themselves. This can happen with *seven*, which is the first two-syllable word in the sequence, and which is consequently sometimes matched to two different objects. A child who counts one short each time whenever there are more than seven objects may well be making this error. Miss Count can be 'organized' to do the same.

Children also need practice at counting objects in different arrays: straight lines are obviously the easiest, while circles or random arrays are the most difficult. Counting out a certain number of objects from a larger collection is a demanding task, because the child must not only count accurately, but must also remember when to stop the enumeration. Some children have difficulty in keeping track of the objects they are counting; it helps if they move each counted object to a new pile. For fixed objects, they need to start in one specific place and enumerate in a particular direction. Miss Count can be used to simulate these difficulties and to provoke discussion about specific keeping-track strategies. However, the teacher needs to practise making each of the errors, as it is quite difficult to counteract all those years spent getting these things right!

Implications for teaching and learning

As discussed above, the literature on errors and misconceptions falls into roughly three camps:

1 teach in such a way as to avoid errors;
2 if your children do make errors, then rectify the situation by teaching in an appropriate manner;
3 use any errors or misconceptions to generate discussion and/or cognitive conflict.

Some advocates of the third approach dismiss the first two, arguing that errors and misconceptions are unavoidable, and so one should '. . . welcome misconceptions as opportunities to engage children in learning through discussion . . .' (Swan 2003: 112). However, I would argue that an enlightened teacher should be able to use all three approaches. An awareness of what research and experience suggest are the most common errors made by young children is an essential prerequisite for the planning of lessons that might help children avoid such errors and misconceptions in the first place. Teachers also need to be aware that some children will inevitably make some of these errors and will develop the occasional 'alternative conception'. They need to have a range of teaching strategies – different from simply correcting the error by explaining the concept once again – in order to deal with these situations. However, they also need to plan lessons in which potential errors and misconceptions are brought to the surface for discussion by the class, with a view to generating information that can be used for formative assessment purposes. It has been suggested that one powerful weapon in the armoury of an early years teacher for such purposes is Miss Count – a numerically-challenged puppet.

References

Ashlock, R.B. (1976) *Error Patterns in Computation*. London: Bell and Howell.

Bell, A.W., (1994) Teaching for the test, in M. Selinger (ed.) *Teaching Mathematics*. London: Routledge.

Brown, J.S. and Burton, R.R. (1978) Diagnostic models for procedural 'bugs' in basic mathematical skills, *Cognitive Science*, 2: 155–92.

DCSF (Department for Children, Schools and Families) (2008) *Independent Review of Mathematics Teaching in Early Years Settings and Primary Schools* www.publications.teachernet.gov.uk/eOrderingDownload/ Williams%20 Mathematics.pdf (accessed June 2008).

DfEE (Department for Education and Employment) (1998) *Teaching: High Status, High Standards. Requirements for Courses of Initial Teacher Training: Circular 4/98*. London: DfEE.

DfES (Department for Education and Skills) (2005) *Supporting Children with Gaps in their Mathematical Understanding*. London: DfES.

Mullis, I.V.S., Martin, M.O., Gonzales, E.J. and Chrostowski, S.J. (2004) *Trends in International Mathematics and Science Study 2003 International Mathematics Report*. Massachusetts: TIMSS & PIRLS International Study Center.

Schaeffer, B., Eggleston, V.H. and Scott, J.L. (1974) Number development in young children, *Cognitive Psychology*, 6: 357–79.

Spooner, M. (2002) *Errors and Misconceptions in Maths at Key Stage 2: Working Towards Success in SATs*. London: David Fulton.

Swan, M. (2003) Making sense of mathematics, in I. Thompson (ed.) *Enhancing Primary Mathematics Teaching*. Milton Keynes: Open University Press.

Teacher Training Agency (TTA) (2003) *Qualifying to Teach: Handbook of Guidance*. London: TTA.

Note

Several practical activities for addressing some of the issues raised in this chapter can be found in the article 'Count it out' (1995), available for downloading at www.ianthompson.pi.dsl.pipex.com (accessed 31 March 2008).

SECTION 7
Towards an early years mathematics pedagogy

The first edition of this book was published in 1997, the year in which the Labour Party won the general election with a landslide victory. As one of its many initiatives, the new government immediately set about increasing services and support for young children and their families. Politicians could call on the plethora of research studies – both international and national – that confirmed the importance of learning in the early years. This research appeared to show quite clearly that the length of time spent in pre-school had a significant and positive impact on attainment in the school situation. In 1997, the annual investment in services for young children and their families was £2 billion; by 2003 this had nearly doubled to £3.75 billion.

The government subsequently produced many reports promising the following:

- free nursery education places for all 4-year-olds whose parents wished to take up the offer;
- Early Excellence Centres that were to serve as models for high-quality practice that integrated early education with child care;
- proposals for the establishment of the Sure Start initiative (a programme to deliver the best start in life for every child), with local programmes to be set up in disadvantaged neighbourhoods to provide community-based support for parents and children under 4;
- the creation of the Foundation Stage for children age 3 to the end of Reception;
- frameworks for this age group along with a complementary one for practitioners working with children under 3;
- a Statutory Framework for the Early Years Foundation Stage focusing on children from birth to 5.

Sue Gifford (Chapter 16) writes in this context of substantial change in early years education, and argues that even though we know young children are mathematically very capable, little is known about helping them learn in pre-school settings. This is important because there are large discrepancies in children's early mathematical experiences which affect their later learning. Research clearly shows that merely providing opportunities for children to learn through play is not effective, and that adults have to be proactive in teaching mathematics. What then are the most suitable ways of teaching mathematics to 3- to 5-year-olds? This chapter reviews recent research into how young children learn mathematics, including evidence from neuroscience, pre-school interventions and home learning. Neuroscientifc evidence points to the importance of frequent and cumulative experience, and endorses multisensory approaches which combine kinaesthetic, visual and verbal learning. This has implications for resources, activities and groupings. Research from pre-school intervention programmes suggests that playful and discussion-based teaching methods, including games, puppets and humour are important. It also suggests the importance of teachers having clear frameworks of mathematical progression. The variation in children's experience and positive examples of home teaching indicates the importance of working with families. Finally, the chapter considers the mathematical framework for the Early Years Foundation Stage.

16 'How do you teach nursery children mathematics?' In search of a mathematics pedagogy for the early years

Sue Gifford

Introduction

Recently 5-year-olds in the USA were asked questions like: 'Which number is bigger, 5 or 4?'. While advantaged children answered correctly 96 per cent of the time, disadvantaged children did so for only 18 per cent (Gersten et al. 2005). The reasons for this disparity may be due to a lack of mathematical experiences at home, or to children's difficulties in linking these to the language of school. In any case, socio-economic status is a major predictor of mathematical achievement, particularly in the UK, and those who start behind tend to stay behind. The good news is that pre-school mathematics education can make a difference (Sammons et al. 2002). What this research also points to is the role of experience rather than innate ability for mathematical achievement.

So what does an effective pre-school mathematics education look like? There has been a recent focus worldwide, with programmes being developed, for instance, in the USA and Australia. However, while we know that young children are mathematically very capable, we are still very ignorant about helping them learn. The overwhelming evidence is that child-initiated play does not work (see Tucker, Chapter 3). A recent review of early years mathematics pedagogy concluded that 'Spontaneous free play, while potentially rich in mathematics, is not sufficient to provide mathematical experiences for young children' (Anthony and Walshaw 2007: 30). Many children do not focus on mathematical aspects of play and neither do many practitioners. What seem to be effective are adult-led, mathematics-focused, group activities with adults actively teaching (Siraj-Blatchford et al. 2002). This approach is not part of traditional early childhood education. It is also not embraced by official UK guidance which emphasizes children learning mathematics through 'child-initiated activities in their own play' (DfES 2007). By referring only briefly to mathematics-focused activities, this gives confusing messages to practitioners, who might want advice about teaching without over-pressurizing young children.

How are we to decide what is appropriate pedagogy? A previous review identified some general principles from research about young children's learning (Gifford 2004). More recent research, including intervention studies and evidence from neuroscience, has added new insights and examples. The aim here is draw on these sources to propose an early years mathematics pedagogy focusing mainly on 3- to 5-year-olds. 'Appropriateness' is considered to include both effectiveness and the fostering of positive attitudes. Anthony and Walshaw (2007) suggest that mathematical communities of practice are needed, with more proactive and knowledgeable practitioners.

What do we know about how young children learn mathematics?

Children's learning has been viewed cognitively, physically, emotionally and socially. Although these are interrelated categories, they are used by researchers and so provide useful headings with which to analyse young children's learning.

Cognitive aspects of learning

Drawing on the theories of Piaget and Vygotsky, young children need to imitate and practise; generalize and make connections; represent ideas (including visualizing, verbalizing and symbolizing); restructure concepts; and use thinking strategies. Therefore, teachers need to provide experiences to help children spot patterns and confront misconceptions, and to model skills and strategies, provoking discussion, problem-solving and exploration.

Recently, neuroscientific evidence has endorsed these processes, according to Goswami and Bryant (2007: 4): their conclusion is that 'cumulative learning is crucial'. Imitation is a basic learning process: newborn babies copy adults putting their tongue out. Parents from many cultures build on this, using 'call and response' to teach children to count, with the child repeating after the parent, or vice versa (see Griffiths 2007). Parents also correct errors, providing instant feedback, as recommended by early years pedagogic research (Siraj-Blatchford et al. 2002). Teaching mathematics to young children, using imitation and instruction, is also part of a Vygotskian approach, whereby children appropriate the culture around them as apprentices learning from experts.

'Cumulative learning' involves babies learning through the frequency of correlations between experiences, which form neural networks in the brain. Children construct prototypes for concepts such as 'dog' or 'three', and compare subsequent experiences to them. This view supports constructivist theory, with children creating their own understanding of mathematical relationships, but also underlines the need for frequency and quantity of experience. Researchers have argued that it is not age or ability which stops young children counting to 100 but a sheer lack of experience. This suggests the need for regular provision via daily routines and the importance of activities with a repetitive structure, such as rhymes and games. Teachers also need to select examples and experiences carefully, and focus attention on key aspects to be linked. Activities which provide checks and feedback, such as puzzles and computer programs or 'find the hidden number' games, also help children make connections.

Learners are reluctant to restructure ideas according to Goswami and Bryant (2007), which explains why children often maintain theories which blatantly do not fit the evidence (such as older children always being taller). They may need a lot of experience and discussion to change their minds. This suggests the need to provide varied examples, such as irregular and regular triangles, and triangles in different orientations, to create rich concepts and avoid misconceptions. The importance of providing cognitive conflict and encouraging discussion has been emphasized by mathematics educators. Using investigation to test the boundaries of ideas, like seeing if counting works in any order, can also expose and clarify misconceptions. Challenging children's expectations with deliberate mistakes also appeals to their humorous delight in incongruity. An example of this approach was used by the US intervention project, 'Big math for little kids' (Greenes et al. 2004). For instance, children were shown a picture of a seesaw with a bear on the high end and a frog on the low end and asked why it was 'funny'. Asking children to explain and 'fix' problems made them clarify their understanding.

The brain presents multiple simultaneous representations of experiences, from visual, auditory, kinaesthetic and other sensory inputs. Young children have very good visual memories, which later link to language and memories of previous experience, so that concepts become complex 'patterns of activation' according to Goswami and Bryant (2007). This endorses the importance of multi-sensory approaches which aim to connect the different modes and also Bruner's theory of presenting new ideas enactively, iconically (visually) then symbolically. For instance, teaching number concepts using fingers and dice builds on young children's kinaesthetic and visual memory. The intervention programme, *Number Worlds*, emphasizes different number images, including objects, dot patterns and number lines (Griffin 2004). Language is important for structuring ideas and organizing memory; carers who elaborate and evaluate children's experience help them to create stronger memories. The emphasis on language in *Big Math for Little Kids* (Greenes et al. 2004) helps children to put non-verbal understanding into words. According to Gersten et al. (2005) helping children link different images, words and symbols is crucial for avoiding later mathematics difficulties. Children's informal recording may also help them to connect spatial and symbolic representations.

Metacognition, or reflection on thinking processes, helps children control learning by focusing, memorizing or checking. This depends on the capacity of working memory, which develops after the age of 6, explaining why young children have difficulty with complex information. According to Goswami and Bryant (2007), metacognition is also linked to language development and self-regulation, which suggests that it is important for adults to 'think aloud' and articulate problem-solving strategies.

In the following example, from Sharp et al. (2002, cited by Anthony and Walshaw 2007: 181) an adult, Joe, encouraged a 4-year-old to reflect on her thinking. They were playing a familiar game requested by the child, which involved sharing cookies between children. Joe adjusted the numbers in two scenarios until they got to seven cookies and four children:

> Leah: That's a hard one, maybe I can't do it.
> Joe: Think about what you did to solve the other two.
> Leah: Whole, whole, whole, whole, then there's three more left. Um, three more cookies left. Then you break up one into halves, then there are two left. And, another into half, half. Break the last one into quarter, quarter, quarter, quarter.
> Joe: Great! How much does each kid get?
> Leah: One whole, one half and one quarter.

This impressive visualization demonstrates what young children can do with practice. It is given as an example of 'sustained shared thinking' (Siraj-Blatchford et al. 2002), which extends children's thinking through a shared focus and mutual understanding. It is also an example of scaffolding, with the adult adjusting the problem according to the child's responses and focusing their attention on key aspects. Coltman et al. (2002) found scaffolding also helped children adopt checking strategies, thereby providing themselves with feedback.

Mathematical learning is therefore the result of sufficient experience of the right kind to help children to make connections and use thinking strategies to solve problems. This requires careful planning, skilled interaction and mathematical understanding.

Physical aspects of learning

Neuroscientific evidence endorses the priority of physical activity and manipulatives for young children. Structured resources such as building blocks and place value cards provide opportunities for children to physically experience mathematical relationships. Large-scale resources and images are effective, such as outdoor number tracks which children can jump along. Rhythmic actons like kicking and hopping help children count to higher numbers than counting objects (see Griffiths, Chapter 4). 'Big math for little kids' (Greenes et al. 2004) found that counting different decades with funny faces and noises for the teens and twisty movements for the twenties encouraged 4-year-olds to count to 100 and beyond.

Generally multi-sensory approaches are supported by research evidence. Mathematical displays can stimulate discussion, for instance with mirrors or giant 100 squares provoking comments on pattern. Sound images may be as powerful as visual images for number, and music can aid memorizing: for instance the BBC *Number Time* counting tune is hard to dislodge. Information and Communications Technology (ICT) is a rich source of such images and has been used creatively in projects, with children controlling robots, designing games and exploring shapes dynamically. However, according to Anthony and Walshaw (2007), ICT is underused in early mathematics (see Higgins, Chapter 13).

Affective aspects of learning

Mathematics anxiety can fill working memory space and prevent learning (Ashcraft 1988). A safe risk-taking environment is therefore needed, emphasizing problem-solving methods rather than right/wrong answers and using playful teaching strategies. Teachers use curiosity and surprise to engage young children, for instance by hiding things in boxes. Making ludicrous mistakes also engages children's sense of humour, while puppets who get into muddles put children into the role of expert and boost their self-esteem (Gifford 2005; Thompson, Chapter 15).

Children's self-image as successful learners is key: according to Dweck (1999) children need to believe that learning depends on effort not ability. Therefore, adults need to encourage children by praising effort not performance, and also by believing that all children can succeed and do not have fixed mathematical ability. Children also learn more effectively if they have some choice and control over activities, which may be just choosing dice for games. Activities need to build on children's interests, whether in ages and birthdays or in activities like scoring goals and 'fishing'. Teachers may therefore need to use observation creatively in order to engage all children in mathematical learning.

Socio-cultural aspects of learning

From a socio-cultural perspective children learn social practices, not ideas. This suggests that settings need to become mathematical communities of practice, where everyone is collaboratively engaged in mathematics. Howe and Mercer (2007) argue that educational success depends on the quality of social and communicative processes in classrooms rather than on teaching techniques or individual ability. Children's mathematical learning therefore requires supportive relationships. Friendships between children can also involve sustained shared thinking and peer teaching, for instance when pairs play games. Howe and Mercer (2007) emphasize the learning power of exploratory talk, where children share ideas, offer alternative viewpoints and jointly solve problems, for instance in construction play. Exploratory talk requires children to listen, challenge each other and accept challenges, requiring self-regulation and collaborative skills.

Grouping raises issues for early mathematics pedagogy in terms of size and composition. Pairs and small groups are effective, but research differs on the benefits of large group activities (Gifford 2004). They can create shared enthusiasm and welcome anonymity for some, but teachers may focus more on management than learning. Therefore, small groups for number rhymes, registration and snack times may provide effective mathematical experiences. In terms of group composition, Sammons et al. (2002) suggest that children learn by mixing with higher attainers and benefit from teachers' higher expectations of them.

A mathematical community of practice also needs to link with children's mathematical experiences from their home cultures. However, according to theories of situated cognition, children may compartmentalize home and school learning. Some children may be able to count in different languages or use fingers to count in threes, but not demonstrate this at school. Some families may regularly discuss mathematics in various contexts, such as money, time, journeys or games, while others do not. Individual homes differ widely in the mathematical experiences they offer and these greatly influence children's confidence and competence (Sammons et al. 2002). Clearly, the potential effect of home learning is so great that working with parents is a key pedagogical strategy. Research shows that many families teach children mathematics effectively in varied but sometimes formal ways (Gifford 2005). Some young children will find it difficult to link home teaching to school play-based learning and teachers may find it hard to endorse the formal home methods. Therefore, it is important for teachers to find out about and build on home learning. This often involves other family members besides parents: grandmothers, uncles or older siblings also sing rhymes, play games or teach sums. Projects with parents that have been found effective include joint sessions for parents and children, as well as sending home kits and games (Anthony and Walshaw 2007). Explaining mathematical progression to parents is important; one way of doing this may be by sharing children's progress.

The adult's role

The quality of adult interaction is crucial, according to research. Emotionally, children need support, with positive expectations and praise for effort. From the cognitive perspective, sustained shared thinking is recommended, but mathematical examples are notably absent from the literature (Siraj-Blatchford et al. 2002). This may be because the negotiation of meanings involves an awareness of misconceptions and learning trajectories. Mathematical conversations with young children therefore require confident subject knowledge. Similarly, scaffolding children's problem-solving requires ongoing assessment and the use of 'increasingly specific hints' to prompt mathematical thinking, as described by the *Building Blocks* project (Sarama and Clements 2004: 186).

Intervention projects like this have found that assessing individual children using mathematical frameworks increases teachers' conceptual knowledge and also their ability to teach mathematics opportunistically (see Wright, Chapter 14). It seems that clear systems of stages, based on research, are particularly effective (Bobis et al. 2005).

The adult also requires a varied repertoire of sensitive interactive skills. Closed questions are not as effective with young children as open-ended ones or speculative comments, like, 'I wonder why . . .' (Gifford 2005). A range of interactive mathematics teaching strategies are listed by Macmillan (2002, cited by Anthony and Walshaw 2007) including 'modelling curiosity', 'inviting imaginative involvement', 'offering challenge' and 'pretending not to know the answer'. Like puppets getting things wrong, this raises children's status to that of experts. 'Topsy-turvy' examples like the 'funny' seesaw are also effective in provoking explanation and reasoning. Practitioners may commonly use strategies like modelling curiosity and making deliberate mistakes with young children, but not usually for mathematics, especially if they do not feel mathematically curious or playful themselves.

The findings derived from research may be summarized as suggesting the following principles of effective pedagogy:

- cumulative learning, with repeated experience and practice;
- mathematics-focused activities, with pair and small-group discussion;
- generalizing – investigating relationships and confronting misconceptions;
- problem-solving, emphasizing processes of predicting, connecting and checking;
- multi-sensory learning, with large-scale activity and resources, rhythm and music;
- connections between images, language and symbols;

- supportive, subtle and playful teaching strategies;
- links with family mathematics.

In general, it seems that a mathematical community of practice requires regular mathematics-focused activities with varied teaching strategies and a clear framework for assessment and planning.

What does a positive pre-school mathematics community of practice look like?

An early years mathematics pedagogy combines a mathematically-rich environment with mathematically-knowledgeable and playful teachers. The former requires planned resources and activities. These include interactive displays, large-scale resources and measuring tools, clocks and calculators to link with home. Visual aids, like fingers, dot patterns and structured apparatus help children to develop subitizing and discover part–whole relationships with numbers and shapes. Activities with repetitive structures like rhymes and games provide practice, links between images, words and symbols, and challenges to predict and check. The use of actions, rhythm and music can help counting, like 'twisting to the twenties'. Adult-led activities can provide playful challenges, like number hunts, sorting mixed-up number staircases, finding how many cookies have been stolen, helping story characters in a muddle or toy animals making mistakes and confronting ludicrous claims like 'There are a million elephants in this box!' Routines like snack time, registration and tidying-up also provide opportunities to discuss problems like 'How shall we share these?', 'How many people are away?' or 'How many scissors are missing?' Adults need to think aloud and scaffold by identifying steps, focusing attention and reminding of strategies. Children can also use mathematics to improve their environment or organize events, designing obstacle courses, role play areas or tea parties. They can vote on themes for role play, cakes to cook or stories to hear. Adults will need to model tools and techniques for purposes like measuring and using calculators.

From these regular experiences, children and adults can develop initiatives and interaction. Children may adapt games to their own rules or choose dice with larger numbers. Outdoors, 4-year-olds can record scores for skittles and indoors can teach each other with games and computers. Four-year-olds can also be encouraged to investigate, for instance, making arrangements for numbers and shapes, taking apart and putting together in different ways. Adults or children may set challenges from stories, like building beds for the bears. Practitioners may develop activities from observing children's interests in numbers and amounts, like making a number line from siblings' ages, seeing how many coins will fill a purse, or counting the number of worms dug up.

The two greatest challenges for settings are to develop the mathematical confidence of all the adults through the use of clear learning frameworks for assessment and planning; and to build on children's mathematical experiences with families, which may also be best achieved by sharing perceptions of children's progress.

Applying the principles

To what extent does the UK Early Years Foundation Stage (EYFS) reflect these features?

The *Practice Guidance for the Early Years Foundation Stage* (DfES 2007) has principles grouped in four themes: a unique child, positive relationships, enabling environments, learning and development. In the oddly named section for mathematics, *Problem-solving, Reasoning and Numeracy*, there is an emphasis on mathematics in child-initiated activity, play and exploration, and on using mathematical language in a variety of activities including daily routines. There is mention of adult-led, mathematics-focused activities and developing mathematics through songs, stories and games (with examples mainly of number rhymes). However, the emphasis on child-initiated rather than planned activity may not ensure 'cumulative learning' for all children.

Multi-sensory learning is advocated in the emphasis on outdoor learning, resources and songs. However, examples such as hopscotch and skittles seem inappropriately recommended for the under-3s rather than the over-4s. There is an emphasis on working with parents, with suggestions such as telling parents how children learn about numbers in the setting and encouraging parents 'to talk in their home language about quantities and numbers' (DfES 2007: 65). There could be more emphasis on learning from and working with families. Some suggestions support a mathematical community of practice, including an emphasis on mathematical language and 'real problem-solving' (such as finding how many spoons are needed, and the use of numbers as labels). The video examples are more engaging than those in the text, with examples of making a bed for a giant and finding the right size wellies.

While the *Practice Guidance for the Early Years Foundation Stage* (DfES 2007) generally recommends 'sustained shared thinking', there are no examples of how practitioners might engage children in thinking mathematically. Although the section title emphasizes problem-solving, there is a lack of examples and interactive strategies. Most problems seem unlikely to engage children's interest, with closed questions such as asking how many children are in the home corner or how many books they have looked at today. While the

Guidance suggests encouraging children 'to be creative in thinking up problems', examples such as, 'suppose there were three people to share the bricks between instead of two', do not exemplify this. Suggestions such as helping children understand that 'two rows of three eggs in the box makes six eggs altogether' do not help adults create a sustainable activity (DfES 2007: 69), and there is no support for developing interactive strategies to foster curiosity or discussion.

However, the main drawback of the EYFS lies in the lack of structure and progression in the mathematics content, supposedly linked to ages and practical examples. For instance, the section on 'Shape, space and measures' includes 'match sets of objects to numerals that represent the number of objects'. This rather verbose statement, which seems to have strayed from the 'Numbers as labels and for counting' section, is next to activities concerned with ordering items by length, playing robots and describing patterns (DfES 2007: 72). Perhaps it relates to data handling, and was thought to go with sorting shapes! However, this jumble of ideas and activities is unlikely to support practitioners in identifying learning trajectories.

Overall, the EYFS advocates some general features of appropriate pedagogy, such as problem-solving, mathematical language, number rhymes and outdoor activity, and emphasizes working with parents. However, it lacks examples of systematically engaging activities and interactive strategies to support problem-solving. These points are endorsed by the Williams review of primary mathematics in the UK (DCSF 2008: 37–8), which emphasizes children's lack of achievement in problem-solving in early years settings and recommends 'direct teaching of mathematical skills and knowledge in meaningful contexts' and 'opportunities for open-ended discussions of solutions, explorations of reasoning and mathematical logic'. Early years practitioners need more inspiring examples and guidance about how to do this, alongside a clearer mathematical framework of likely progression, so that they can provide all children with a confident start in mathematics.

References

Anthony, G. and Walshaw, M. (2007) *Effective Pedagogy in Mathematics/pangarau: Best Evidence Synthesis (BES)*. Wellington, NZ: Ministry of Education www.educationcounts.govt.nz/publications/series/ibes/5951 (accessed 31 March 2008).

Ashcraft, M.H., Kirk, E.P. and Hopko, D. (1988) On the cognitve consequences of mathematics anxiety, in C. Donlan (ed.) *The Development of Mathematical Skills*. Hove: Psychology Press.

Bobis, J., Clarke, B., Clarke, D., Thomas, G., Wright, R., Young-Loveridge, J. and Gould, P. (2005) Supporting teachers in the development of young children's mathematical thinking: three large-scale cases, *Mathematics Education Research Journal*, 16(3): 27–57.

Coltman, P., Petryaeva, D. and Anghileri, J. (2002) Scaffolding learning through meaningful tasks and adult interaction, *Early Years*, 22(1): 39–49.

DCSF (Department for Children, Schools and Families) (2008) *Independent Review of Mathematics Teaching in Early Years Settings and Primary Schools* www.publications.teachernet.gov.uk/eOrderingDownload/ Williams%20Mathematics.pdf (accessed June 2008).

DfES (Department for Education and Skills) (2007) *Practice Guidance for the Early Years Foundation Stage*. Nottingham: DfES www.publications.teachernet.gov. uk/eOrderingDownload/eyfs_guide12_07.pdf (accessed 31 March 2008).

Dweck, C. (1999) *Self-theories: Their Role in Motivation, Personality and Development*. Philadelphia, PA: Psychology Press.

Gersten, N., Jordan, C. and Flojo, J.R. (2005) Early identification and interventions for students with mathematics difficulties, *Journal of Learning Disabilities*, 38(4): 293–304.

Gifford, S. (2004) A new mathematics pedagogy in the early years: in search of principles for practice, *International Journal of Early Years Education*, 12(2): 39–49.

Gifford, S. (2005) *Teaching Mathematics 3–5: Developing Learning in the Foundation Stage*. Milton Keynes: Open University Press.

Goswami, U. and Bryant, P. (2007) *Children's Cognitive Development and Learning* (Primary Review Research Survey 2/1a). Cambridge: University of Cambridge Faculty of Education.

Greenes, C., Ginsburg, H.P. and Balfanz, R. (2004) Big math for little kids, *Early Childhood Research Quarterly*, 19(1): 159–66.

Griffin, S. (2004) Building number sense with number worlds: a mathematics program for young children, *Early Childhood Research Quarterly*, 19(1): 173–80.

Griffiths, R. (2007) Young children counting at home, *Mathematics Teaching*, 203: 24–6.

Howe, C. and Mercer, N. (2007) *Children's Social Development, Peer Interaction and Classroom Learning* (Primary Review Interim Reports 2/1b). Cambridge: University of Cambridge Faculty of Education.

Sammons, P., Sylva, K., Melhuish, E., Siraj-Blatchford, I., Taggart, B. and Elliot, K. (2002) *Technical Paper 8a: Measuring the Impact of Pre-school on Children's Cognitive Progress over the Pre-school Period*. London: Institute of Education, University of London.

Sarama, J. and Clements, D. (2004) Building blocks for early childhood mathematics, *Early Childhood Research Quarterly*, 19(1): 181–9.

Siraj-Blatchford, I., Sylva, K., Muttock, S., Gilden, R. and Bell, D. (2002) *Researching Effective Pedagogy in the Early Years* (REPEY) (Research Report 356). London: Department of Education and Skills.

Index

Related books from Open University Press

Purchase from www.openup.co.uk or order through your local bookseller

---

CHILDREN'S MATHEMATICS 4–15
LEARNING FROM ERRORS AND MISCONCEPTIONS

Julie Ryan and Julian Williams

The mistakes children make in mathematics are usually not just 'mistakes' – they are often intelligent generalizations from previous learning. Following several decades of academic study of such mistakes, the phrase 'errors and misconceptions' has recently entered the vocabulary of mathematics teacher education and has become prominent in the curriculum for initial teacher education.

The popular view of children's errors and misconceptions is that they should be corrected as soon as possible. The authors contest this, perceiving them as potential windows into children's mathematics. Errors may diagnose significant ways of thinking and stages in learning that highlight important opportunities for new learning.

This book uses extensive, original data from the authors' own research on children's performance, errors and misconceptions across the mathematics curriculum. It progressively develops concepts for teachers to use in organizing their understanding and knowledge of children's mathematics, offers practical guidance for classroom teaching and concludes with theoretical accounts of learning and teaching.

Children's Mathematics 4–15 is a groundbreaking book, which transforms research on diagnostic errors into knowledge for teaching, teacher education and research on teaching. It is essential reading for teachers, students on undergraduate teacher training courses and graduate and PGCE mathematics teacher trainees, as well as teacher educators and researchers.

Contents
Acknowledgements – Introduction – Learning from errors and misconceptions – Children's mathematical discussions – Developing number – Shape, space and measurement – From number to algebra – Data-handling, graphicacy, probability and statistics – Pre-service teachers' mathematics subject matter knowledge – Learning and teaching mathematics: towards a theory of pedagogy – Appendix 1: Common errors and misconceptions – Appendix 2: Discussion prompt sheets – Glossary – References – Index.

2007   264pp
978–0–335–22042–7 (Paperback)   978–0–335–22043–4 (Hardback)

LANGUAGE FOR LEARNING MATHEMATICS
ASSESSMENT FOR LEARNING IN PRACTICE

Clare Lee

Assessment for learning is a powerful way to raise standards and improve learning. However, as this book shows, effective assessment for learning in the mathematics classroom depends on pupils being able and willing to use mathematical language to express their ideas. When discussion, negotiation and explanation are encouraged, teachers use assessment for learning creatively, the work quickly becomes more challenging and the pupils come to see themselves as successful learners.

Many pupils find it difficult to express ideas in mathematics because of problems with the language that is used to convey mathematical concepts. This book shows teachers how to help pupils express what they really know and understand, so that assessment for learning can be used. The book:

- Discusses what mathematical language is, and what it is not
- Suggests practical approaches to introducing more discourse into the classroom
- Explores the ideas of assessment for learning – rich questioning and dialogue, effective feedback, and peer and self assessment – and suggests how these can be used effectively in mathematics classrooms to improve learning

Language for Learning Mathematics is key reading for teachers and trainee teachers in mathematics, as well as assessment advisors at LAs.

Contents
Acknowledgements – How this book tells its story – Increase discourse: Increase learning – Mathematical Language: What it is and what it isn't – Starting to talk in the mathematical classroom – Assessment for learning – Going further with purposeful communication in mathematics – The source of the ideas: Delving into theory – Looking at practice more deeply – References – Index.

2006   136pp
978–0–335–21988–9 (Paperback)   978–0–335–21989–6 (Hardback)